Strategic Management in a Hostile Environment

Strategic Management in a Hostile Environment

Lessons from the Tobacco Industry

Raymond M. Jones

QUORUM BOOKS
Westport, Connecticut • London

Library of Congress Cataloging-in-Publication Data

Jones, Raymond M., 1942–
Strategic management in a hostile environment : lessons from the tobacco industry / Raymond M. Jones.
p. cm.
Includes bibliographical references and index.
ISBN 1–56720–158–X (alk. paper)
1. Tobacco industry—United States—History. 2. Tobacco industry—Moral and ethical aspects—United States. 3. Tobacco—Health aspects—United States. 4. Social change—United States. 5. Antismoking movement—United States. I. Title.
HD9135.J66 1997
338.7′6797′0973—dc21 97–5884

British Library Cataloguing in Publication Data is available.

Library of Congress Catalog Card Number: 97–5884
ISBN: 1–56720–158–X

First published in 1997

Quorum Books, 88 Post Road West, Westport, CT 06881
An imprint of Greenwood Publishing Group, Inc.

Printed in the United States of America

The paper used in this book complies with the Permanent Paper Standard issued by the National Information Standards Organization (Z39.48–1984).

10 9 8 7 6 5 4 3 2 1

Contents

Illustrations

FIGURES

TABLES

Acknowledgments

This book is the culmination of a significant amount of learning over a number of years from many and varied sources. First and foremost, my appreciation goes to Lee Preston at the University of Maryland, who continually narrowed my focus and refined my thoughts on both the facts and the concepts. Without Lee, there would not have been a book. My debt to the intellectual contributions of MBA classmate Michael Porter will be obvious to the reader.

Other academics who directly and indirectly impacted either my thinking, my knowledge, or my writing were Anil Gupta, Marty Gannon, Tom Greer, Judy Olian, Ken Smith, the late Parker Fielder, Ming Jer Chen, Norman Berg, Sam Hayes, Page Keeton, Cynthia Montgomery, Tony Mento, Roger Kashlak, John Cotner, Ellen Hoadley, John Burbridge, Fred Derrick, Eleanor Donaghue-Kimrey, Harsha Desai, Harry Sapienza, Mancur Olson, Neng Liang, and Robert Nozick. My gratitude goes also to the undergraduate, graduate, and executive classes of the University of Maryland and Loyola College who have sharpened my viewpoint with their questions and comments. Specific thanks go to Kevin O'Hara both for his overall assistance and for his drafting of the appendix on the UST firm. I was fortunate to have the research assistance provided by Mahinder Kingra and Kristen Frey. The computer skills of Dee Hoeck were invaluable and most appreciated.

I have likewise benefited from various business relationships (to include consultants, lawyers, and politicians) that have significantly impacted the way I view things. For example, the impact of the late Armand Hammer and Marvin Watson on my understanding of corporate political economy in practice cannot be overestimated. Other sources of learning from this community have been Dave White, Joe Baird, Jim Christie, Jan Ahart, Jack Dorgan, the late A. P. Gates, Alice Howard, Jerry Muro, Gene Buccarelli, Sam Dominick, Antoine Savary, John Anderson, Gerry Jones, Bob Holland, the late Charley Torem,

Bonnie Shepard-Clark, Bob Goldfarb, Michael Kentor, Bill Vance, Matt Platania, Mick Ginnings, Chris Reale, and Joe McDonough. I also need to thank the staff of the Library of Congress as well as those at Loyola College, Duke University, the University of Maryland, and the Department of Agriculture Library at Beltsville, Maryland. Ron Anton, Bob Margenthaler, and Eddie Jacobs were always there with an encouraging word.

My daughters, Andrea and Audra, lent their support as well as their legal and business experience to the venture. Nothing can ever erase my debt to my wife Bobbie. This book is dedicated to my father and my deceased mother. My appreciation to them and to all, named and unnamed, who contributed to this work. Any mistakes or errors of judgment remain with me.

Chapter 1

Overview

The cigarette industry has undergone three major shifts in its historical environment. The first was a structural change wrought by the government when it dissolved James B. Duke's tobacco trust in 1911. The break-up of the trust resulted in four successor companies (American Tobacco, R.J. Reynolds, Liggett and Myers, and the P. Lorillard Company), all of which are still active in the industry in 1995.

The second major environmental shift was that from a consumer demand for dark Turkish tobacco cigarettes to a preference for lighter American blend tobacco-type cigarettes. This change in consumer preference was facilitated by World War I. The war interrupted the supply of Turkish leaf from the Mid-east and hence the production of dark cigarettes. Thus, the masses of men undergoing the military socialization process were introduced only to lighter American blend-type cigarettes. This was the cigarette habit the doughboys came home with after the war. This dissemination of lighter blend cigarette preference, combined with the action of the cigarette companies' national advertising campaigns for their respective major brands, triggered the tremendous growth experienced by the cigarette manufacturers between 1915 and 1950. A similar shift from dark to light tobacco has occurred on a global basis over the last thirty-five years of the century.

The third major impact on the industry was the modern anti-smoking movement that commenced in the 1950s and continues unabated today. The first wave of anti-smoking activities (publicity by health organizations, the surgeon general, and activists; advertising bans for the industry) led to the search for a safer cigarette. This search has resulted in the consumption of filter cigarettes rather than nonfilters. In 1995, filter cigarettes accounted for 97.2% of cigarette consumption as opposed to essentially 0% in 1950. This desire for a safer cigarette has also resulted in a low-tar type of filter cigarettes reaching a 59.7% market share in 1995, again from a 1950s base of 0%.

The second wave of the anti-smoking movement went beyond negative publicity and advertising bans. It was aimed at banning smoking, especially to protect a non-smoking bystander from being forced to suffer the effects of a smoker's sidestream smoke. The effect of these smoking bans, combined with the socialization process away from cigarette smoking caused by the first wave of negative publicity resulted in the maturity and decline of the number of cigarettes smoked in the United States. Figure 1.1 demonstrates this graphically.

Figure 1.1
U.S. Cigarette Consumption, 1950–1995

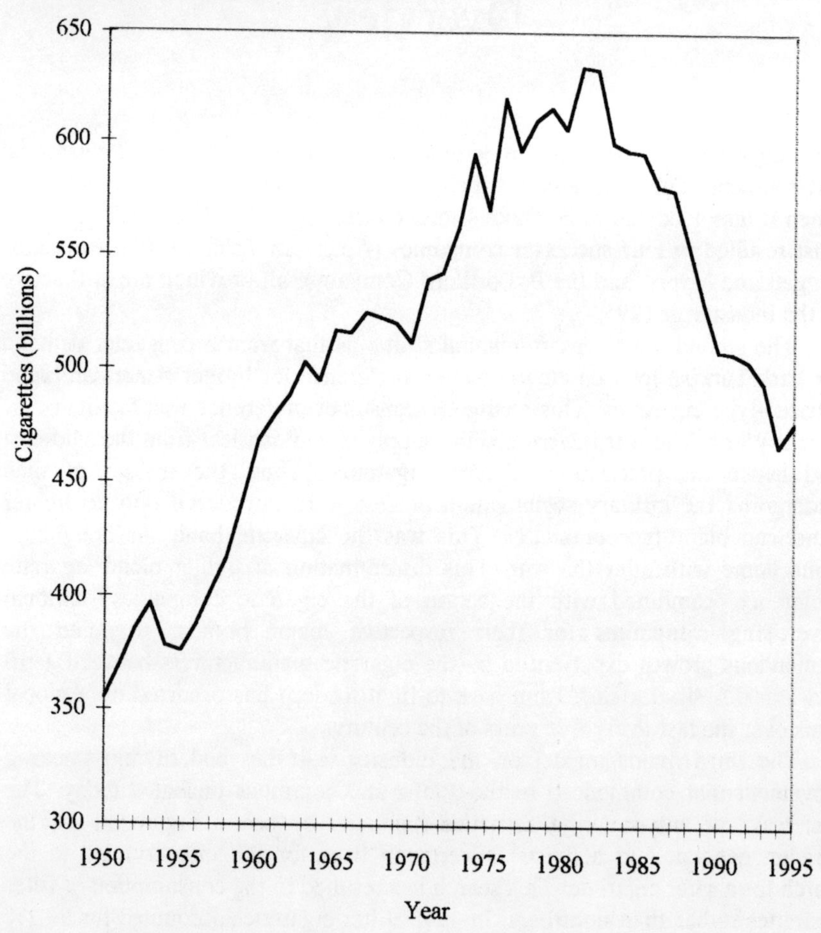

Source: Tax Burden on Tobacco, 1995.

Two new characteristics of the anti-smoking movement have appeared as the fin de siècle approaches. The first is the issue of fraud. It is now alleged that the cigarette firms had lied concerning their knowledge of the harm caused by cigarettes, the addictive nature of tobacco, and the manipulation of nicotine in their products. This fraud issue, a 1996 presidential election agenda item, will influence the mind-set of the American public—the pool for potential juries in the future cigarette lawsuits. Even if fraud is not proven, the American public's historic reluctance to "reward" smokers for damages when they continue to engage in behavior known to be hazardous to your health will begin to fade. The second complementary approach is an extremely clever issue-framing argument by the government. The surgeon general has declared cigarettes to be addictive. The Food and Drug Administration (FDA) has labeled smoking a childhood disease, owing to the age most commence smoking. The case then made is that children cannot make an informed decision concerning the decision to smoke because of their age and that by the time they can do so they have become addicted. This inability to make a reasoned decision would only be compounded by any finding that the industry, by committing fraud, had withheld information concerning cigarettes' addictive or disease-causing additives. The plaintiff in such a lawsuit will no longer be viewed as a tawdry lotto seeker whose own behavior inflicted the damages but rather as a deserving victim of an evil, dishonest industry cabal. The cigarette firms have stated that the intent of these fin de siècle approaches is not regulation, as stated by their advocates, but rather as the extinction of cigarettes and their producers.

An unintended consequence of the anti-smoking movement is the predominance of people from the lower socioeconomic population segments among the remaining smokers. Statistically, they are significantly over-represented among smokers in 1995. This group of blue-collar, less educated whites and blacks, did not stop smoking in the same percentage numbers as did the rest of the population. In terms of both health and social status, they suffer from the present stigma of still smoking. The spending power of this demographic segment, which has been more or less enforced (albeit unintentionally) on the industry because of the anti-smoking movement, is obviously not as high as is the population's in general. Thus, while the cigarette firms raised prices significantly faster than the consumer price index (CPI) rose during the 1980s to more than compensate for lower unit volumes, they were simultaneously forced to introduce discounted price-value brands to serve that demographic market segment that was not declining as fast as was the market as a whole. The price-value brand segment of the domestic cigarette market had peaked at 36.8% of the market in 1993 from almost nothing in 1980. If this price-value market trend were to have continued to the point where filter tips sales have gone, it would have created a "commodity" impact on the profitability of the firms. As opposed to filters, which reduced the cost of manufacturing a cigarette because less tobacco was required, price-value brands are estimated by investment analysts who follow the cigarette industry to reduce operating profit margins in half. Particularly hard hit was Philip Morris's franchise brand Marlboro. From a 26.3% share of the market in 1990, Marlboro had fallen below 24% in early 1993, and the firm's management had projected it to dip below 20% by year-end if the then-current trend continued. On March 2, 1993, henceforth known as Marlboro Friday, Philip Morris reduced the price of a pack of Marlboros by $.40. This attempt to protect the investment in brand name equity appears to have been successful for the industry and especially so for Philip Morris, whose Marlboro brand had increased its market share to 30.1% by 1995. Simultaneously, price-value brands have decreased to a 30% share of the total market.

DOMESTIC MARKET

The industry's domestic environment has grown increasingly hostile for the cigarette firms owing to the smoking and health issue over the forty-five years of this study. In the forty-five years prior to this study, a consistency in market growth, in product type, and in the market share rankings of the firms was maintained once the trust had been dissolved and the consumer preference for lighter blend cigarettes had been established around 1920. On the other hand, the modern anti-smoking movement has played the major role in changing the industry's product types (filter, low-tar and price-value), in the maturation and decline of the market's consumption (per capita consumption dropped 30% from its peak), and in drastically changing the ranking of firms' market shares because of either failure or success in adjusting to the changing environment. Success for a cigarette firm required first and foremost an awareness of these consumer trends. Knowledge of these consumer trends then needed to be exploited by product innovation and development, by an ability to develop and sustain leading brands, by an efficient distribution network, and by creative promotion programs. Success came to those firms who recognized a consumer mass-market or niche trend and then exploited it with an appropriate product type that was creatively promoted to build and sustain brand loyalty. Brand loyalty has, historically, created high psychic switching costs for the consumer. The most successful firms exercised the most successful brand leadership strategy. However, with the decline of overall cigarette consumption, coupled with a skewed distribution of remaining smokers from the lower socioeconomic population segments, price-value brands have entered the marketplace as a basis of competition. Even with the success of Marlboro Friday, prices have not kept pace with the trend established in the 1980s and early 1990s.

MARKET DIVERSIFICATION

In response to the maturity and decline of their domestic markets, the industry's firms turned to market diversification for an avenue of growth. In the international markets, three trends have affected the cigarette companies' progress. First was, and is, a trend away from the dark Turkish-type cigarettes toward the lighter American blend product-type. It is the exact consumer preference metamorphosis undergone in the U.S. market, although with a significant time lag.

Part of the reason for the time lag was the second international trend. Overseas cigarette markets were opening up slowly. Tariff and quota barriers, state-owned enterprise monopolies, and the closed block of Communist countries all contributed to a restrained market potential for the international cigarette firms. From 1950 to 1995, this study's time frame, trade barriers were liberalized and communism fell. Accordingly, the cigarette firms' access to worldwide markets has grown from an estimated 25% level to a 90% level by 1990.

The third overseas factor is a negative one—excise taxes. Foreign excise taxes are two to three times U.S. excise taxes as a percentage of the retail sales price. In 1995, for example, Philip Morris's international sales in dollars were less than twice its domestic sales. In absolute dollar terms, its foreign excise taxes were over two and a half times as large as they were in the U.S. The net effect of these international factors has been to provide an avenue of growth for participating firms, albeit at a profit level reduced from that enjoyed in the United States. However, international cigarette profit levels are still higher than those found in most other products sold in the U.S. or abroad.

Operating profit margins for cigarettes are uniquely attractive. In the United States, full-price brands are in the 32% to 40% range, whereas price-value brands are half of those figures. Overseas, these margins are reduced to the 30% range. The upper end of these ranges is enjoyed by those who have exercised market leadership and have thus enjoyed economies of scale in manufacturing and marketing. For example, Marlboro's absolute advertising dollars are twice that of any other top ten brand but are a minimum 25% less on a per unit basis due to its leadership position. However, the most significant point is that the worst of these cigarette operating profit margins is at least as good, if not better, than those enjoyed by those businesses into which the firms have entered through their product diversification efforts.

Success in the international markets required the same sensitivity to consumer trends and the same ability to build and sustain brand loyalty that was needed in the domestic markets. Additionally, a leading firm was required to gauge the changing consumer preferences for global versus local brands and adjust its product portfolio offerings accordingly. Finally, a firm would have had to adjust its production and marketing operations to suit the demands of the host country. The host country demands (e.g., state-controlled distribution channels) changed during the course of this study, and the most successful firms adjusted their strategies in response. A successful international firm was acutely aware of shifting trends, both consumers' and host government's, and it managed its brands, from both a marketing and production standpoint, to align itself with those trends.

PRODUCT DIVERSIFICATION

All six major cigarette companies (Philip Morris in 1918 and Brown & Williamson in 1927 joined the trust's four successor companies in the marketplace) were ranked in Fortune's first "500" rating in 1955. Such a ranking necessitated acquisitions that were large if the sales of these firms were to be diversified. The extraordinary profits of cigarette operations dictate an almost 3:1 ratio of noncigarette sales to cigarette sales in order to obtain a roughly equal diversification of operating profits. By 1995, the industry had a higher percentage of sales in noncigarette products than in cigarettes, although cigarette sales contributed higher margins.

THE STUDY'S METHODOLOGY

Strategy scholar Michael Porter posits three causes of an industry's decline. One, there could be a technological innovation that makes the industry's product obsolete, as in the case of the transistor replacing the vacuum tube. A second potential cause of decline could occur with a change of demographics that affects the demand for the industry's products—e.g., the effect of a birthrate drop on the baby food producers. The third cause is a shift in demand for sociological reasons. This is the case of the cigarette industry where former Surgeon General Koop attributed the decline of smoking in the U.S. to the "social revolution" instigated by the anti-smoking movement. A *New York Times* article was headlined, "Smoking Is Deviant Behavior." Such phraseology is usually reserved for the social control section of texts in sociology.

The social strategies employed by the industry were, broadly speaking, waged from an industry association vantage point rather than that of the individual firms. The industry consistently converted cigarette-related issues into issues that were either pan-business (e.g., rule-making authority of government agencies) or free speech (commercial advertising) or civil rights (the rights of non-smokers). They were skillful in their ability to build unlikely coalitions, as was the case where the industry enlisted the president of the Affirmative Action Association to speak out on the rights of non-smokers as a civil rights issue. These social strategies and related tactics are not the focus of this study. The social strategies appear only as necessary to facilitate the analysis of the industry. As such, and in accordance with Porter's work on industry analysis, the social cause of decline is pertinent in how it affected the demand for the industry's product. The strategies of concern in this hostile environment are those concerned with the marketplaces.

In his industry analysis research, Michael Porter has also developed a framework for mature and declining industries. A particular aspect of interest is his contention that the firms in such industries will follow one of four possible strategies: leadership, niche, harvest, or exit. In the cigarette industry, we will determine from a case history of each individual firm what type of strategy it did follow. Additionally from Porter's writings on diversification, both geographically and by product, we will hypothesize what a firm's diversification efforts will be, based in part on what strategy the firm has chosen as the domestic cigarette market matured and then declined.

The study can be conceptualized as, first, the effect of the anti-smoking movement on the industry's overall demand and on the specific demand for particular product types (e.g., "safer"). Second, based on Porter's frameworks, hypotheses are developed with respect to both domestic market and diversification strategies. Third, these strategies are then tested against the firms' actual choices that are contained in each firm's case history. Analysis of results and conclusions is the final element. Porter's framework was based on case studies dealing with industries declining, essentially because of substitute products. The purpose of his case studies was to generate theory. The methodology in this study is the use of multiple case studies to attempt to replicate, in a quasi-experimental sense, Porter's research in an industry whose maturity and decline has been brought about by hostile social factors concerning the industry's product. The analysis is intended to test theory and is an explanatory and predictive multiple case analysis.

STUDY STRUCTURE

Chapter 2 outlines the activities of the anti-smoking movement from 1950 to 1995. Chapter 3 details industry responses, in terms of product types, to the evolution of the smoking and health issue. Chapter 4 then draws upon the work of Michael Porter to develop hypotheses of how the individual firms will respond to the challenges of the smoking and health issue. The overall driving research question is, What strategies have the cigarette firms developed to operate in such a hostile environment and with what results? Figures 1.2 and 1.3 demonstrate this graphically. Chapter 5 tests the Porter-derived hypotheses against the actions of the individual firms. The final chapter, Chapter 6, collects the hypotheses together, analyzes the results, and states conclusions. Porter's tenets on domestic rivalry, on international expansion, and on diversification are tested over a forty-five year time frame by the strategic choices of the six cigarette firms as they act, react, and interact in the hostile environment of the anti-smoking movement. A prospective scenario of industry life under a tobacco accord is then sketched.

Figure 1.2
Growth, Maturity, and Decline in the U.S. Domestic Cigarette Industry, 1930–1995

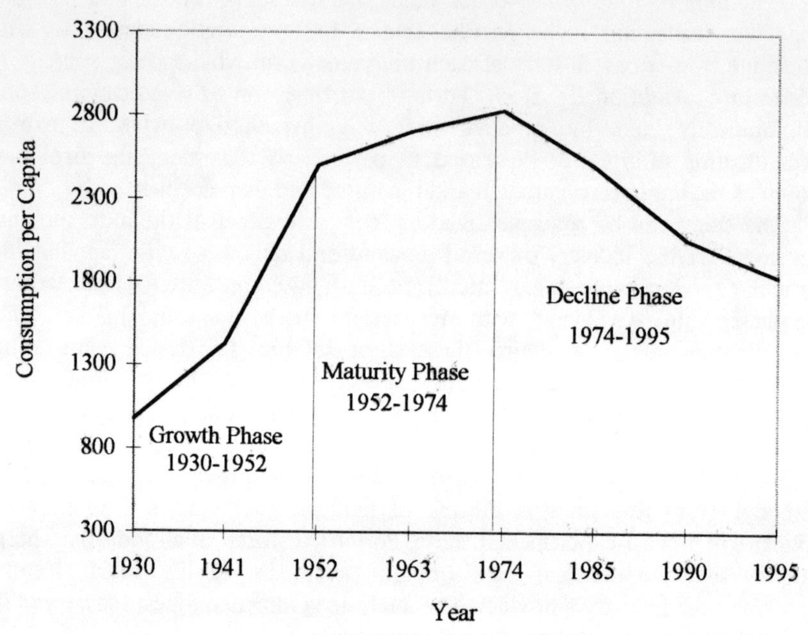

Note: Per capita differs from U.S. Department of Agriculture (USDA) figures, which show data for eighteen-years+ population.
Source: Tax Burden on Tobacco, 1995.

Figure 1.3
Evolution in the Cigarette Industry

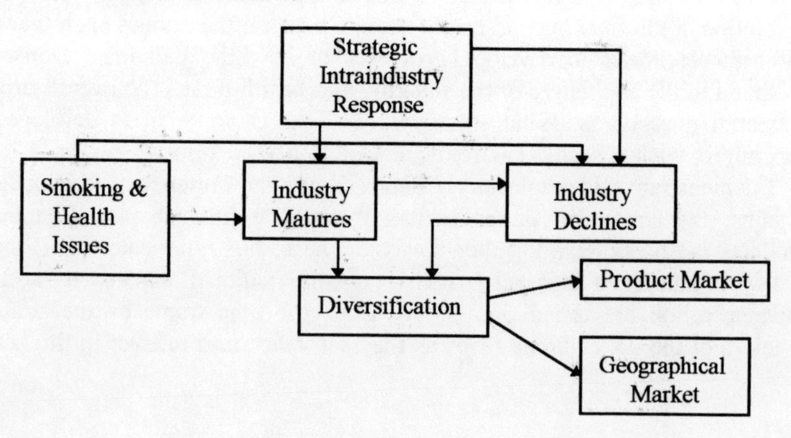

Chapter 2

The Smoking and Health Issue

Public policy developments concerning the cigarette industry have been usefully characterized by Richard McGowan (1988, 1995) as occurring in three waves:

First Wave (1911–1950)	Issue: Industry structure—monopoly/ oligopoly Policy Response: Antitrust suits
Second Wave (1950–1972)	Issue: Health of the smoker Policy Response: Advertising bans, excise taxes
Third Wave (1972–1995)	Issue: Rights of the non-smoker; the cost of the smoker Policy Response: Advertising bans, excise taxes, smoking bans, lawsuits

THE FIRST WAVE: INDUSTRY STRUCTURE—MONOPOLY/OLIGOPOLY, 1911–1950

The modern cigarette industry began with the 1883 invention of a new cigarette-making machine, the Bonsack, which halved production costs while significantly increasing both throughput and quality of the product (A. Chandler, 1977). Utilizing the competitive advantage of an exclusive U.S. lease on the new machine, James B. Duke built a tobacco trust that between 1885 and 1911 dominated the industry completely. So successful was the trust, with an approximate 90% market share, that it was dissolved in 1911 under the provisions of the Sherman Antitrust Act.

For the next twenty years after the breakup of Duke's trust, numerous companies competed in the cigarette industry. By the mid-1930s, however, the number of market competitors had been essentially reduced to six companies: R.J. Reynolds (RJR), Philip Morris, Brown & Williamson (B&W), American, Lorillard, and Liggett & Myers (L&M). The antitrust action had effectively changed the structure of the industry from a monopoly to an oligopoly.

Thirty years from the date of the first trust suit, a second antitrust action was brought by the federal government in 1941. This action charged the major cigarette companies with monopolistic practices in purchasing tobacco leaf and with a trust conspiracy to set retail prices. Although the conviction on these charges was upheld by the Supreme Court in 1946, a lack of any type of effective redress (e.g., another splintering of the industry as followed the 1911 action) left the industry's oligopolistic structure intact. Antitrust actions have played no further role in the cigarette industry; nonetheless, antitrust legislation does act as a deterrent to the acquisition of a smaller cigarette firm by one of the more dominant companies. Therefore, when American Brands sold its U.S. cigarette operations in late 1994, a possible sale to either Philip Morris or R.J. Reynolds was out of the question. Even Brown & Williamson, the acquirer, was required by the Federal Trade Commission (FTC) to divest certain submarket brands when it was deemed that competition could have been negatively impacted. Thus, the chronicler of the early economic history of the cigarette industry, Richard B. Tennant, wrote in 1950 that the essential character of the industry in 1950 was determined in the early decades of the twentieth century.

THE SECOND WAVE: THE HEALTH OF THE SMOKER, 1950–1964

Health concerns about smoking were far from recent. In an often-quoted treatise published in 1604, England's King James I wrote that smoking was "a custom loathsome to the eye, hateful to the nose, harmful to the brain, dangerous to the lungs, and in the black stinking fume thereof nearest resembling the horrible Stigian smoke of the pit that is bottomless" (Dillow, 1981). At the turn of the century in America, anticigarette associations and pressure groups had succeeded in getting anti-smoking legislation on the books in all states except Wyoming and Louisiana. However, by 1927, all states had repealed such laws, and cigarette sales skyrocketed in the 1930s. These early anti-smoking efforts were most concerned with the "moral health" of the smoker. In the 1950s, concerns of a different nature about health and cigarettes arose.

In 1949 and 1950, four scientific reports were published, all of which drew the same conclusion: A relationship existed between smoking habits and the occurrence of lung cancer in males. *Reader's Digest*, long an anti-smoking crusader, in 1952 published an article called "Cancer by the Carton" (Norr, 1952). In 1952, the *British Medical Journal* carried a study of 1,465 lung cancer patients and showed a close correlation between heavy smoking and the disease (U.S. Department of Health and Welfare [USDHW], 1964). At the end of 1952, *Time* magazine indicted cigarettes as a major cause of lung cancer, and in a widely read article in *Reader's Digest* titled "Can the Poisons in Cigarettes Be Avoided?" cigarettes were bluntly accused of shortening the smoker's life (Lieb, 1953). Most significant and far reaching of all was the

1953 Sloan-Kettering Report, which soberly and scientifically confirmed links between lung cancer and cigarette smoking. In the November 1953 issue of *Cancer Research*, Ernest Wynder at the Sloan-Kettering Institute of New York's Memorial Hospital published his findings showing that he had produced a skin cancer in mice by using tobacco tars from a cigarette smoking machine. This concerted and well-publicized campaign to tie cigarette smoking to health issues had an immediate effect. Cigarette sales fell 4.6% from 396.7 billion cigarettes in 1953 to 378.4 billion in 1954; between 1954 and 1955, sales fell another 1% to 376.1 billion. The effects of this drop in sales were, for the most part, immediate and short-lived. In 1956, sales had climbed 3% to 387.3 billion, and by 1957, sales had reached an all-time high of 402.7 billion.

In 1955, the federal government entered the smoking-health controversy for the first time, as the FTC established advertising guidelines for the cigarette industry. Broadly, the guidelines aimed at discouraging cigarette makers from targeting children and minors with their advertisements and from attributing to their products healthful properties. Until the language of these guidelines was strengthened in 1960, the FTC depended on the self-regulation of the industry. In 1957, the U.S. Public Health Service issued a warning against excessive smoking. These events foreshadowed the much greater involvement of the U.S. government in the smoking-health issue and anticipated the landmark 1964 Surgeon General's Report (USDHS, 1964).

However, cigarette consumption was continuing apace, each year setting new sales records despite the increasingly hostile atmosphere surrounding smoking. At the end of 1959, *Business Week*, in its annual cigarette industry survey, declared that the industry's prospects were "the brightest in several years." The cancer scare, while causing occasional ripples in the stock market, seems to have lost its deterrent effect on smoking. Even the release of fresh studies linking smoking to several diseases and degenerative conditions apparently had no effect on cigarette consumption" (*Business Week*, 1959, p. 87). In the absence of any authoritative evidence, and given the number of contradictory reports published in these years, the indifference with which new anti-smoking reports were greeted was not surprising.

The early 1960s saw new strategies developed in the smoking and health arena. In 1962, a number of groups and public officials led a concerted effort to use the information published over the last decade to persuade youths not to begin smoking. New York State issued a pamphlet distributed throughout the school system warning youngsters that cigarette smoking was "a serious health hazard." At the same time, an association of high school teachers approached professional athletes to convince them to stop their endorsement of cigarettes and liquor. Finally, and most damagingly, the president of the National Association of Broadcasters, Leroy Collins, openly criticized television advertising that portrayed smoking in such a way as to make it enticing to youths. In 1963, Collins brought American Tobacco to task for its Lucky Strike ad campaign ("Luckies separates the men from the boys, but not from the girls").

While the above anti-smoking advocates targeted youth, other movements were also afoot. The most far-reaching of these was the announcement in late 1962 that the U.S. surgeon general was assembling a panel of scientists and doctors to produce an authoritative report on the decade-old discussion of health and smoking issues. In anticipation of the 1964 report, other bodies introduced further evidence and action against cigarette smoking. In December 1963, at a meeting of the American Medical Association (AMA), the American Cancer Society (ACS) made public new statistical evidence supporting its previous claims about the link between smoking and cancer. The ACS also launched an advertising anti-smoking campaign aimed at youngsters featuring prominent athletes. Also in 1963, pharmacies in New Jersey voluntarily removed cigarettes from prominent display and discontinued "point-of-sale" promotions.

THE SECOND WAVE: THE HEALTH OF THE SMOKER, 1964–1972

The following year, however, witnessed the significant turning point for the cigarette industry. On January 11, 1964, U.S. Surgeon General Luther L. Terry released the report of the Advisory Committee to the Surgeon General on smoking and health (USDHW, 1964). The 1989 Surgeon General's Report, *Reducing the Health Consequences of Smoking: 25 Years of Progress*, summarizes the contents of that landmark document:

> On the basis of more than 7,000 articles relating to smoking and disease already available at that time in the biomedical literature, the Advisory Committee concluded that cigarette smoking is a cause of lung cancer and laryngeal cancer in men, a probable cause of lung cancer in women, and the most important cause of chronic bronchitis. The Committee stated that "cigarette smoking is a health hazard of sufficient importance in the United States to warrant appropriate remedial action" [although] what would constitute "appropriate remedial action" was left unspecified. (U.S. Department of Health and Human Services [USDHHS], 1989, p. 14)

The immediate reaction to the Surgeon General's Report was less dramatic than the reaction to the Sloan-Kettering Report and other early 1950s anticigarette publicity. Cigarette sales declined only 1.6% from 1963 to 1964 (503 billion cigarettes sold in 1963; 495 billion in 1964). By 1965, sales had climbed again to a record of 517 billion cigarettes, an increase of 4.4%.

However, the 1964 U.S. Surgeon General's Report did have a profound long-term significance on the cigarette industry, the effects of which are still being felt. Most important, the interest of the U.S. surgeon general legitimized later government involvement in the cigarette industry. He heralded the "Second Wave" of government intervention in the cigarette industry that involved the "remedial actions" alluded to in the first Surgeon General's Report. The report allowed/encouraged/demanded the government to take an active role in the regulation of the cigarette industry along health issue lines. But the federal government was never of one mind in its involvement with cigarettes. Congress's initiative in anti-smoking regulation was tempered by the opinions and votes of senators and representatives of tobacco states such as North Carolina, Virginia, and Tennessee. The attempt to reduce the number of smokers also divided the executive branch: The Surgeon General's office, Health, Education, and Welfare (HEW) and the FTC pushed the federal government into taking increasingly extreme anti-smoking positions, while the Departments of Agriculture and Commerce supported the cigarette companies and the tobacco industry in opposing further regulation (McGowan, 1988, 1995). The highlights of this Second Wave were thus largely congressional legislation. In 1964, the FTC Advertising Code was passed and required the following warning label to appear on every package of cigarettes: "Caution: Cigarette smoking may be hazardous to your health." This language was strengthened in 1980, and different warnings were rotated on packages, e.g., "Warning: Cigarette smoke contains carbon monoxide."

In 1967, a series of highly effective anti-smoking TV advertisements were first broadcast, given free air time on television stations around the country due to an ingenious appeal to the Federal Communication Commission's (FCC) "Fairness Doctrine." Previously applied only to political viewpoints, the FCC allowed the request, and so effective were the ads that the industry experienced a 5.7% decline in per capita sales from 1967 to 1970. Indeed, when rumors first spread that Congress was contemplating a ban on television advertising for the cigarette companies, some in the industry saw that as a welcome escape from the anti-smoking propaganda. *Business Week* interviewed an unnamed industry executive admitting, "I'd like to see us legislated out of TV. Then the networks would not be compelled to run these anti-smoking spots—and that would help a great deal" (*Business Week*, 1968, p. 67). Despite remarks such as this and denials about the importance of advertising (our advertising does not attract new smokers; its only value is to switch away those who smoke competing brands), the cigarette companies in 1969 spent $201.8 million on TV advertising alone. The December 1969 congressional decision to ban broadcast—TV and radio—advertising hurt the industry's media plans. The TV/radio ban went into effect on January 1, 1971, and the last week of 1970 saw a flurry of cigarette ads on TV pushing new brands rushed onto the market for the occasion. In the years following the ban, the industry redistributed their advertising dollars to newspapers, magazines, and outdoor and transit ads.

INDUSTRY REACTION TO THE SECOND WAVE

The involvement of the U.S. government gave the industry a focal point for its activities, especially the industry's Tobacco Institute, an already established lobby organization. Between its founding in 1958 and the release of the first Surgeon General's Report, the Tobacco Institute had emphasized the inconclusiveness of the evidence linking smoking to cancer or other ailments. Despite growing statistical evidence, the industry emphasized the clinical lack of cause and effect. The Institute's first challenge was the FTC's attempt to introduce its health warning labeling rule. In political tactics that would be duplicated over the coming years, the Tobacco Institute, headed by former Senator Earle G. Clements, side stepped the health issue altogether (Kluger, 1996). Rather, "the strategy of the tobacco men was to question Federal Trade authority to make policy involving a cigarette health warning" (Fritschler, 1975, p. 54).

Turning the industry-specific issue of cigarette package labeling into a constitutional issue in which the FTC's attempt to make policy threatened the democratic form of government was imaginative (Miles, 1982). In the end, however, the Tobacco Institute encouraged its industry benefactors to accept health warning labels in exchange for "unfettered media advertising and a prohibition against states developing their own health warnings" (Miles, 1982, p. 70). Nonetheless, the strategy of enlarging an industry-specific issue to a pan-business issue had been established and was next applied to the congressional ban on cigarette broadcast advertising. Arguing that the abridgment of the cigarette companies' freedom of commercial speech threatened to erode the Constitution, lawyers for the industry took their case to the U.S. Supreme Court, where in 1972 the ban was upheld as constitutional. In fact, the effects of the advertising ban have been uncertain. The rationale behind the ban was that cigarette advertising successfully attracted new smokers, and thus, if advertising were banned, then cigarette sales would ultimately drop (McGowan, 1988, 1995). The continued increase in absolute sales of cigarettes after 1971 has led some (e. g., Blum, 1986) to argue that the ban indeed had the opposite effect of what was intended and that sales increased because the ban on broadcast cigarette advertising also brought an end to the Fairness Doctrine—supported anti-smoking ads. This argument is, however, complicated because although absolute sales did increase after the ban, adult per capita sales continued to fall.

THE THIRD WAVE: THE RIGHTS OF THE NON-SMOKER, THE COST OF THE SMOKER, 1972–1995

In addition to the Supreme Court's upholding of the broadcast ban, the early 1970s witnessed further events troubling for the industry. The Second Surgeon General's Report, released in 1972, stated that breathing other people's smoke is dangerous to the non-smoker's health. The environmental tobacco smoke (ETS) issue would resurface anew after 1984 and has proved one of the most damaging issues to the tobacco industry. The Second Surgeon General's Report also declared that low-tar cigarettes were not as dangerous as full-tar brands, driving up sales of cigarettes with 15 milligrams of tar or less. Also in 1972, health warnings were made mandatory in all cigarette advertising. In addition, a health-oriented excise tax was proposed in Congress in 1972, but the bill was defeated. Finally, in 1972, all airline companies volunteered to establish no-smoking sections on their flights. This move followed the Interstate Commerce Commission's (ICC) 1971 banning of smoking on all interstate buses excepting the last five rows. In 1973, the airlines' voluntary actions were formalized into regulation by the Civil Aeronautics Board (CAB).

More problematic for the cigarette industry was Arizona's 1973 decision to ban smoking in public places. It was the first state to do so. By 1974, twenty-seven states had passed similar laws. And by 1976, forty-eight states had introduced 423 pieces of legislation regulating cigarette smoking in public places (Miles, 1982). This wave of legislation was a direct response to the Second Surgeon General's Report discussing the dangers of ambient smoke, or ETS. A second wave of public policy activism on the "sidestream" smoking issue followed in the late 1980s. By 1989, forty-one states had passed laws that restricted smoking in public places, and a 1988 New York City law restricted smoking in restaurants, stores, theaters, hospitals, museums, and "virtually all other public places" (Quimpo, 1990). At least 400 municipalities had enacted laws that restricted smoking in the workplace (Rosewicz & Karr, 1990).

Private firms felt that they could realize savings in health, absenteeism, and lost productivity by their enforcement of a smoking ban in the workplace. Because of potential compensation claims, the USG company, an insulation and tile manufacturer, has banned smoking both on and off the job. The firm believes that smoking compounds the likelihood of lung cancer, a claim to which they were already vulnerable because of the mineral fiber nature of their products (*New York Times*, 1988). A survey of private and government employers conducted by the Administrative Management Society in 1990 showed that 68% of U.S. employers had some type of restrictive smoking policy, while 38% banned smoking entirely (Quimpo, 1990). This public and private activism spurred the federal government into further action. Prompted by a 1993 Environmental Protection Agency (EPA) report classifying ETS as a Class A carcinogen, the Occupational Safety and Health Administration (OSHA) has proposed an overall ban on indoor smoking in the workplace with minor exceptions. The industry has responded with lawsuits challenging both the EPA's finding and the proposed OSHA ban. In 1996, the FDA, claiming jurisdiction over cigarettes as a drug delivery system, promulgated regulations affecting the sale of cigarettes to minors, vending machine sales, and advertising. The industry has filed suit stating that the FDA has no power of regulation and, furthermore, that advertising restrictions violate their First Amendment rights. A federal court found that the FDA had the power to regulate, but not to restrict, advertising. The suit is being appealed by both parties. Cynics feel that if the regulation is successful, people will continue to smoke and that expenditures formerly spent on advertising will fall to the bottom line.

REVIEW

Reviewing the past 25 years of anti-smoking activism, C. Everett Koop, U.S. Surgeon General from 1981 to 1989, stated in the preface to his 1989 report, "These developments have changed the way in which our society views smoking. In the 1940s and 1950s, smoking was chic; now, increasingly, it is shunned... The ashtray is following the spittoon into oblivion" (USDHHS, 1989). Broadly, this hostile environment toward the cigarette industry created since the early 1950s has had four basic components: First are restrictions on advertising and promotion, beginning in 1955 with the FTC's first guidelines on cigarette advertising, continuing through the passage of the Federal Cigarette Labeling and Advertising Act of 1965, resulting in the Public Health Cigarette Smoking Act of 1969, which banned cigarette advertising from broadcast media. Recent developments on this front have been the public outcry about the use of target advertising of minorities and women on billboards and in specialty magazines and the 1990s controversy about the appeal to children of RJR's cartoon camel mascot for its Camel brand cigarettes and B&W's Kool brand penguin mascot (Lipman, 1991; Brody, 1990). *New York Times* Health Correspondent and Harvard School of Public Health Fellow Philip J. Hilts (1996) has stated that the Joe Camel campaign to attract young smokers was carried out "with a style and ferocity unmatched in tobacco marketing history."

Second are restrictions on smoking in public places beginning with the ICC ban on smoking in all interstate buses in 1971, continuing with Arizona's 1974 ban on smoking in public buildings, and continuing up through New York City's 1988 sweeping legislation. The growth of the ETS issue since 1985, especially as taken up by the U.S. Surgeon General's Office and the EPA, has intensified efforts to ban smoking in public places as well as in private workplaces. Following the 1972 Surgeon General's Report detailing the dangers of "secondhand smoke," some companies voluntarily banned smoking in their offices. Companies have felt that by eliminating smoking from the workplace, they are both protecting their employees from ETS as well as realizing savings in health, absenteeism, and lost productivity. The evidence has been growing about the harmfulness of ETS. In May 1991, the EPA released a report that concluded that secondhand cigarette smoke kills 53,000 non-smokers a year. In 1993, the EPA classified ETS as a carcinogen.

OSHA has recommended that all employers "ban smoking in the workplace, offer classes to help workers stop smoking and offer incentives to encourage them to stop." The FDA has declared jurisdiction over the cigarette industry and has proposed restrictions on advertising and vending machine sales. The industry has instituted legal proceedings against these actions. Anti-smoking grassroots organizations like ASH (Action on Smoking and Health) and GASP (Group against Smoking Pollution) have emerged as active participants working with government on the ETS issue.

Third, both the federal government and nearly every state (the tobacco-growing states of Kentucky, North Carolina, South Carolina, and Virginia being obvious exceptions) have used taxes to make smoking financially unattractive. At the same time, states and the federal government have realized significant revenues from the sale of cigarettes and their ever-increasing "sin" taxes. In 1980, federal and state governments collected $6.3 billion in cigarette taxes; by 1995, their combined tax revenue reached $12.9 billion. Of course, the danger of these tactics is that the federal and state governments are cutting off their own revenues even as they collect higher and higher amounts of cigarette taxes.

Finally, the fourth component of the hostile, anti-smoking environment has been the lawsuits filed against cigarette makers for health complications brought about by cigarette smoking. Over 300 suits of this nature have been filed cumulatively between 1950 and 1988, when the late Rose Cipollone was awarded $400,000 in damages by a federal jury. The industry had never lost a case previously. The high cost of the trial for the plaintiff—$3 million—put a worried industry at ease, as did the 1990 reversal of the decision handed down by the U.S. Court of Appeals for the Third Circuit. Such decisions favorable to the industry had reduced the number of cases pending in the industry from a peak of 157 in 1986 to a total of 53 in the fall of 1990 (Crovitz, 1992).

On June 24, 1992, the U.S. Supreme Court ruled, in the Cipollone case, that the 1965 Federal Cigarette Labelling and Advertising Act did not preempt damage suits based on common-law actions like fraud; that is, if the tobacco industry "deceived" smokers about the danger of smoking, preemption by federal regulation would not protect them, otherwise, it would do so. The assumption of risk by the smoker is a strong defense versus any post-1965 plaintiff. Absent an ability to prove fraud by the industry with respect to the health issue, the case-by-case nature and expense of lawsuits are not extremely prejudicial to the industry. Securities analysts have calculated that Philip Morris's after-tax income would be reduced by only 6% if it were to lose 1,000 lawsuits at $750,000 in damages per lawsuit (Collins, 1996).

However, the lawsuit horizon is far from clear for the cigarette manufacturers. Even though the Supreme Court decision in the Cipollone case was a victory, it signaled that fraud was a potentially fruitful avenue of attack. The Justice Department has since launched a criminal probe against the industry. It is a attempting to prove that the firms deliberately withheld or falsified information given to Congress and/or federal agencies or in their advertisements vis-à-vis their knowledge of nicotine addiction and ETS health risks. Discovery procedures, leaks of internal industry documents, and whistle blowers have unveiled an unprecedented opportunity to view the private internal workings of the industry's firms. Activist University of California Professor Stanton A. Glantz, who himself received several thousand unsolicited documents from a Brown & Williamson source, has likened the situation to that of the Pentagon Papers—that is, the public has been given the opportunity to see the secret knowledge, doubts, and workings of the industry in this smoking and health war. This information has been made generally available through both print and Internet media. Successful asbestos plaintiff lawyer Norwood Wilner utilized such B&W information in obtaining his $750,000 judgment against B&W in mid-1996. The Florida judgment has been appealed. Meanwhile, Wilner, by himself, now has over 200 cases pending—a far cry from the 1990 industry figure of 53 such suits. Yet these are single-plaintiff cases.

By mid-1997, at least forty states, with more sure to follow, had filed class action suits to recoup the health care costs paid by the state because of smoking-related illness and diseases. Class action suits frightened securities analysts because such suits play against the industry's ability to wear individual plaintiffs down financially. It was with relief, then, that analysts greeted the appeals court decertification of the Castano case class action, where sixty of the major plaintiff law firms had banded together financially and otherwise to sue for all American smokers who claim to be addicted to nicotine. It was with trepidation that these same analysts viewed the December 1996 action by a Florida judge to allow a charge of racketeering to be entered into the class action Medicaid case brought under a 1994 Florida statute that permits statistical proof of the harm caused by smoking and disallows the assumption of risk defense. Although the analysts' concerns are mitigated by the statute's applicability to only post-1994 damages, the concerns are enhanced by the allowance of treble damages in a successful racketeering charge.

To date, the socialization process has created more effect on the demand side of the smoking issue than either regulations or lawsuits have had on the supply side. However, a slow socialization process of potential jurors has commenced. The state of New Jersey's Medicaid suit contains a RICO action (the New Jersey Racketeer Influenced and Corrupt Organizations Act) alleging that the industry constituted an enterprise whose purpose was to enhance sales through fraudulent claims—e.g., the firms actually knew smoking was harmful and addictive. The effect of "the cigarette firms lied" feeling begins to combat the traditional feeling of jurors that smokers knew what they were doing and that they should not get rich from their own mistakes. Adding to the potential change in the logic of future juries are mounting health and moral responsibility issues against the cigarette industry: (1) the surgeon general has declared that nicotine is a drug; (2) the FDA has declared that smoking is a childhood disease; (3) a child cannot make an informed adult decision; (4) the FDA and surgeon general both point out that individuals commence smoking in their teens when they cannot make an informed decision (especially in light of possible fraud by firms hiding their knowledge concerning potential harm and addiction); and (5) by the time an individual can make an informed decision, that person has likely become addicted. Thus, a future plaintiff can be portrayed as a victim rather than as a fortune hunter. Such framing by plaintiffs' lawyers will occur and absent an effective counterargument, it could be decisive with future jurors.

THE EFFECTS OF THE THREE WAVES

The above narrative provided a context for various aspects of the anti-smoking movement. Next follows a discussion of the effects this movement has had on the industry.

Tax Effect

As shown in Figure 2.1, total federal and state tax collections from cigarette sales increased from $1.66 billion in 1950 to $12.9 billion in 1995. Beginning in 1970, the states' portion of tax collection surpassed that of the federal government. This is seen more clearly in Figure 2.2, where we see federal, selected states, and a fifty-one state average tax rate from 1950 to 1995. Michigan's rate was 3.1 times that of the federal government's whereas North Carolina's was less than one-fourth.

Figure 2.3 shows a microview of the tax policies in four states: California, a traditional trend-setting state; Michigan, a rustbelt representative; North Carolina, a leading tobacco producer; and Connecticut, a Boston/Washington representative. Percentage increase, from 1970 to 1995, varied from 582% for Michigan to 150% (from $.02 to $.05) for North Carolina. If California, Michigan, and Connecticut are trend states, the all-state 1995 average of $.567 per pack will continue to grow. The industry points out the tax rates outpace the consumer price index and place a regressive burden on smokers. This is especially pertinent when we see the effect that the anti-smoking campaign has had on industry customers.

Figure 2.1
Federal and State Tax Collection, 1950–1995

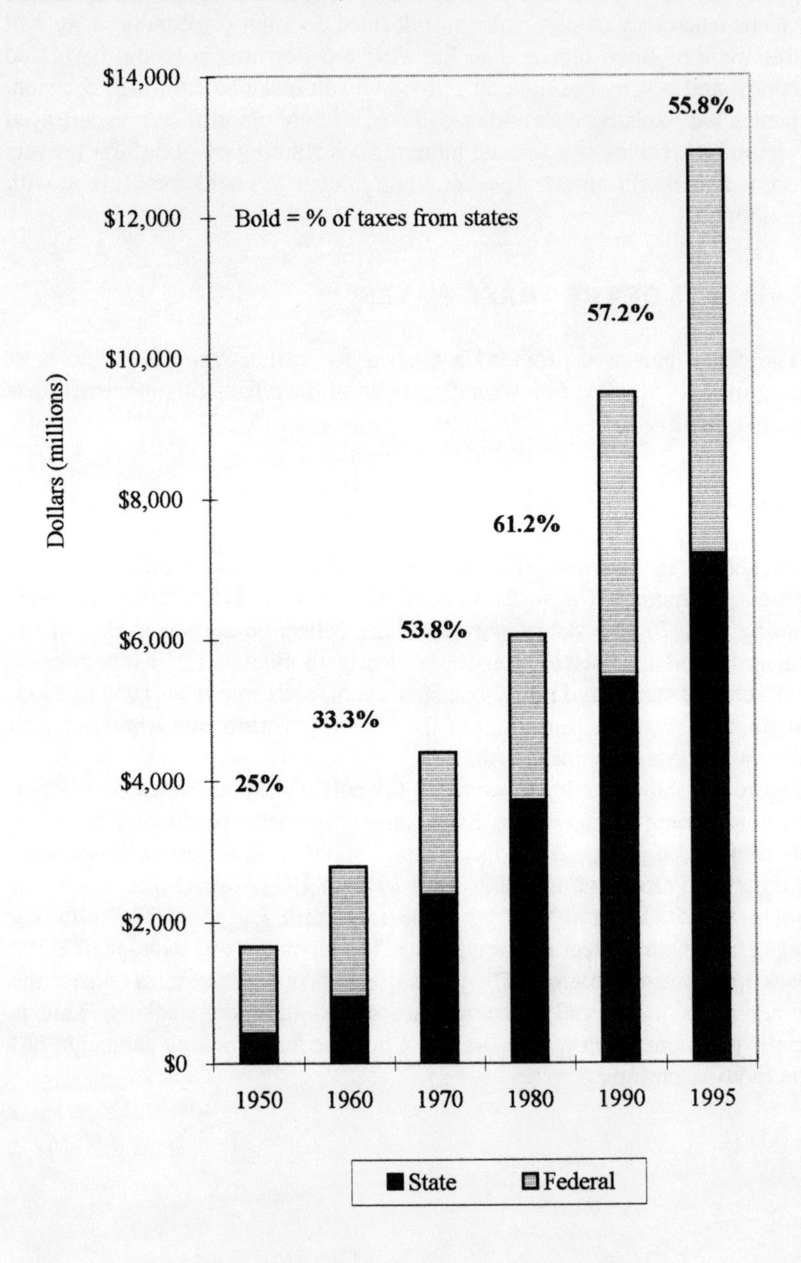

Source: Tax Burden on Tobacco, 1995.

Figure 2.2
Tax Rate per Package, 1950–1995

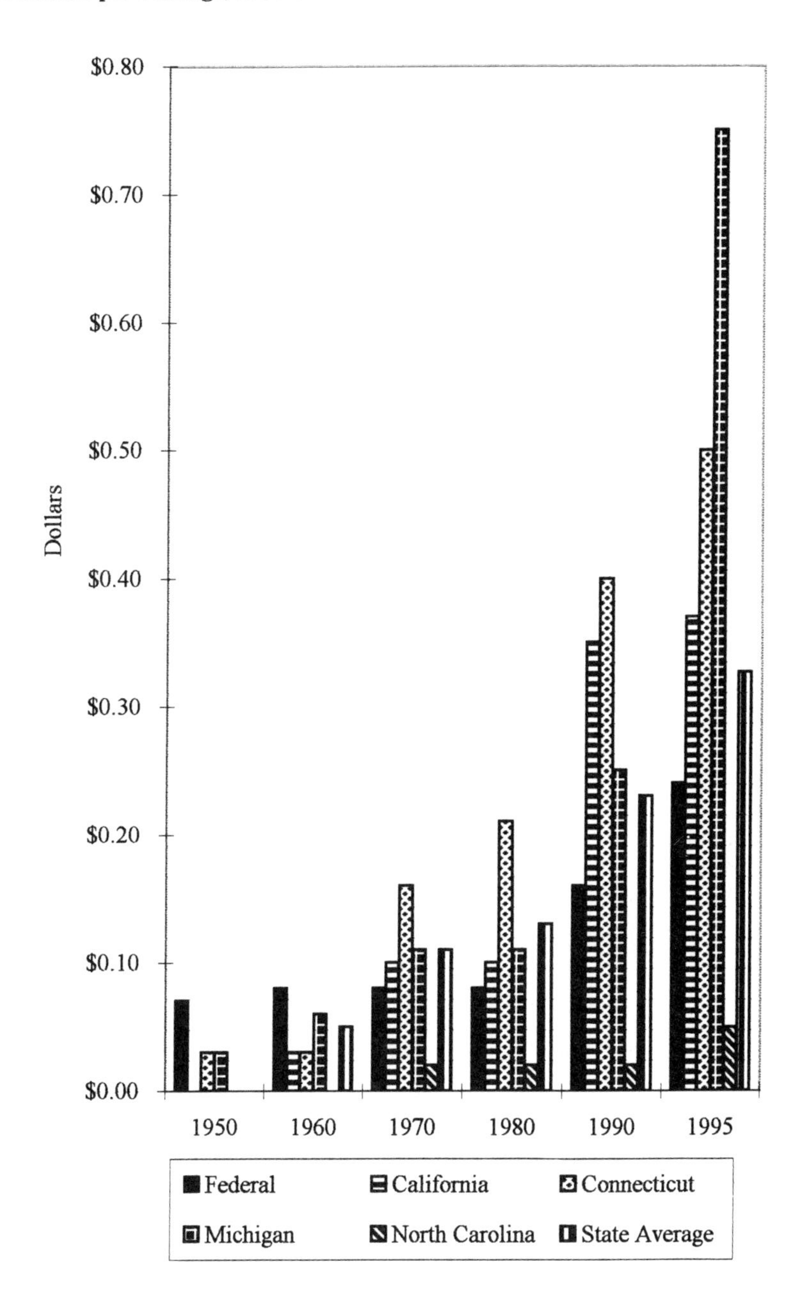

Source: Tax Burden on Tobacco, 1995.

Figure 2.3
Combined Federal and State Cigarette Taxes per Package in Four States, 1970, 1980, 1990, and 1995

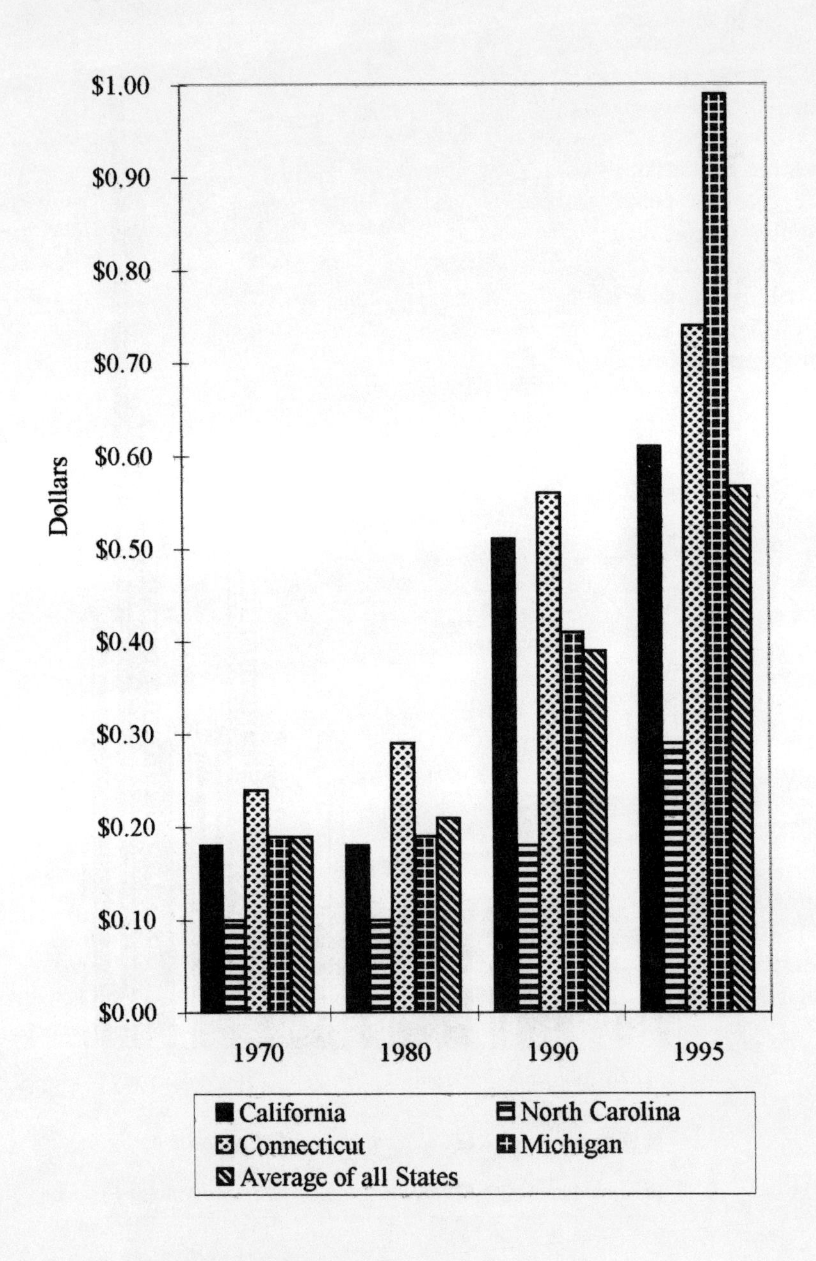

Source: Tax Burden on Tobacco, 1995.

Demographic Effect

The effect of the concerted information campaign to publicize the dangers of smoking is clearly seen in Figures 2.4 and 2.5. The number of former smokers by age group has dramatically increased over a twenty-eight year span. The increase in former smokers aged forty-five and over is particularly dramatic. Both sexes enhanced the ranks of former smokers over the 1965 to 1993 time frame. The higher percentage for females must be discounted somewhat because of its lower base, as shown in Figure 2.9.

Figure 2.6 clearly indicates a more precise demographic shift among cigarette smokers. For both males and females, fewer smokers are found in those households with income of $30,000 or more. Similarly, Figure 2.7 shows that the percentage of college graduates who smoked was halved between 1966 and 1987, while the percentage of those smokers with less than a high school degree essentially remained the same over the same time period.

Figure 2.8 points this out with its dramatic lower ratios (14% for males; 10% for females) of smokers in 1994 for those people who have completed 16 or more years of education. Figure 2.9 reveals further demographic shifts. It shows for 1988 a higher proportion of smokers among the black population-both male and female—than among the white population. This was a reversal from 1965. However, in 1993 and continuing for 1994, white female smokers had surpassed black female smokers. Figure 2.10 shows that whites—both men and women—are more likely to be former smokers than blacks.

It is apparent from these statistics that the anti-smoking campaign has had uneven results. The 1989 Surgeon General's report concluded as much. It noted that despite the social revolution which has occurred since the 1964 Surgeon General's report "the prevalence of smoking remains higher among blacks, blue-collar workers, and less educated persons than in the overall population. The decline in smoking has been substantially slower among women than among men" (USDHHS, 1989). While the data since then shows an improvement with respect to gender, all other aspects of the 1989 report have held true. In effect, a set of demographics has been enforced on the industry, i.e., the anti-smoking movement has limited the industry's market to a demographic segment that is not particularly attractive (financially speaking) relative to the population as a whole.

Figure 2.4
Former Smokers by Age, 1965–1993

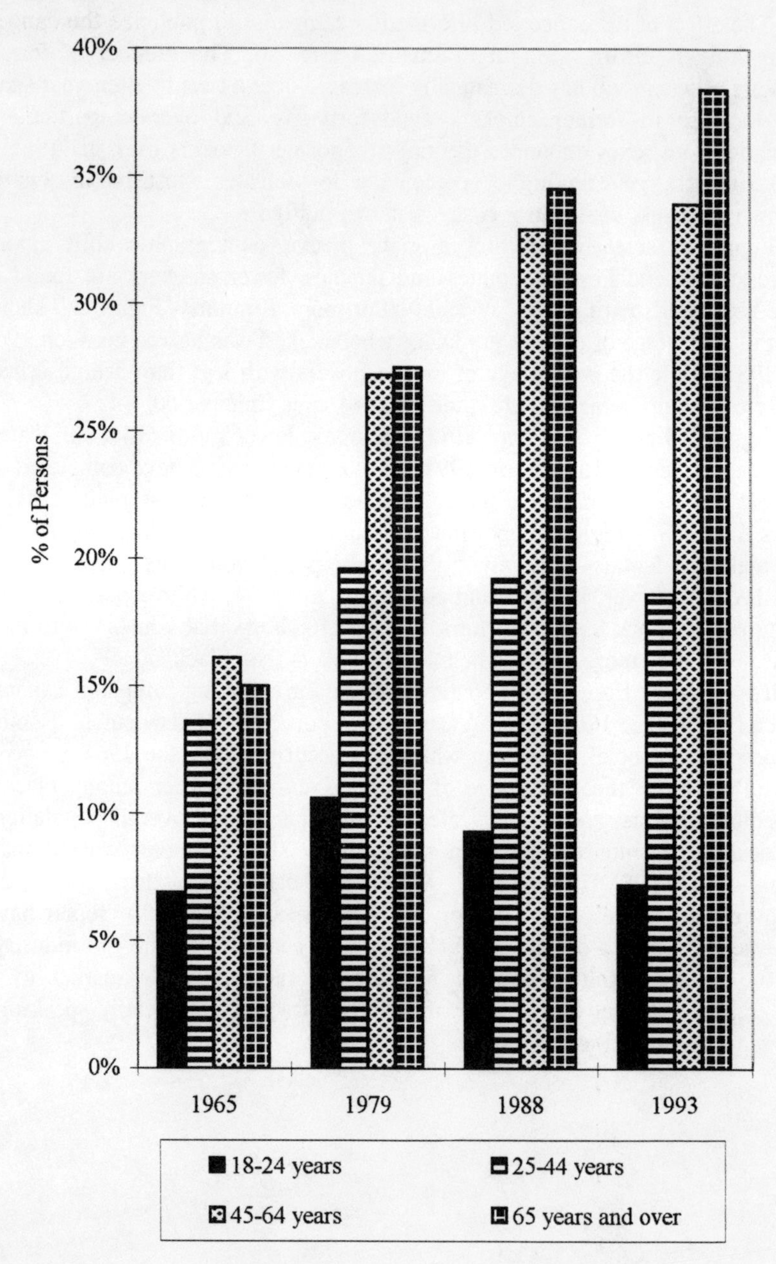

Source: National Center for Health Statistics, 1996.

Figure 2.5
Former Smokers by Sex, 1965–1993

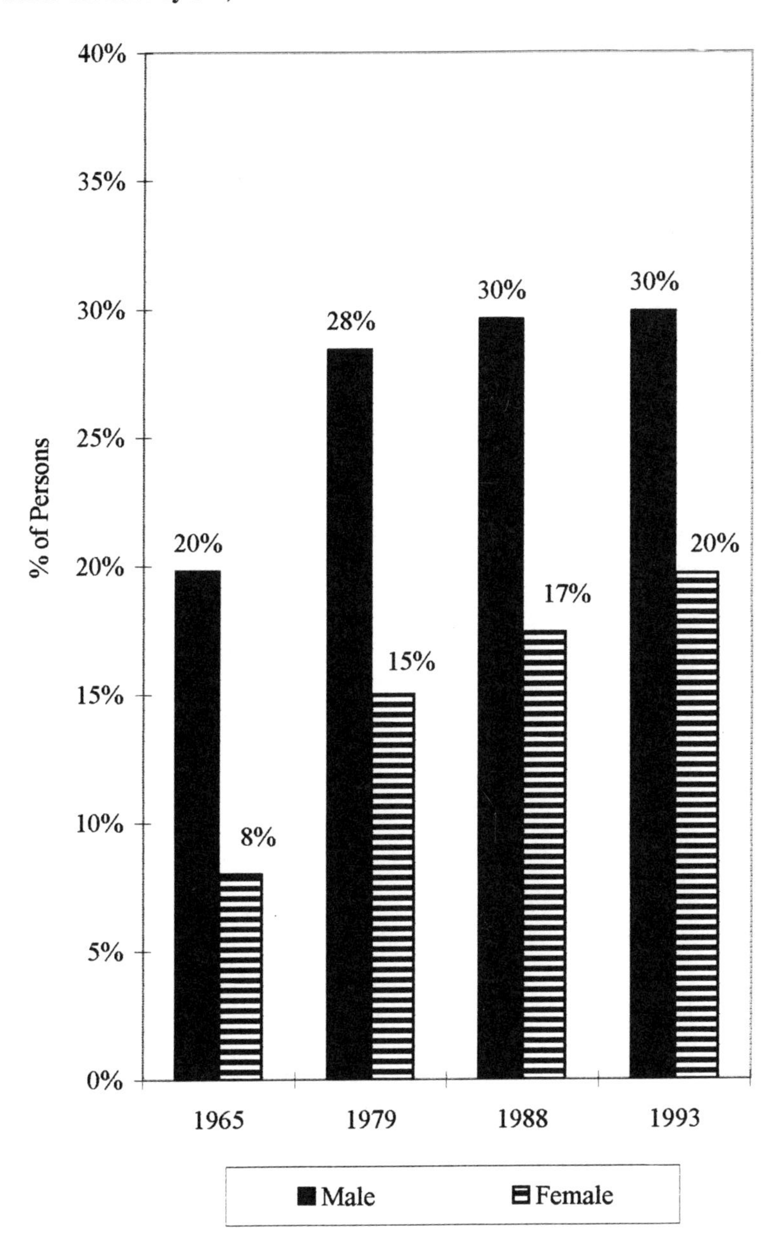

Source: National Center for Health Statistics, 1996.

Figure 2.6
Demographics of Smoking—Household Income, 1986

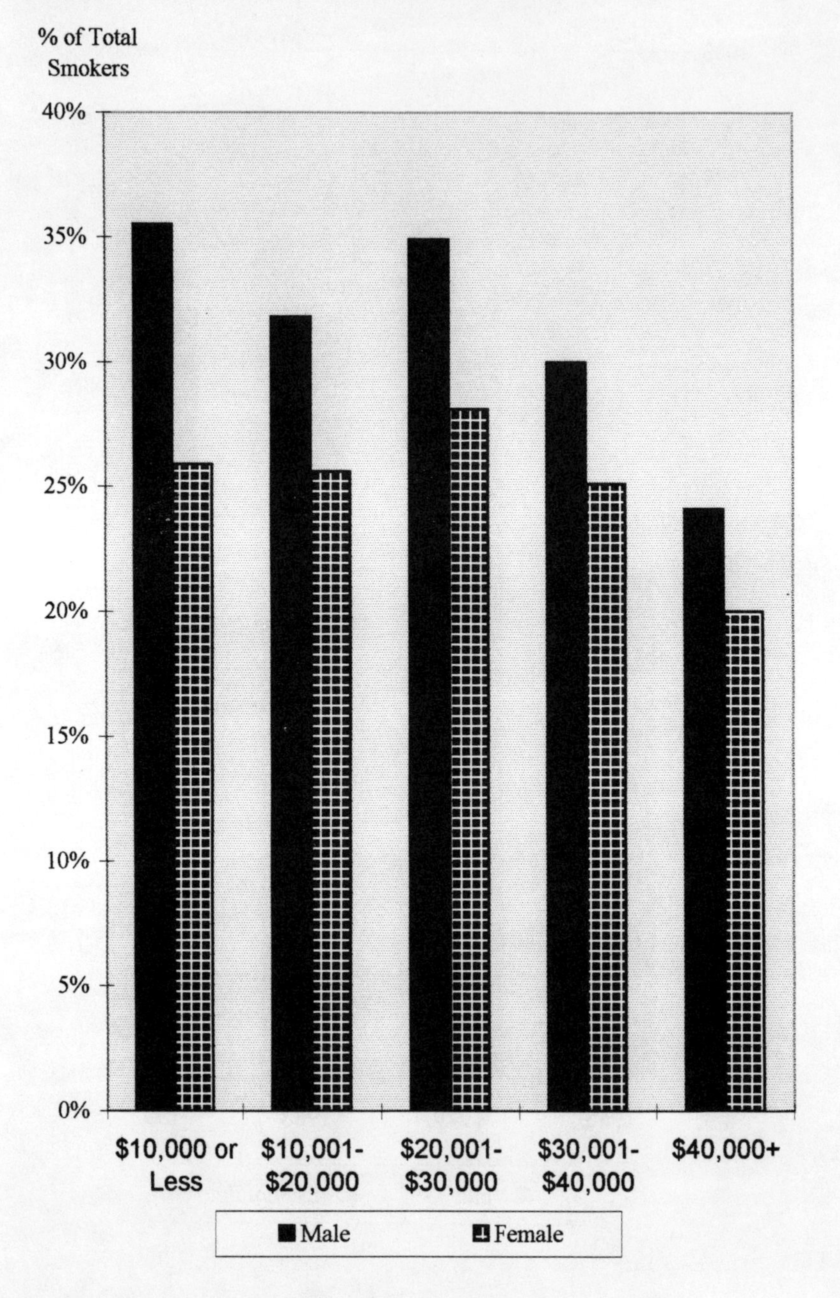

Source: National Center for Health Statistics, 1996.

Figure 2.7
Demographics of Smoking—Education, 1966–1994

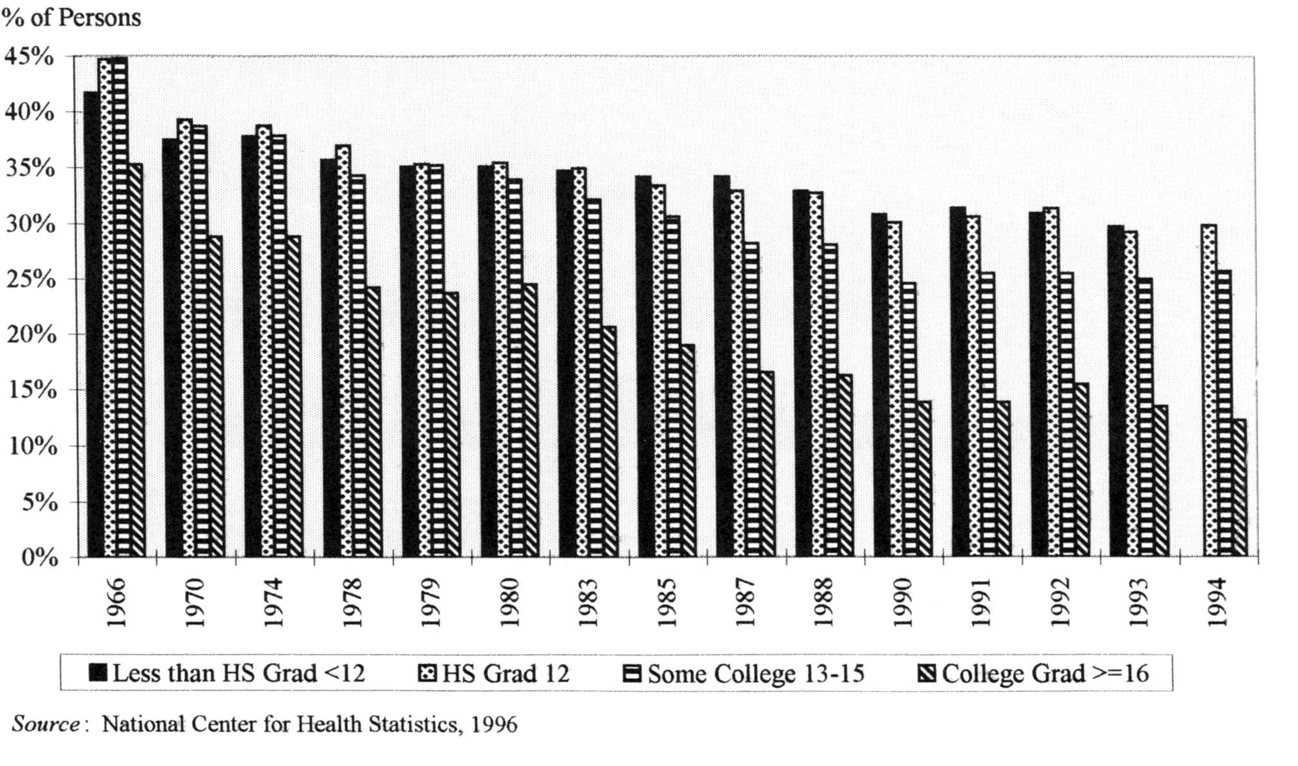

Source: National Center for Health Statistics, 1996

Figure 2.8
Demographics of Smoking—Education, 1994

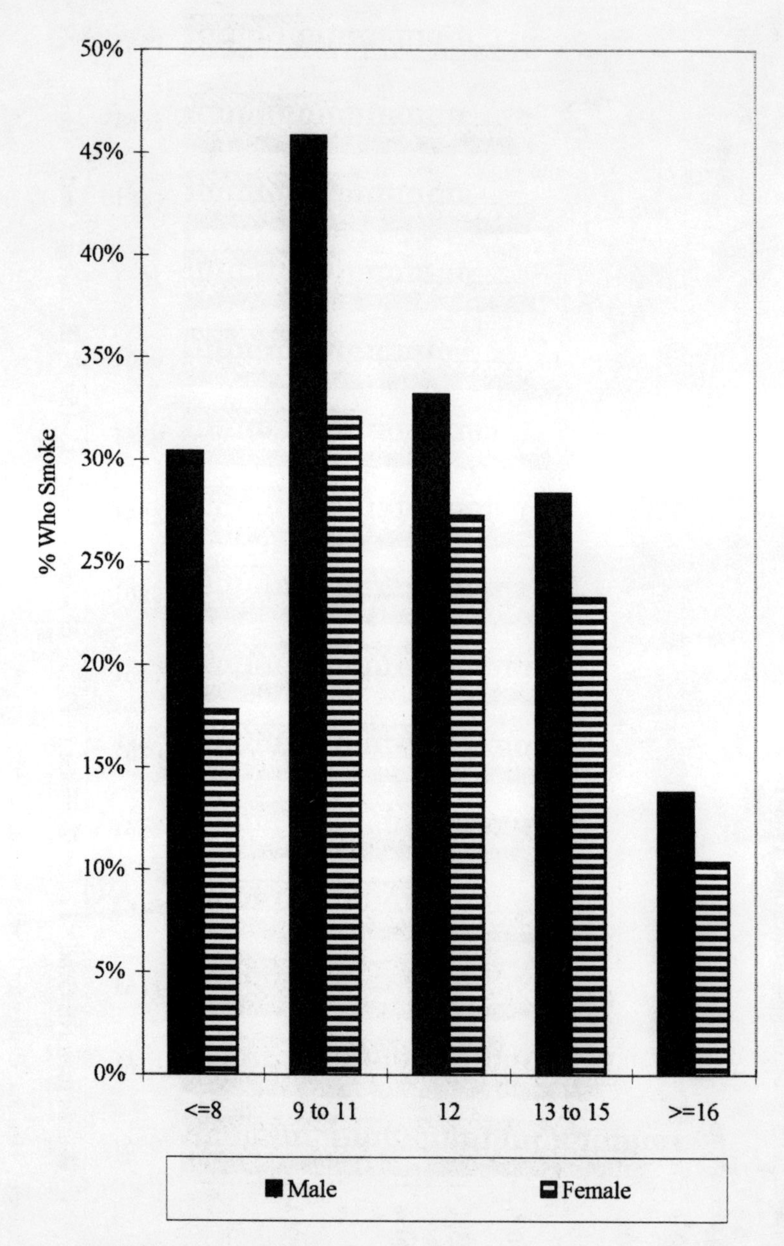

Source: National Center for Health Statistics, 1996.

Figure 2.9
Current Smokers by Race and Gender, 1965–1994

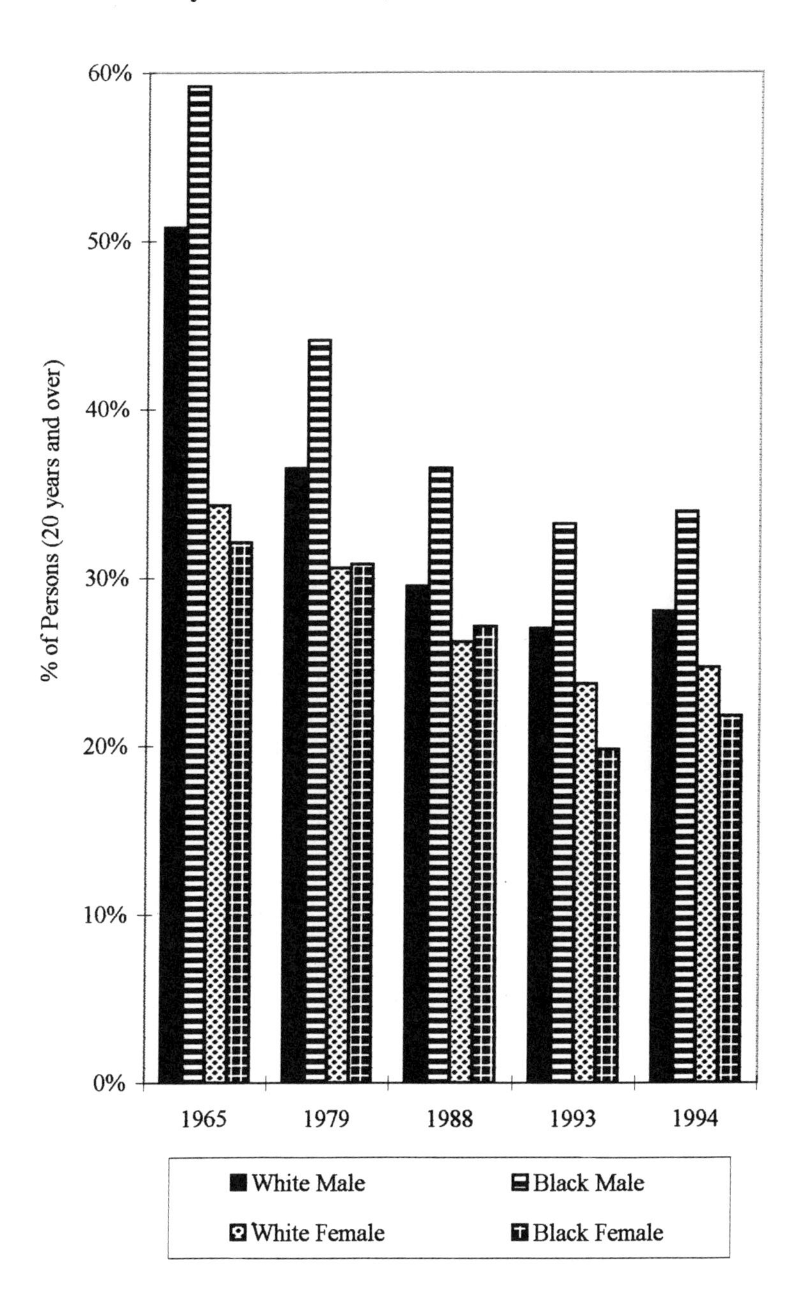

Source: National Center for Health Statistics, 1996.

Figure 2.10
Former Smokers by Race and Gender, 1965–1993

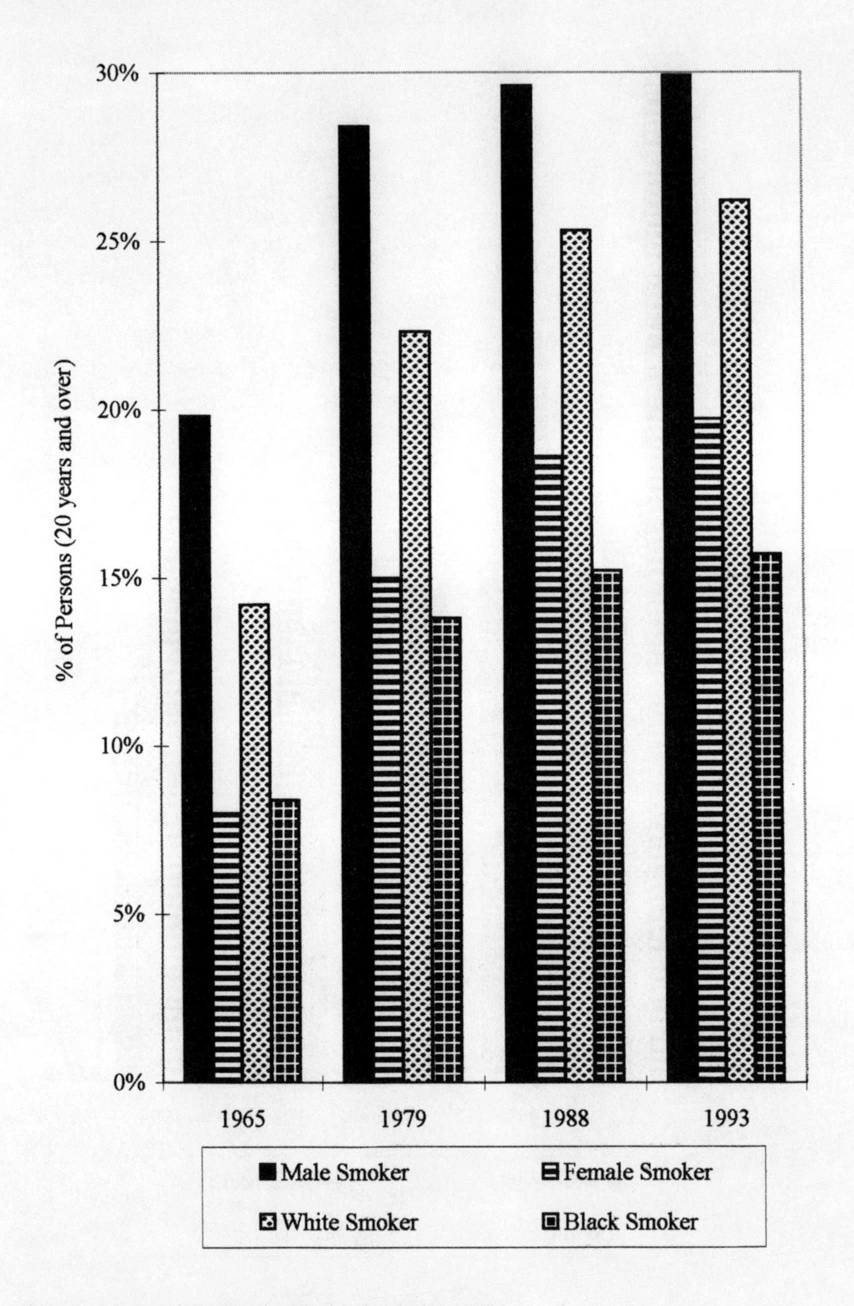

Source: National Center for Health Statistics, 1996.

EFFECT ON CIGARETTE ADVERTISING

Figures 2.11, 2.12 and 2.13 show the distribution of advertising over years 1970 to 1993. The effect of the TV/Radio ban is obvious. The total outlays are staggering—$6 billion expended in 1993, a seventeen-fold increase over the 1970 figure when TV/Radio advertisements were still allowed.

Figure 2.14 gives a micro-picture of particular advertising tactics, that of sponsoring sport and music events and of couponing. Lacking access to the mass media, the industry has had to contrive means to get its brand names in front of the public. The industry's expenditures on this indirect advertising have grown from $500,000 in 1970 to $125 mm in 1990. Its decrease over the next three years has been more than overshadowed by the increase in couponing and discounting (retail value added). This type of increased expenditure, which was over $2.5 billion in 1993 demonstrates the industry's awareness of the demographic shift towards a low-income smoking population.

Figure 2.11
Distribution of Cigarette Advertising Expenditures, 1970–1977

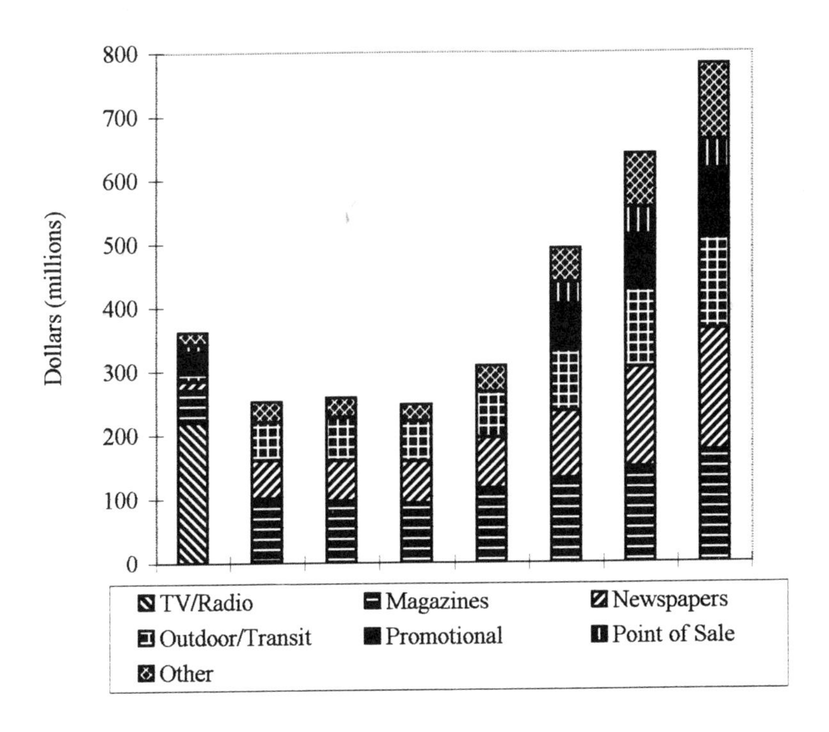

Source: FTC Report to Congress for 1993.

Figure 2.12
Distribution of Cigarette Advertising Expenditures, 1978–1985

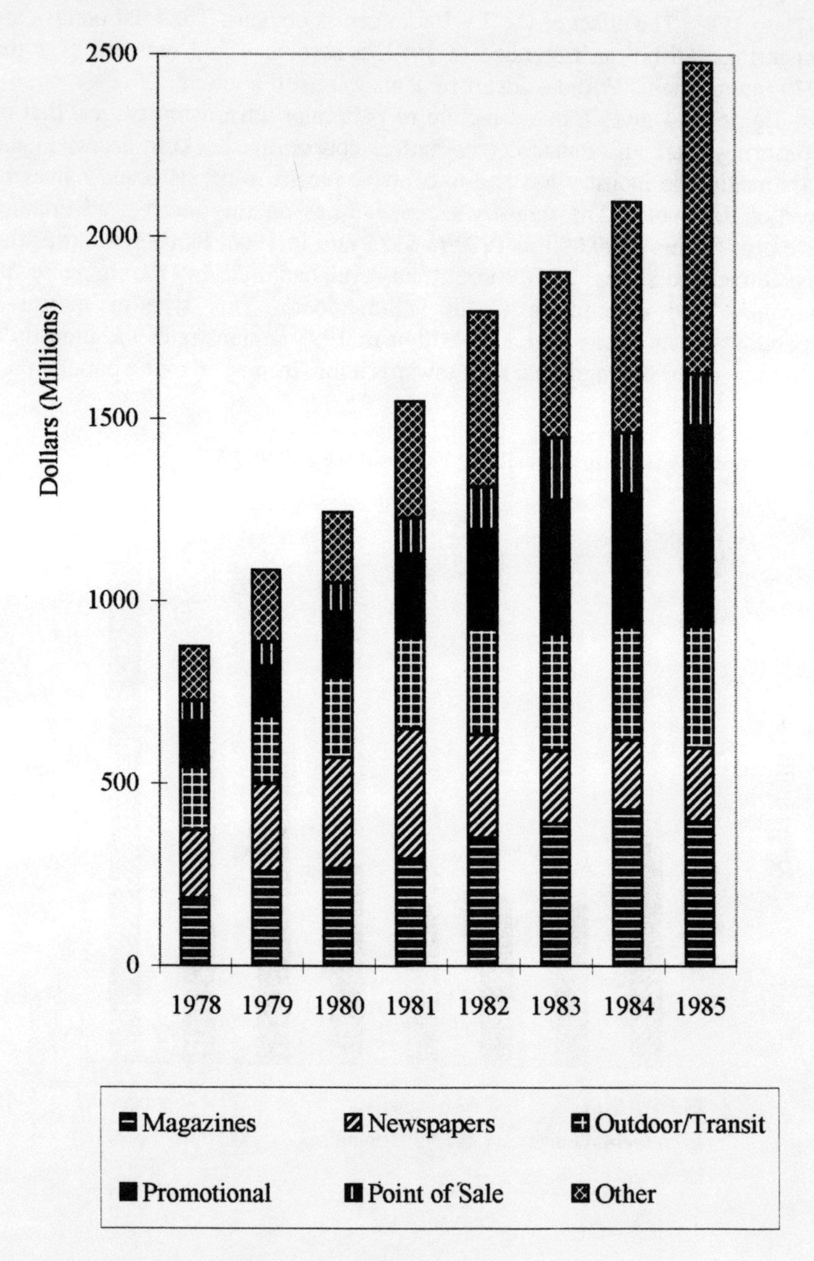

Source: FTC Report to Congress for 1993.

Figure 2.13
Distribution of Cigarette Advertising Expenditures, 1986–1993

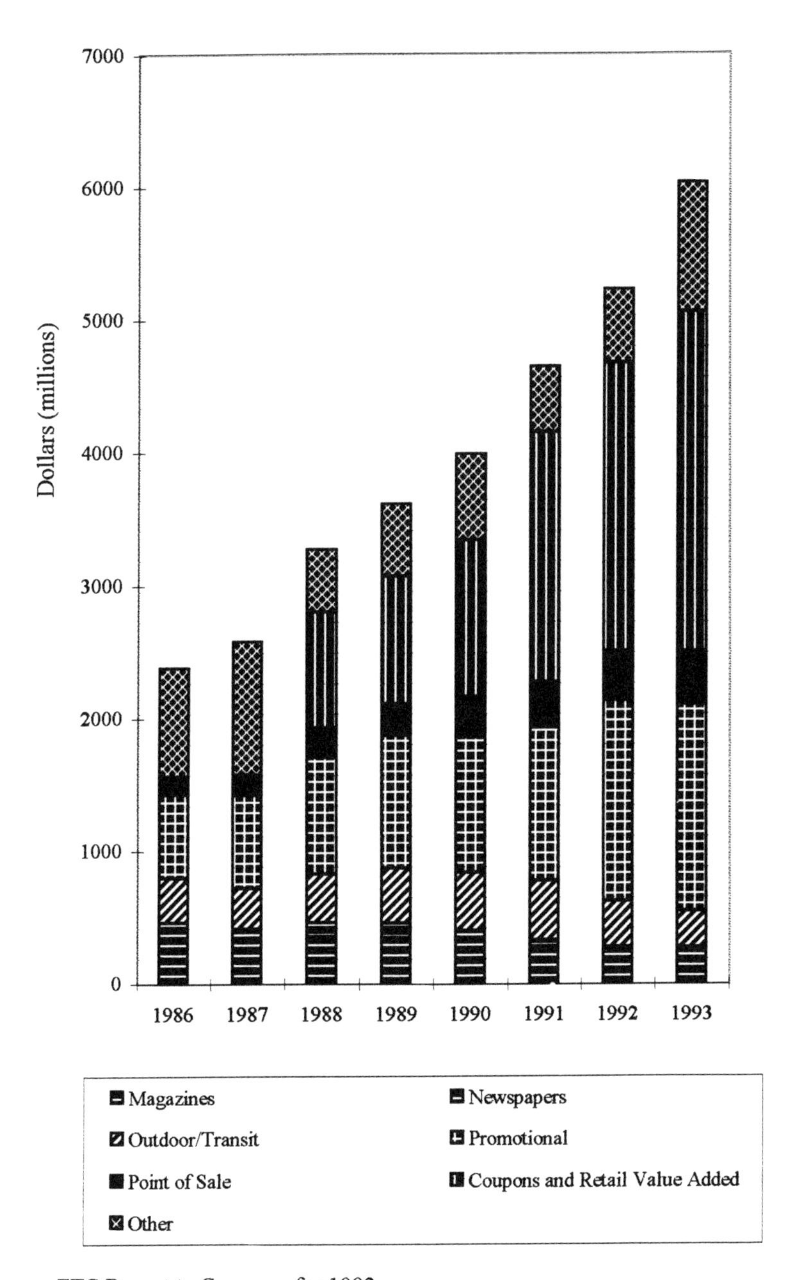

Source: FTC Report to Congress for 1993.

Figure 2.14
Cigarette Industry Expenditures on Public Entertainment and Coupons, 1970–1993

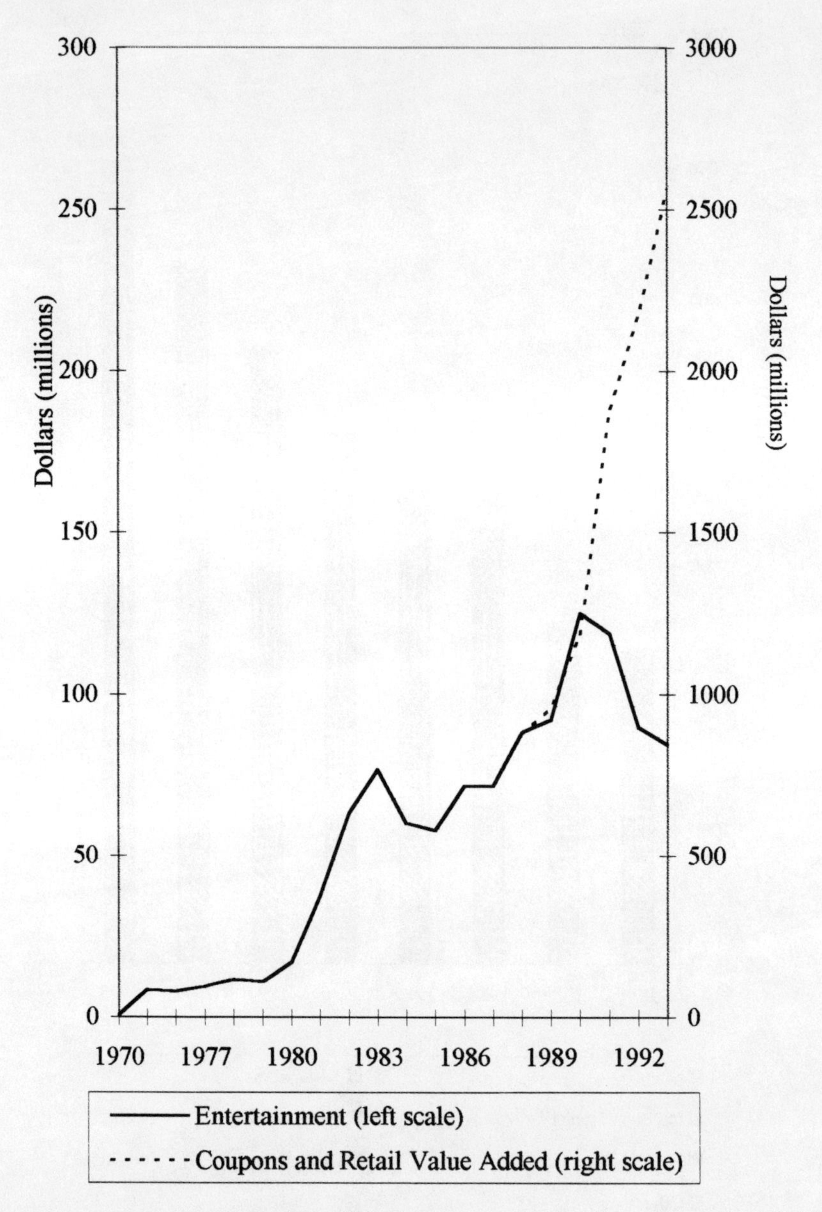

Note: Entertainment is primarily sporting and music events.
Source: FTC Report to Congress for 1993.

EFFECT ON OVERALL CONSUMPTION

The effect of the anti-smoking movement on the consumption of cigarettes in the U.S. market is shown on overall basis in Figure 2.15 and on a per capita basis in Figure 2.16. Gross consumption peaked in 1981 whereas per capita consumption hit its high in 1963. The rate of decrease both in overall and per capita consumption has slowed in the 1990s, with a slight uptick in 1995. On a longitudinal basis, however, the anti-smoking movement has clearly been successful. Not only has the prevalence and per capita consumption been drastically reduced over the past forty-five years, but the ethos of smoking has changed for the vast majority of Americans. In 1985, an individual, upon entering a restaurant, would have asked doubtfully whether there was a smoke-free area. In 1995, an individual would now be asking doubtfully and sheepishly if there was a smoking area. The socialization process has successfully reduced the incidence of smoking. The next chapter will consider how this success has affected the industry as a whole.

Figure 2.15
U.S. Cigarette Consumption, 1950–1995 (Taxable Sales Only)

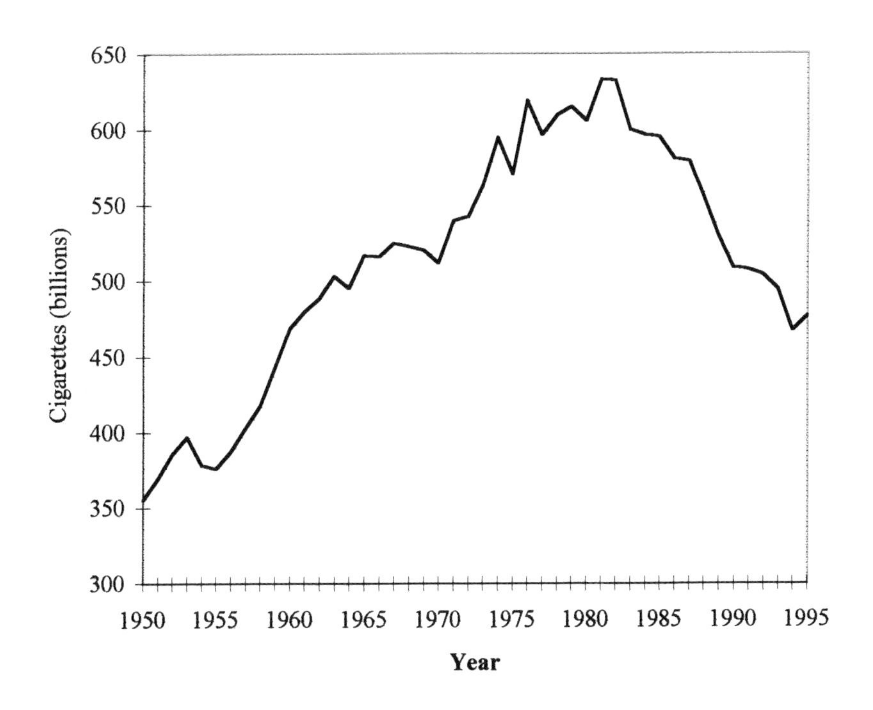

Source: Tax Burden on Tobacco, 1995.

Figure 2.16
U.S. Cigarette Consumption per Capita, 1950–1995

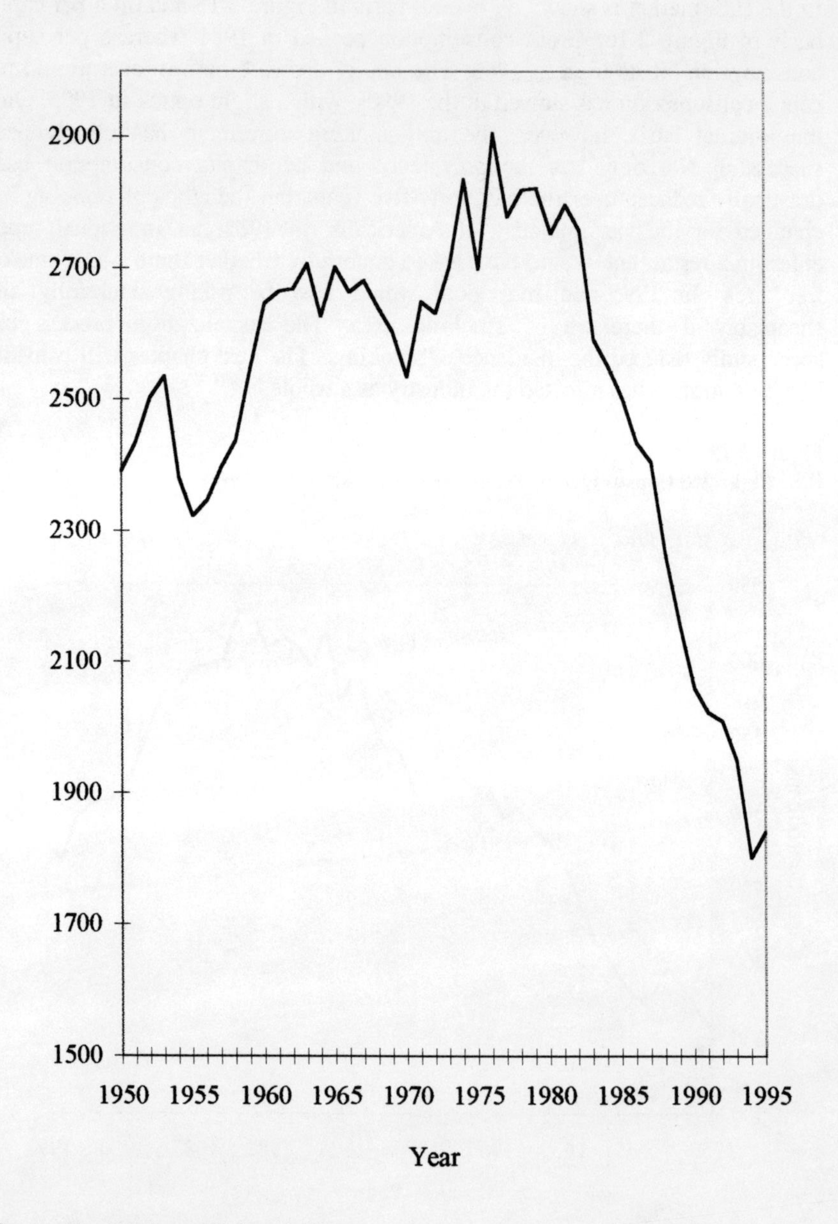

Source: Tax Burden on Tobacco, 1995.

Chapter 3

Industry Response to Smoking and Health Issues

The anti-smoking crusade, between 1950 and 1995, had three fundamental effects on the cigarette industry. First, by causing smokers to question the healthfulness of traditionally popular brands, it forced the industry to develop "safer" types of cigarettes. Second, the campaign against smoking brought about a significant demographic shift among the smoking population away from the affluent, well-educated white, male population toward both a lower-income, blue-collar constituency and a larger number of women and minorities, predominantly blacks. This demographic shift caused the industry to redirect advertising and promotion campaigns towards the new smoking population, devise new brands, and reconsider the traditionally oligopolistic pricing policies. Finally, the anti-smoking crusade succeeded in influencing millions to quit smoking and discouraging millions more from taking up the habit, bringing the domestic adult per capita consumption of cigarettes down from the 1974 peak of 2,835 to 1,840 in 1995, far below even the 1950 figure of 2,390.

The industry has turned elsewhere to counter the threat of a declining market. In the international cigarette market, exports of U.S. cigarettes to the rest of the world have increased from "limited" exports "mostly...to U.S. armed services personnel overseas" in 1950 (Miles, 1982) to over 29 billion cigarettes in 1970 and finally to over 231 billion cigarettes in 1995. Figure 3.1 graphs this trend. The 1995 volume in exported cigarettes contributed a favorable $5.33 billion to our balance of trade. Given that exports have increased 40% over the last five years, it is reasonable to project that U.S. cigarette production destined for export will exceed that for domestic consumption. Exports were not the only growth area for the cigarette firms. The industry has likewise searched for growth in business areas other than cigarettes. The industry's "specialization ratio" (i.e., the percentage of annual net sales accounted for by cigarette sales) has declined from virtually 100% in 1950 to 75% in 1970 to 45% in 1995, indicating a process of intensive diversification into businesses other than cigarettes. Both international expansion and diversification will be discussed in relation to the strategic decision made by individual companies in Chapter 5. In this chapter, domestic industry-specific responses to the smoking and health issue will be considered: product innovations that have aimed at creating safer cigarettes; advertising and marketing strategies devised to exploit the new demographic base of the smoking population; and paradoxical pricing policies both to compensate for declining consumption and to cater to the lower-income level of the average smoker.

Figure 3.1
U.S. Tobacco Industry Export of Cigarettes, 1950–1995

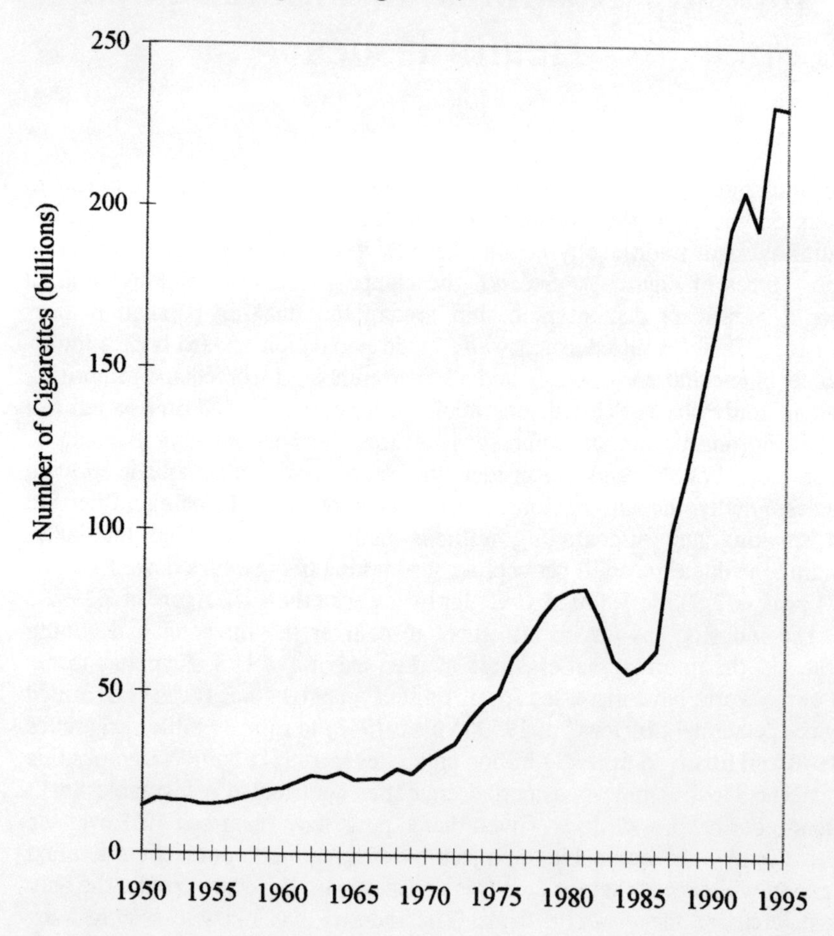

Source: Maxwell, 1983, USDA.

EVOLUTION OF THE INDUSTRY: AN OVERVIEW

The body of this chapter details the various industry-specific responses to the anti-smoking movement introduced above. However, Figure 3.2 provides a useful overview of the major trends within the industry between 1930 and 1995.

Figure 3.2
Growth, Maturity, and Decline in the U.S. Domestic Cigarette Industry, 1930–1995

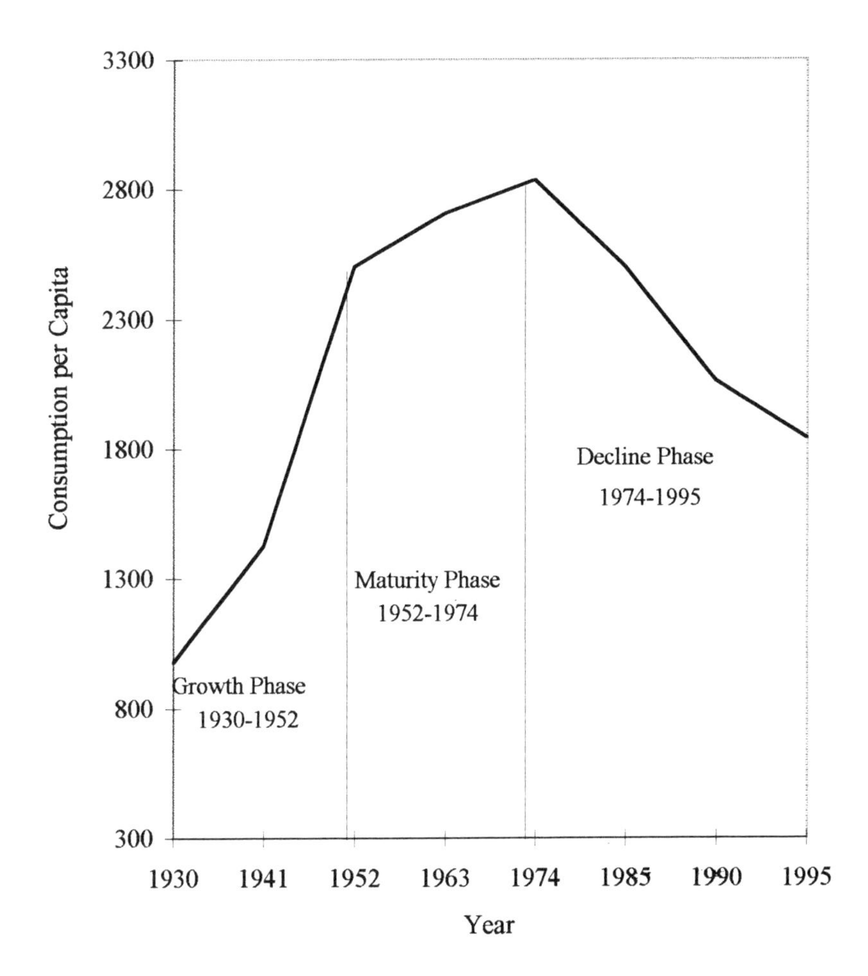

Note: Per capita differs from U.S. Department of Agriculture (USDA) figures, which show data for eighteen-years-+ population.
Source: Tax Burden on Tobacco, 1995.

As a series of "snapshots" of the leading brands (those with more than a 2% market share) taken at twenty year increments, Tables 3.1 and 3.2 reveal the following insights.

Table 3.1
All Brands Greater Than 2% Market Share, 1930, 1950, 1970, and 1990

	1930	1950	1970	1990
Lucky Strike	34.9 (1)	22.7 (2)	3.0 (12)	
Camel	28.5 (2)	27.2 (1)	6.3 (6)	4.1 (6)
Chesterfield	21.3 (3)	17.9 (3)	2.0 (14)	
Old Gold	6.9 (4)	5.4 (6)		
Other	8.4	2.4	13.3	21.6
Philip Morris		11.1 (4)		
Raleigh (VP)		2.1 (9)	3.1 (10)	
Tarreyton (K)		2.3 (8)	4.0 (8)	
Pall Mall (K)		6.4 (5)	11.0 (2)	2.4 (13)
Kool (M)		2.5 (7)	8.3 (5)	5.4 (4)
Salem (M)			8.5 (4)	6.2 (3)
Winston			15.7 (1)	9.0 (2)
Marlboro			9.9 (3)	26.3 (1)
Benson & Hedges			2.8 (13)	3.9 (7)
Kent			5.3 (7)	
Viceroy			3.8 (9)	
L & M			3.0 (11)	
Newport (M)				4.6 (5)
Merit				3.8 (8)
Vantage (VP)				2.9 (11)
Virginia Slims (F)				3.2 (10)
Doral (VP)				3.7 (9)
Cambridge (VP)				2.9 (12)
Basic (VP)				
Forsyth (VP)				
GPC (VP)				
Private Label (Philip Morris)				
Monarch				
Best Value				
Total	100.0	100.0	100.0	100.0
Filters	0.0	0.0	79.7	95.8
Low-tar	0.0	0.0	3.6	56.2
Price-Value	7.0	2.1	3.1	17.2

Source: Nicholls; *Business Week* Surveys; Maxwell
VP = Coupon or price-value.
K = King.
M = Menthol.
F = Female.
(#) = Brand ranking for that year.

Table 3.2
All Brands Greater Than 2% Market Share, 1991–1995

	1991	1992	1993	1994	1995
Lucky Strike					
Camel	3.0 (9)	3.2 (8)	3.0 (8)	4.0 (7)	4.4 (7)
Chesterfield					
Old Gold					
Other	27.8	29.0	22.2	24.6	21.2
Philip Morris					
Raleigh (VP)					
Tarreyton (K)					
Pall Mall (K)					
Kool (M)	4.7 (6)	4.4 (6)	3.0 (9)	3.6 (9)	3.6 (9)
Salem (M)	5.5 (3)	5.0 (3)	3.9 (7)	3.8 (8)	3.7 (8)
Winston	7.7 (2)	7.0 (2)	6.7 (2)	5.8 (2)	5.8 (3)
Marlboro	25.8 (1)	24.4 (1)	23.5 (1)	28.1 (1)	30.1 (1)
Benson & Hedges	3.2 (7)	3.1 (9)	2.5 (13)	2.4 (11)	2.4 (12)
Kent					
Viceroy					
L & M					
Newport (M)	4.8 (4)	4.9 (4)	4.8 (5)	5.1 (5)	5.6 (5)
Merit	3.1 (8)	3.0 (10)	2.3 (16)	2.4 (12)	2.4 (11)
Vantage (VP)	2.0 (13)				
Virginia Slims (F)	2.8 (10)	2.6 (11)	2.3 15)	2.4 (13)	2.4 (10)
Doral (VP)	4.7 (5)	4.5 (5)	4.6 (6)	5.1 (4)	5.7 (4)
Cambridge (VP)	2.8 (11)				
Basic (VP)		2.3 (12)	5.3 (3)	4.7 (6)	4.7 (6)
Forsyth (VP)			3.0 (10)	2.5 (10)	2.2 (13)
GPC (VP)	2.1 (12)	4.3 (7)	5.1 (4)	5.5 (3)	5.8 (2)
Private Label (Philip Morris)		2.3 (13)	2.9 (11)		
Monarch			2.5 (12)		
Best Value			2.4 (14)		
Total	**100.0**	**100.0**	**100.0**	**100.0**	**100.0**
Filters	96.3	96.6	96.9	97.2	97.2
Low-tar	58.2	58.4	59.2	59.1	59.7
Price-Value	24.9	30.2	36.8	32.5	30.1

Source: Nicholls; *Business Week* Surveys; Maxwell

VP = Coupon or price-value.
K = King.
M = Menthol.
F = Female.
(#) = Brand ranking for that year.

Brand Proliferation. In 1930, the top three brands held an 84.7% share of the nation's market, but by 1995, their market power had been more than halved to 41.7%. This decentralization of market power was in part due to the proliferation of cigarette types and brands in response to consumer demand for safer cigarettes in light of the smoking and health issue. The introduction of new cigarette types (filter, hi-fi, low-tar, etc.; see below) drove the number of brands and their extensions from eighteen in 1950 to over 450 in 1995 and reduced the market share of the top three brands to as low as 35.5% in 1993.

Market Segmentation. In the early years of the modern cigarette industry, the market was essentially a composite of regional brands. In the 1920s, however, the transformation of Camel and Lucky Strike brands in particular into national brands signaled the beginning of massmarketing aimed at a monolithic consumer base. By 1950, some segmentation had occurred with regard to cigarette size (king-size brands grabbed a 1950 market share of 8.7%), flavor (menthol brands had a 2.5% share), and value (the coupon-oriented Raleigh held a 2.1% share). After 1950, market segmentation exploded with the entry and dramatic use of filter cigarettes, which grew from less than 1% of the market in 1950 to 79.7% in 1970 to 97.2% in 1995. As a result of the health issue, filter cigarettes expanded from a submarket into a defining characteristic of the market as a whole. At the same time, other market segments—menthol and low-tar brands—became more and more significant submarkets. Figure 3.1 also indicates that market segmentation became more sophisticated, as a "women's" brand of cigarette, Virginia Slims, joined the leading brands after 1970 with a 3.2% market share.

Demographic Shift. The entry of four price-value brands into the ranks of the leading cigarettes of 1990 reveals industry sensitivity to the demographic shift among the smoking population to lower-income groups discussed in Chapter 2. By 1993, this type of cigarette had peaked with a 36.8% market share. Marlboro Friday has reduced the market share held to 24.9%. A comparison between the 3.1% market share of this cigarette type in 1970 and the 1990s figure is somewhat inaccurate, given that the Raleigh brand offered coupons with which to purchase numerous consumer goods; the later price-value brands simply sold at lower prices than other brands. As a brief overview of the developments in the cigarette industry since 1930, Table 3.1 shows some change in the status quo between 1930 and 1950. While the figure indicates some market segmentation between 1930 and 1950, mainly king-size and menthols, more significant is the segmentation change brought on by the post-1950 cancer scare. Table 3.2 shows that segmentation continued in the 1990s owing to the growth of price-value brands due to the aforementioned "enforced demographics." The remainder of this chapter will detail the changes wrought by the smoking and health issue since 1950.

EVOLUTION OF THE INDUSTRY, 1911–1950

The years after the dissolution of the tobacco trust witnessed a number of fundamental transformations in the content, packaging, and marketing of cigarettes. Introduced in 1913, the Camel brand of cigarette was the first to feature a new, lighter blend of tobacco—made from a combination of Maryland, Virginia, Turkish, and Burley tobaccos—which soon replaced the harsher, largely Turkish blend of tobacco as the American consumer's tobacco of choice. The Camel brand's regional popularity led to national distribution, the first cigarette so marketed. Unlike other regularly priced cigarettes, the Camel brand was sold at a reasonable price and in packs of twenty cigarettes, a practice previously reserved for premium-priced brands only. Heavily supported by national newspaper and billboard advertising, Camel gained a phenomenal 45% share of the national market by 1923.

Other brands soon followed Camel's successful pattern into the national market, and by 1926, Chesterfield, Lucky Strike, and Old Gold brands had been introduced along lines similar to Camel. In 1933, the Philip Morris eponymous brand's tobacco blending was made to resemble Camel's and its competitors more closely. By 1950, these five brands accounted for 84.3% of the market. Thus, the industry's status quo of 1950 had, as Tennant (1950) argued (see Chapter 2), been established in the early decades of the century. In short, this 1950 status quo can be described as follows: Each U.S.-based competitor backed with its advertising resources a single cigarette brand that was packaged by twenties and priced oligopolistically. Maintenance of this status quo was, in 1950, perceived as the key success factor in profitable competition within the cigarette industry.

PRODUCT INNOVATION AFTER 1950

In 1950, five major brands, all of them "regular" brands (i.e., unfiltered 70 millimeter cigarettes), dominated the market with an 84% market share. "king-size" brands (i.e., 85 millimeter unfiltered) constituted another 10% of the total market. Within the king-size submarket, Pall Mall, introduced in 1939, was the leading brand, with a 65% share. "Menthol" brands, among which the Kool brand was the submarket leader, made up another. "Price-value" brands, primarily the Raleigh brand, constituted 3.0% of the total market. Essentially, then, the 1950 cigarette market was dominated by a remarkably small number of cigarette brands: five regular brands (Camel, Chesterfield, Lucky Strike, Old Gold, and Philip Morris), a menthol (Kool), a king-size (Pall Mall), and a price-value brand (Raleigh). Together, these eight brands accounted for 95.3% of the total market.

King-Size and Filter Brands

Sales of king-size cigarettes continued to grow in the early 1950s due to (1) the "more is better" syndrome and (2) the industry-promoted belief that the greater amount of tobacco itself acted as a filter and made the cigarette milder and hence safer in the mind of the consumer. Brand extensions of Philip Morris, Old Gold, Chesterfield, and Raleigh into the king-size submarket by 1953 was proof of the popularity of this cigarette type. The early 1950s also saw sales of "filter" brands, primarily Parliament, Viceroy, and Kent, rise, "further indication," according to *Business Week*, "of health consciousness on the part of smokers" (*Business Week*, 1952). Filter cigarettes had first been sold in the 1930s, advertised along lines that stressed mildness, and most commonly sold regionally.

Upon the release of the Sloan-Kettering Report, which linked cigarette smoking to lung cancer and capped several years of anti-smoking activity, sales in 1953 increased 2.9% over 1952 sales; filter sales increased 132.1% over the same period.

By the end of 1953, the four major filter brands (Kent, L&M, Parliament, and Viceroy) had grabbed 3.2% of the cigarette market. All benefited from the health claims made by their advertising in light of the Sloan-Kettering Report, as did king-size brands. Unfiltered king-size brands constituted approximately 28% of the total market in 1954. By 1955, however, the health merits of unfiltered king-size cigarettes came into question, and their sales began to plummet. By 1974, the market share held by unfiltered king-size brands had fallen to 8.1%, to 2.4% in 1988 and by 1995 unfiltered king-sized brands had shrunk to 1.8% of the market. Also by 1995, sales of unfiltered cigarettes of all sizes constituted only 2.8% of the market. Filtered cigarettes, on the other hand, continued to spiral upward as all of the major firms hurried to introduce filtered brands into the market. Sales of filter cigarettes were again boosted by a 1954 *Reader's Digest* article that suggested that filters could reduce the health dangers of smoking (Miller & Monahan, 1954).

Among filter cigarettes, the early entry brands, particularly Viceroy and Kent, were marketed with extensive health-oriented advertising and enjoyed early success. Kent was marketed with the assurance that its "protection" was priceless (Corina, 1975). However, despite impressive initial sales (1952: 0.7 billion; 1953: 3.0 billion; 1954: 4.0 billion), Kent was found to be not only priceless but also tasteless. Former unfiltered brand smokers, while concerned for their health, still wanted a good taste to their cigarettes. Although Viceroy's advertising similarly emphasized its "20,000 filter tips" rather than taste, it managed to sell 14.9 billion units in 1954 and 20.1 billion in 1955; demand became so great that it quickly outstripped supply. Despite this formidable competition, the Winston brand was introduced in July 1954 to exploit the weakness of flavorlessness. It was advertised as the filter cigarette that had a "satisfying" tobacco taste, to contrast it to both Kent and Viceroy (Wooten,

1979). In 1955, Viceroy's advertising campaign was refocused, and in 1957, Kent was reformulated and reintroduced with more tar and nicotine. By 1956, however, Winston had already become the leading filtered brand, selling 31.0 billion units in that year, compared with 25.4 billion units of Viceroy and 3.0 billion of Kent.

The success of filtered cigarettes precipitated a proliferation of filtered brands by 1955, with cigarette manufacturers hoping to gain a share of the booming market. In order to draw attention to their filtered brands, industry members pursued several marketing strategies. Some introduced filtered versions of best-selling unfiltered brands (for example, Kool, and Old Gold) in order both to capitalize on brand recognition and to discourage brand defection. Winston was marketed with an eye to the failings of other filtered brands, as was Marlboro. Both emphasized "full flavor" rather than health.

Marlboro was aimed at a new market niche—"the filter cigarette for macho men" (Mahar, 1990). Market research had shown that despite the health risks men were reluctant to switch to filtered cigarettes, which were seen as "effeminate." Indeed, when the Marlboro brand was first introduced in the 1930s, the brand was aimed at women with its "Mild as May" slogan. Reintroduced in 1955 in a distinctive flip-top, red-and-white cardboard box, the Marlboro marketing campaign soon centered around the Marlboro Man—still an icon of masculinity—and by 1956, Marlboro had become the tenth best-selling brand in the U.S. In 1995, Marlboro was the best-selling brand in America—selling 144.9 billion units and accounting for 30.1% of all cigarettes sold. Plain filters had captured 71.6% of the 1995 market. Filters overall constituted 97.2% of the market.

Also profiting from the "flavorlessness" of the first-generation filters was the menthol filter submarket. Salem, the first menthol filter cigarette, was introduced in 1956. The Kool brand, an early menthol cigarette, was given a filter in late 1956, following the success of the Salem brand. Newport and Oasis entered the market in 1957; Belair joined the menthol submarket in 1960. Emphasizing a strong menthol flavor to compensate for the flavor filtered out on other brands, and benefiting from a long-term attribution of medicinal properties to menthol, menthol filter cigarettes gained a significant share of the total cigarette market, averaging between 27% and 29% from 1974 to 1989. In 1994 and 1995, market share had stabilized at 25.2%.

Hi-Fi and Charcoal Brands

Another reaction to the description in smoking trends brought about by the Sloan-Kettering Report was a series of much-publicized research and development programs that resulted in the creation of new filter types believed to better screen out the harmful elements of cigarette smoke. In 1957, Lorillard reintroduced its Kent filter brand with an extensive promotion campaign emphasizing its "new micronite" filter, a high-filtration ("hi-fi") cigarette. According to a 1957 *Reader's Digest* survey, the reformulated Kent had the lowest tar and nicotine content of all brands tested (Wootten, 1957). The success of Kent (sales of Kent increased 316.7% from 1956 to 1957), due to the favorable publicity in *Reader's Digest*, set off a so-called tar derby. New brands were released boasting lower and lower tar and nicotine contents. Brands such as Alpine, Hit Parade, and Parliament Hi-Fi with a recessed filter constituted a new "hi-fi" submarket that began to decline after a December 1959 FTC ruling that cigarette advertisements could no longer make claims as to low tar and nicotine content. In the early 1960s, most hi-fi cigarettes gradually increased their tar and nicotine content to match the levels of plain filters.

In 1963, Lark brand joined Tarreyton Dual Filter in boasting a charcoal filter. The success of Tarreyton and especially Lark, largely due to a 1963 article in the *New England Journal of Medicine* that endorsed Lark's charcoal filter as a more effective filter than regular filters, sparked off a proliferation of charcoal filter brands (e.g., Tempo and Carlton). The charcoal filter submarket peaked in 1965 with 34.8 billion units sold, or 6.8% of the total cigarette market. By 1995, charcoal filtered cigarettes accounted for only 0.4% of the total market. Other marketing fads were similarly engineered: Fifty-Fifty, a cigarette composed of half filter and half tobacco: and the Waterford brand, a cigarette with "water capsules" in its charcoal filter, supposedly giving it the same kind of taste improvement as a hookah. Such devices were not unique to the 1960s. As recently as 1989, Lorillard was test-marketing a lemon-flavored cigarette.

Low-Tar Brands

In 1966, the FTC's decision to publish periodic reports on the tar and nicotine contents of every cigarette brand created the most successful cigarette submarket after the regular and the plain filter submarkets—the low-tar submarket. The FTC defines any cigarette with less than 15 mg of tar as a "low-tar" cigarette. Capitalizing on the built-in publicity surrounding government-approved tar content figures, the cigarette industry rushed into the new field. The first entry low-tar brand was True, which was introduced in April 1966. The brand enjoyed immediate success in the tar-conscious climate, with sales increasing 180.8% between 1966 and 1967. However, as with early plain filter brands, True's tastelessness opened the submarket to competition based on "flavorful" low-tar brands. The success of two other early entries into the low-tar submarket, Doral (introduced in 1969) and Vantage (introduced in 1970), was attributed in the industry to their ability to deliver flavor. Other low-tar brands followed in 1971, including Carlton and a brand extension, Marlboro Lights. A large percentage of the sales of low-tar brands in the late 1960s and early 1970s came from established smokers of regular filters brands.

These smokers had been made more aware of the health issues surrounding smoking by the highly effective television advertising campaign made possible by the FCC's "fairness doctrine" in 1968. Increasingly, the cigarette companies themselves conducted promotional campaigns for low tars (and later ultra-low tars) that explicitly invoked health issues. Vantage ads in the early 1970s revolved around a headline that read "Think." Established brand names were also used to capitalize on the market's low-tar trends. Popular brands like Kent and Marlboro utilized product extensions, Kent Golden Lights and Marlboro Lights, in order to carry brand loyalty into the lower-tar submarket. By 1995, low-tar cigarettes accounted for 59.7% of the industry's market, up from a 3.6% market share in 1970. For an alternative "safer" approach to the cigarette, see the historical evolution and potential of smokeless tobacco in the appendix.

Demographic Segment Brands

Since its early days, the cigarette industry's marketing had targeted particular groups. The entry of women into the ranks of smokers had prompted the introduction of "womens' brands," like the 1927 version of the "Mild as May" Marlboro brand. The introduction of Virginia Slims in 1968 signaled the adaptation of a traditional strategy for "enforced demographics" reasons. While the proportion of U.S. adults who regularly smoked was declining, and the percentage of adult white men was similarly declining, the percentages of women and minorities who smoked were decreasing at a slower rate as fewer women and minorities were quitting smoking than white males. Among some groups, percentages actually increased during some periods (see figures, Chapter 2). Government figures cited in *Business Week's Annual Survey of the Cigarette Industry (1980)* revealed that in 1979 white male smokers twenty-one and older outnumbered female smokers by 26.2 million to 22.0 million, the number of new male smokers increased only 3.4% between 1975 and 1979, while the female smoking population increased 7.8%. More significantly to the cigarette industry, looking for long-term customers, the number of male teenage smokers dropped 25% to 1.5 million during that period, while the number of female teenage smokers increased 40% to 1.7 million (*Business Week*, 1981).

As per capita cigarette consumption declined, the cigarette industry looked to those groups defying the general trend. The successful 1968 launch of Virginia Slims, whose promotional campaign tied cigarette smoking to sexual equality ("You've come a long way, baby"), was quickly followed in 1968 by Silva Thins, in 1969 by Embra, and in 1970 by Eve 120s. In addition to advertising campaigns aimed at women, the cigarettes themselves were designed with the intention of attracting female smokers. Longer and slimmer than plain filter and king-size filter brands, "feminine" cigarettes were further modified—in color, for example. More Lights, introduced in 1981, featured beige paper on the assumption that the beige had a "tremendous feminine appeal" (*Business Week*, 1981). The Eves St. Laurent logo was added to the premium-priced women's brand Ritz, while another premium-price brand, Satin, featured a filter that felt like satin. Virginia Slims remains the most successful women's brand, with a 1995 market share of 2.4%, enough to make it the tenth best-selling brand in the country.

Marketing segmenting was not limited to women. Since the late 1950s, cigarette companies have been aware of the higher proportion of black men and women smoking regularly (see figures in Chapter 2) and have been donating funds to black arts and political groups, most prominently the various Kool Jazz Festivals held around the country. The popularity of menthol filters among blacks caused the Newport, Kool, and Salem brands to redirect advertising and promotional campaigns to this niche—advertising in magazines catering to blacks and on billboards in minority areas. In large part, cigarette manufacturers have been content to target existing brands, especially menthols, to blacks. However, in 1990, after much market analysis, Salem manufacturers announced plans to test-market a new brand—Uptown—designed to appeal specifically to blacks. Uptown was developed according to marketing information gathered about black smokers: The brand had a lighter menthol flavor than Salem menthol brand, and because many Newport smokers opened their packs upside down, Uptown's packaging was designed to be opened in that fashion. However, medical authorities and black leaders in the test-market city—Philadelphia—began a vociferous campaign that caused the firm to withdraw the brand with an estimated loss of $10 million (Koeppel, 1990a).

Although other ethnic groups—Hispanics and Asians, in particular—show no special preference for any brand or type of cigarette (Ramirez, 1991a), cigarette manufacturers have attempted to discover or invent other marketing niches. In 1981, a so-called regional brand that used ante-bellum southern scenes in its advertising to attract smokers in the Southeast was test-marketed. In 1982, a regularly priced Benson & Hedges Deluxe Ultra Lights brands, packaged in an embossed, metallic-colored box and foil liner to attract upscale smokers, was introduced. In 1985, the English Dunhill brand and a Ritz brand, both premium-priced brands with a marketing campaign aimed at upper-class smokers, were introduced to compete in the potential market niche. However, this strategy failed largely because of the demographic shift of cigarette smoking away from better-educated and higher-income individuals to lower-income groups (see Chapter 2). This same demographic shift was behind a 1988 decision to license the Harley-Davidson brand name and attach it to a brand that was niche-targeted to young, male, blue-collar workers, with whom the motorcycle name was assumed to be popular. In 1995, Harley-Davidson had achieved a 0.3% market share, with 1.39 billion units sold.

Price-Value Brands

The income shift among smokers, combined with health-issue-inspired federal and state tax increases on cigarettes (see Chapter 2), resulted in the introduction in 1980 of a new generation of price-value brands, the first of which were generic cigarettes. The history of pricing in the cigarette industry up to 1980 had been oligopolistic, with all six of the majors agreeing on monolithic price increases. But in 1980, an industry member was approached by generic-product distributor Topco with a plan to manufacture generic cigarettes that Topco would then sell at a discount under store labels. The plan ran contrary to all conventional wisdom in the industry, which believed that cigarette sales were wholly dependent on the image provided by advertising and packaging. However, sales of generic cigarettes skyrocketed as new supermarket food chains signed on with Topco. By 1984, 20 billion generic cigarettes were being produced annually. Thus, their share in the market had climbed to 5.7% in 1984 from 0% in 1979.

The surprise success of generics inspired the creation of a new price-value category introduced in 1984 with the entry of the Doral brand into the market: the so-called branded generic, or a lower-priced branded product. Selling at $.25 to $.40 a pack less than full-priced brands, as against generics, which sold for $.40 to $.70 less per pack, branded generics aimed at catering to lower-income smokers who nonetheless were willing to pay more to avoid the supposed social onus of carrying generic cigarettes. Other branded generics followed. Cambridge, Alpine, and Viceroy were some examples.

In 1984, the introduction of Richland and Century brands marked another price-value strategy. Each pack of these "value 25" brands contained twenty-five cigarettes instead of the traditional twenty. "Value 25" brands were inspired both by the prevalence of lower-income smokers, and by market research that revealed that a typical smoker consumes an average of twenty-three cigarettes per day.

In 1988, the entry of the Pyramid brand into the market heralded a new price-value category: the "subgeneric," which in 1990 sold for $.70 to $.90 a pack, well below even generic cigarette prices. Cigarette industry analyst John C. Maxwell called Pyramid brand "one of the most successful cigarettes introduced recently" (Lowenstein, 1990). Overall, the price-value submarket has itself proven remarkably successful, which is not surprising given the enforced demographic shift the anti-smoking movement created toward lower-income smokers. The increased anti-smoking taxes imposed by both state and federal governments threatened to make smoking among this new demographic base an inaccessible, expensive habit: thus the introduction of a price-value submarket. By 1993, the price-value market constituted 36.8% of the total U.S. market. The previously described Marlboro Friday actions have subsequently reduced that market share to 24.9% in 1995.

REVIEW

The industry has responded to the smoking and health issue in a number of ways. Tables 3.1 and 3.2 show the proliferation of cigarette brands and types that occurred after 1950 as the industry attempted to provide safer and more appealing cigarettes in light of the cancer issue. Figure 3.3 shows the market share held by the top single, three, five, ten and twenty brands from 1950 to 1995. The erosion in the combined market share of the top three brands from 1950 to 1995 and the more significant declines over the same period for the top five and ten brands indicate trends of both brand proliferation and market segmentation, as the numerous new brands found market niches.

Figure 3.3
Brand Proliferation—Market Shares of Top 1, 3, 4, 10, and 20 Brands, 1950–1995

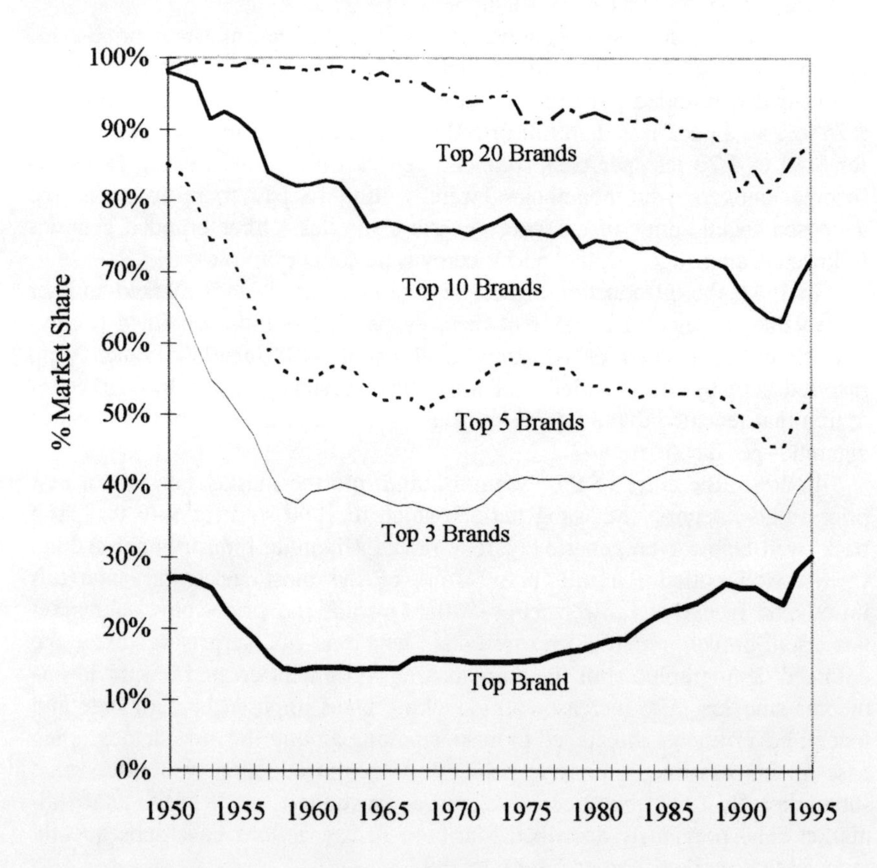

Source: Business Week (1952-1990), Maxwell, 1996.

Figure 3.4
Share of U.S. Market by Cigarette Type, 1950–1995

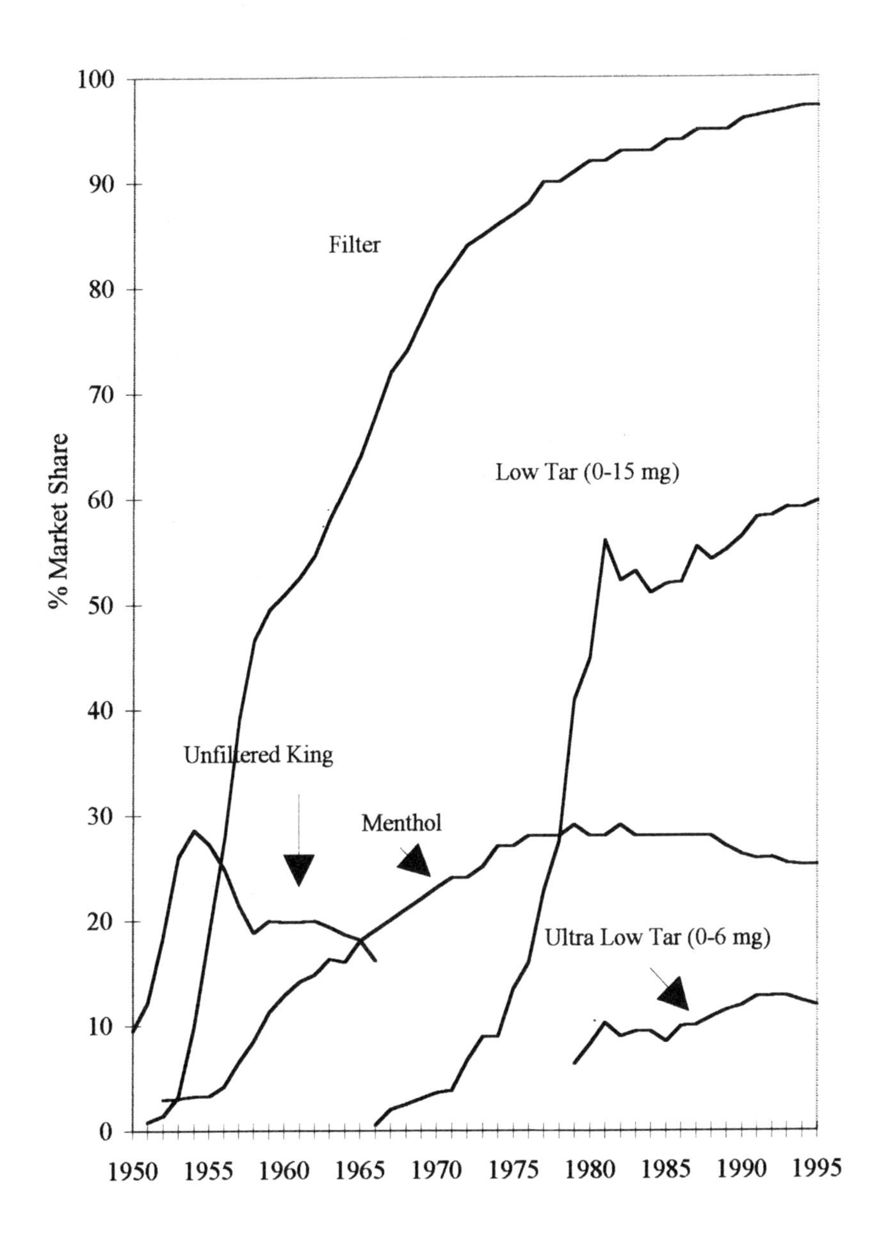

Source: *Business Week*, 1952-1990; Maxwell, 1983, 1996, FTC Report to Congress for 1993.

Figure 3.4 reveals more directly the impact of the anti-smoking campaign on the industry. Awareness of the health dangers of high-tar cigarette smoke drove consumers to find new types of cigarettes less harmful than regular unfiltered brands. The phenomenal growth of the filter submarket—from virtually nothing in 1950 to 9.9% in 1954, the year after the Sloan-Kettering report, to 64.4% after the release of the 1964 U.S. Surgeon General's Report, to the 1995 figure of 97.2%—has nearly been matched by the dramatic increase of the low-tar market—from nothing in 1965 to 59.7% in 1995. The failure of the ultra-low tar segment to duplicate the success of low-tar brands in general indicates that despite health warnings consumers still demand the flavor provided by tar.

The short-lived, health-related increase of unfiltered king-size brands, abandoned by consumers after their safety was called into doubt, was not repeated by menthol brands, which have an equally dubious claim to healthfulness. Instead, menthol brands have, over the past two decades, held a constant market share of approximately 25%. If the early increase in sales of menthols was due to the medicinal properties associated with menthol, its continued market share is due to demographic market segmentation. Figure 3.5 indicates that menthol brands are the overwhelming choice of cigarettes for black smokers. Sixty-nine percent of the black smoking population smoke menthols. Given the demographic shift in the general smoking population, the continued market strength of menthol brands is hardly surprising. Equally unsurprising are the marketing tactics the cigarette industry has employed to exploit this market niche. In addition to the industry sponsorship of black-oriented events discussed above, the cigarette industry has targeted advertising toward this group. Thus, cigarette advertising as a percentage of the total advertising in black-oriented magazines is significantly above that of the national average for all magazines (e.g., 10.2% in *Jet* compared with a national magazine average of 6.1%).

Nor have other niche markets been ignored by the industry. Cigarette manufacturers' have been sensitive to the demographic shift among the smoking population toward women. Women's magazines have, since the 1970s, received a significant amount of advertising attention from the cigarette industry. Cigarette advertising constitutes a higher percentage of the advertising in magazines such as *Mademoiselle* (3.1% greater than national magazine average) and *Cosmopolitan* (2.7% greater).

Figure 3.5
1989 Market Share Among Black Smokers

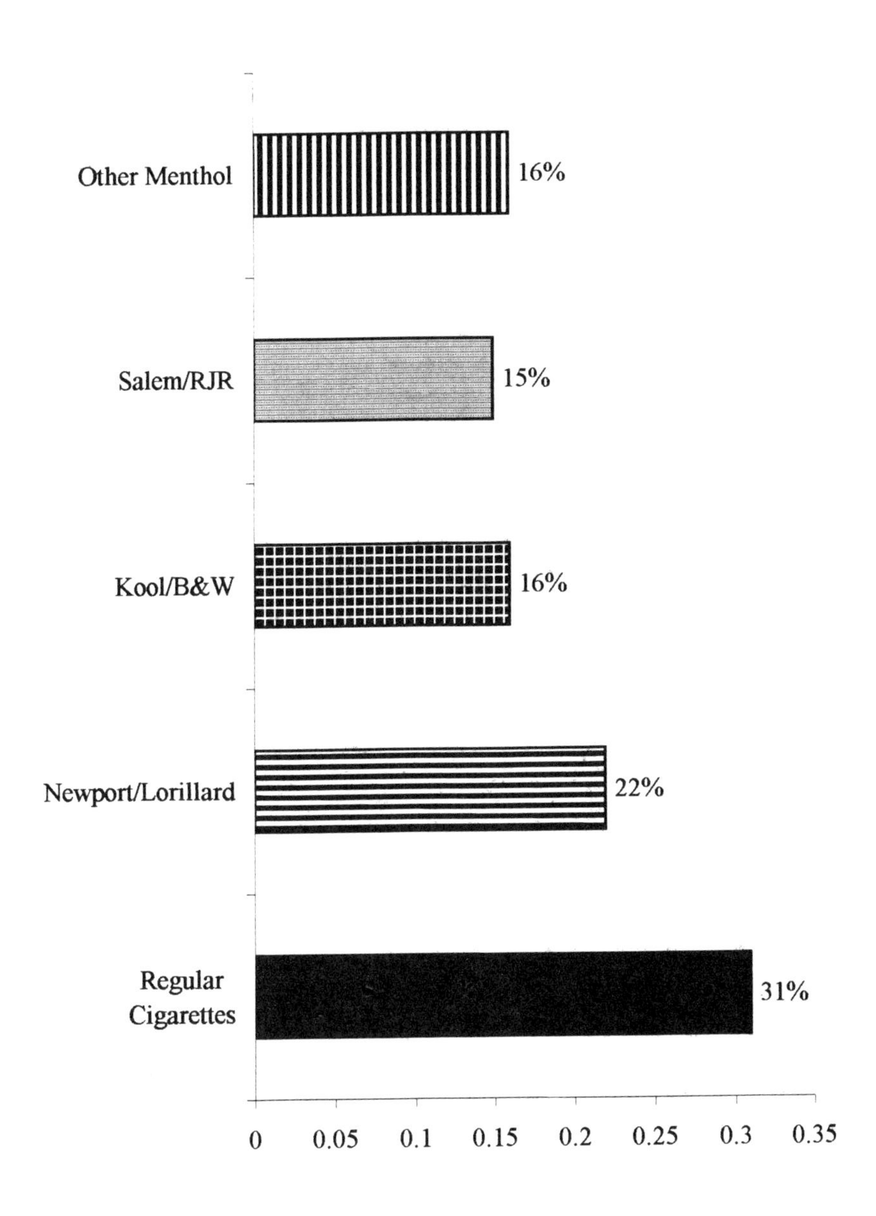

Source: New York Times, January 12, 1990, p. D-1.

Figure 3.6
Total Domestic Tobacco Sales, 1980–1995

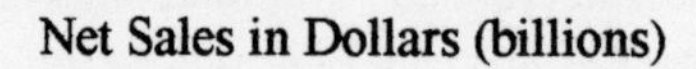

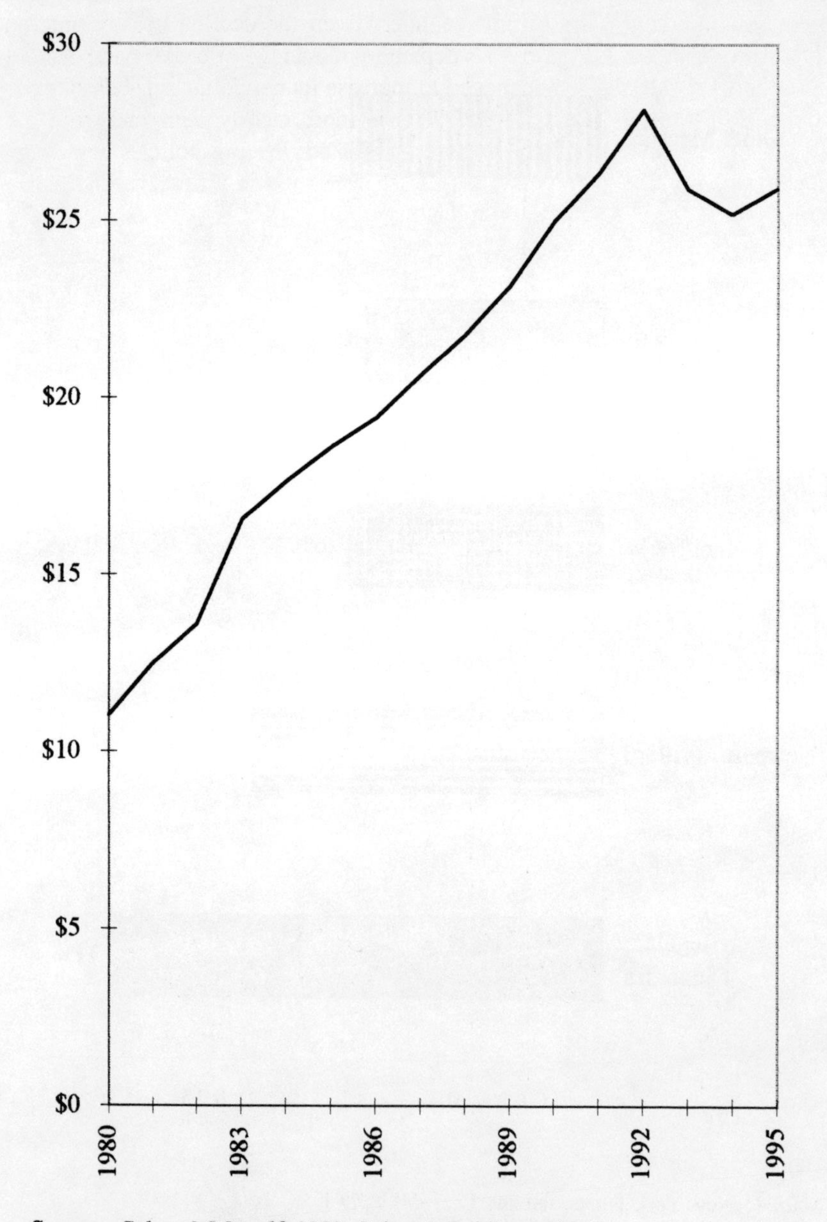

Sources: Cohen & Metcalf, 1990; Cohen & Reidinger, 1995.

Figure 3.6 shows the total manufacturing dollar value of domestic cigarette sales from 1980 to 1995. Between 1980 and 1992, there was a 155% increase from $11 billion to $28.1 billion. In 1993, decreasing volume and Marlboro Friday pricing policies resulted in an 8% decline to $25.9 billion. After a further decline in 1994, total sales reached the 1993 level in 1995 due to price increases and a slight rise in unit volume. Given the decline in consumption discussed in Chapter 2, Figure 3.7's depiction of average price per pack demonstrates how the industry has managed to increase its net dollar sales despite the drop in unit volume through 1992. This is more clearly seen in Figure 3.8 where the price and volume trends are contrasted. Pricing policies associated with Marlboro Friday and its aftermath are seen in both figures from 1993 to 1995.

Figure 3.7
Weighted Average (Median) Price per Package, 1954–1995

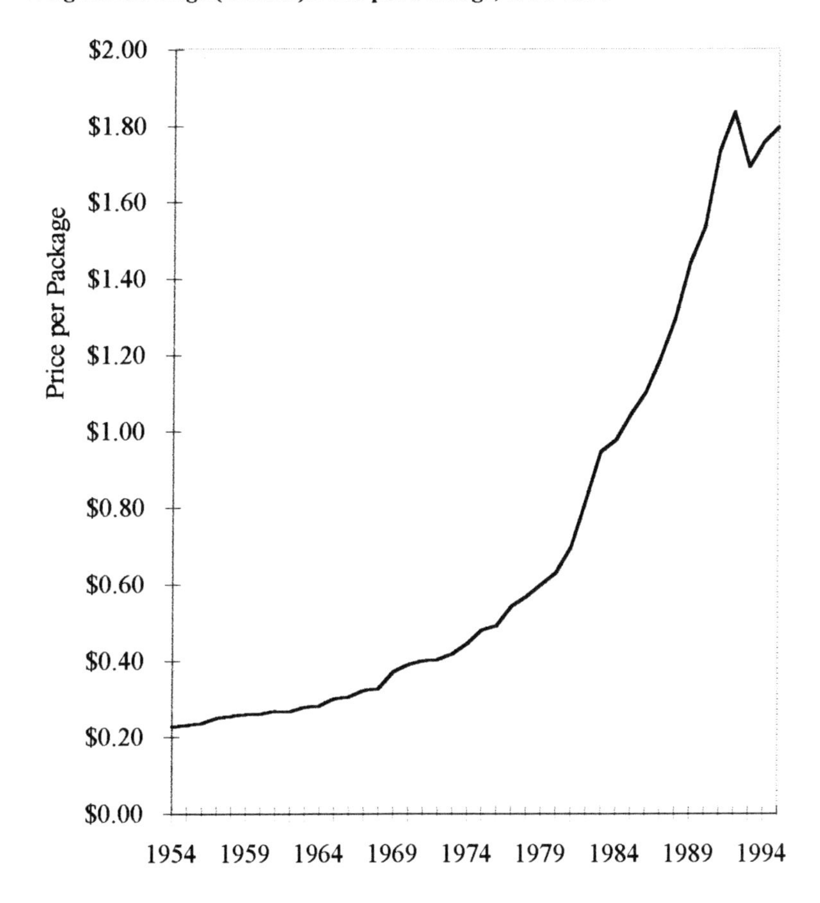

Source: Tax Burden on Tobacco, 1995.

Figure 3.8
U.S. Cigarette Consumption versus Average Price per Package, 1955–1995

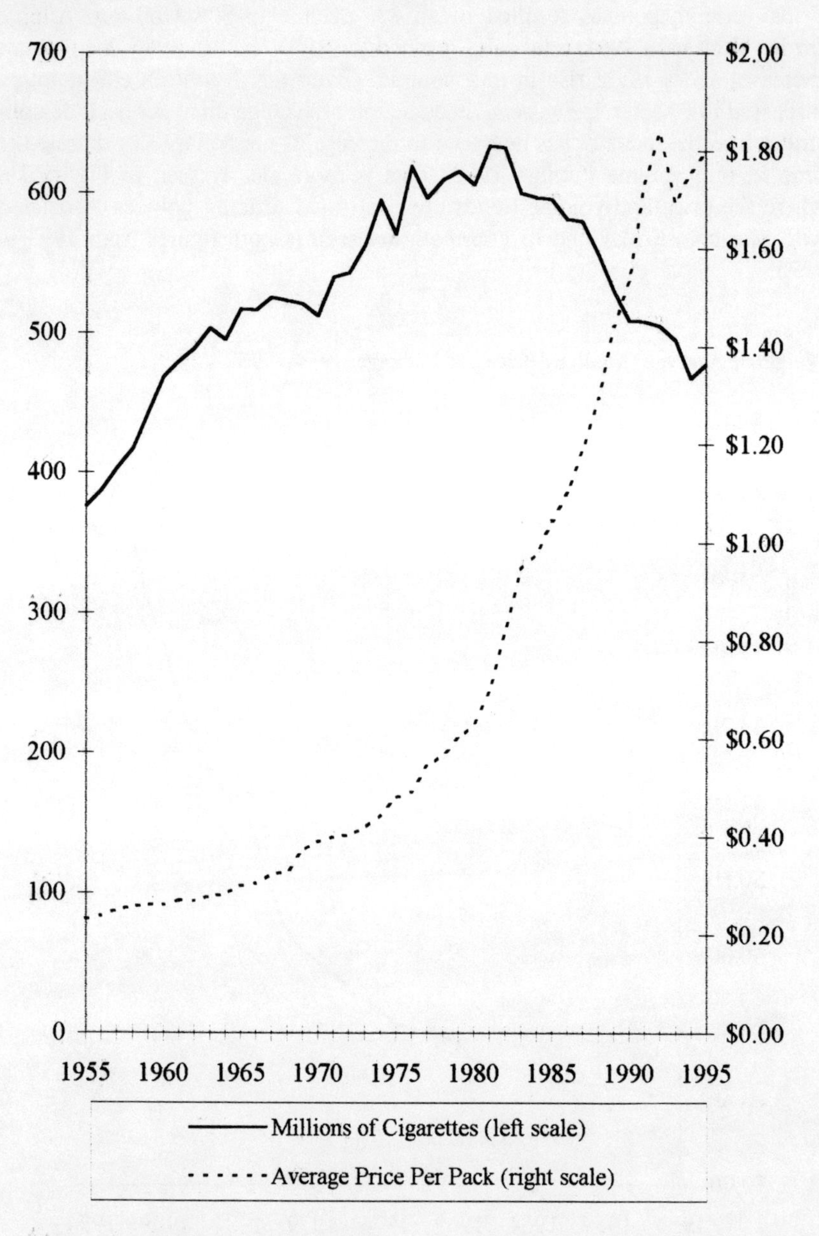

Source: Tax Burden on Tobacco, 1995.

Figure 3.9
Percentage Increase in Retail Price versus CPI, 1981–1995

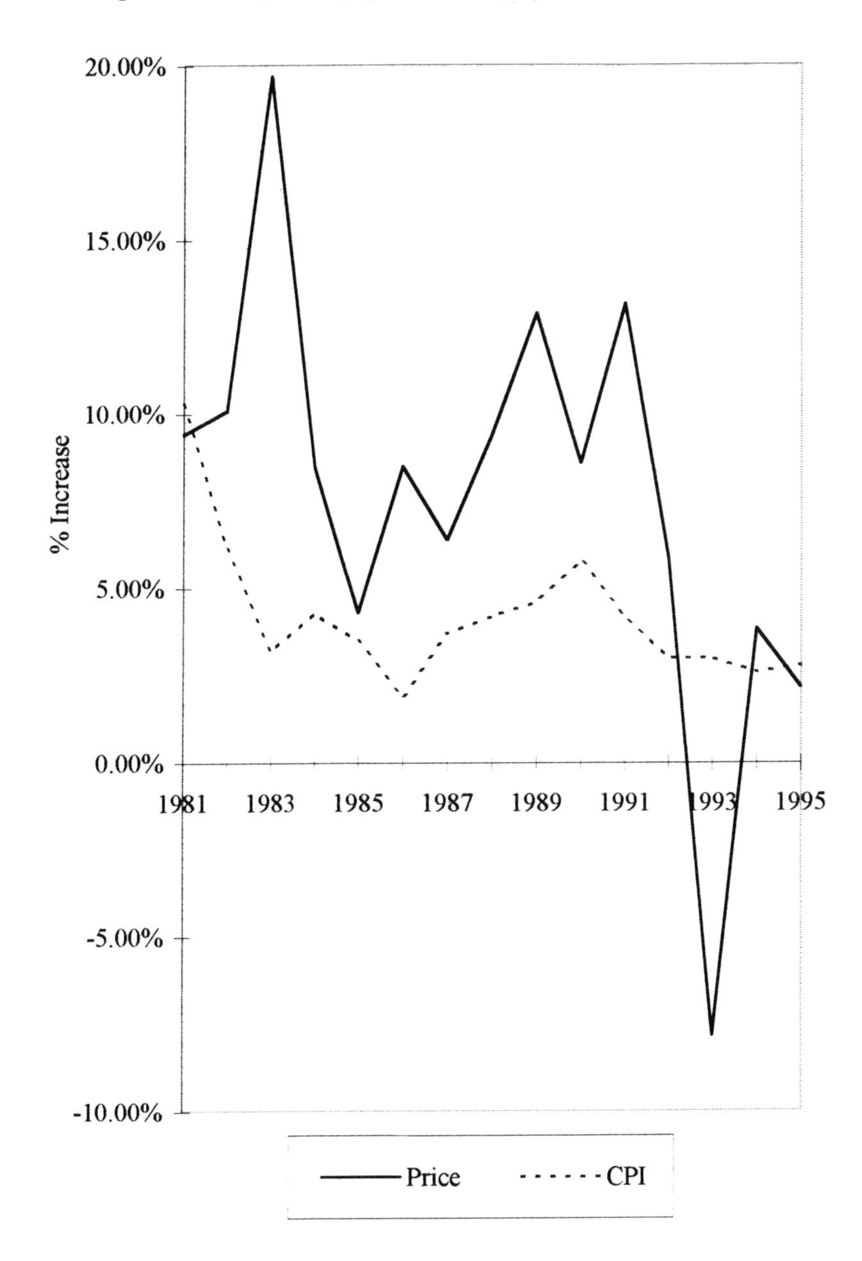

Source: Author's calculations.

Figure 3.9 shows the cigarette pricing outstripping the consumer price index for most of the last decade and a half. Until 1993 and Marlboro Friday, the industry has compensated for the slowdown and decline in unit sales due to health concerns with price increases that have exceeded inflation.

Given the prior discussion of the demographic shift to the less affluent and the less educated enforced on the industry by the smoking and health issue, it is no surprise to see in Figure 3.10 the dramatic growth of the price-value submarket to a 36.8% market share in 1993 from less than 1% in 1981. The enforced demographic shift appears to have overcome the industry's oligopolistic price tendencies. Even though Marlboro Friday's accomplished purpose was to protect brand name investment, it did, in reality, also reduce prices.

Finally, Figure 3.11 examines recent developments in the cigarette market. The three price-value brands among the top twenty brands (Basic, Doral, and GPC) saw significant annual growth rates in each year between 1986 and 1993. In 1994 and 1995, their growth rates, while still positive, were negatively impacted by Marlboro Friday.

Figure 3.10
Price-Value Brands—Share of Total Cigarette Market, 1982–1995

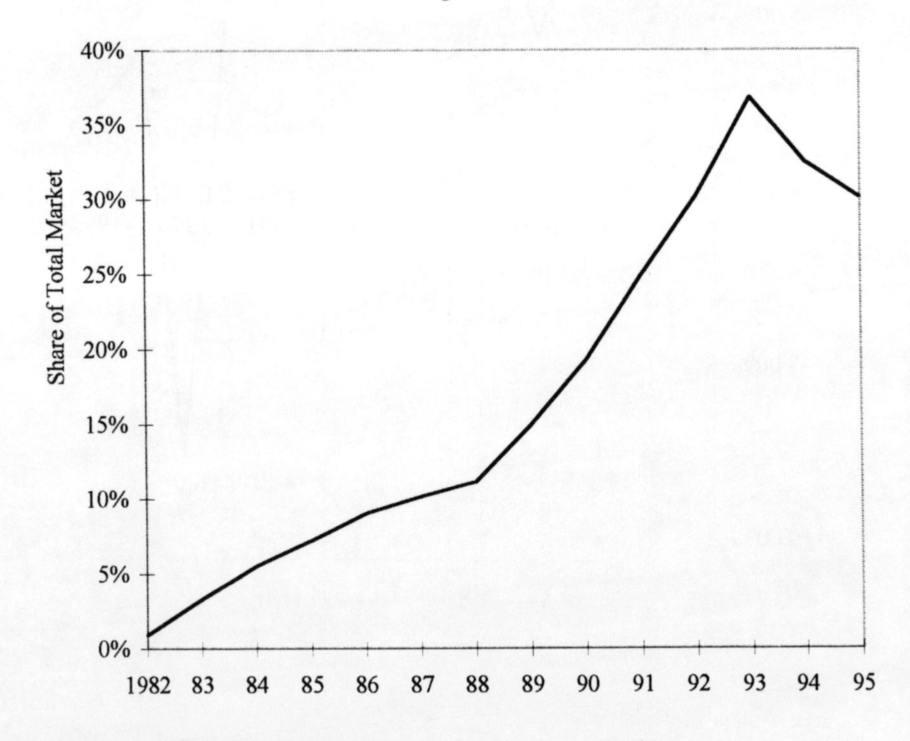

Source: Maxwell, 1989, 1996, *Business Week*, *Advertising Week*.

Figure 3.11
Annual Growth Comparison, 1986–1995: Top Twenty Brands, Full-Price Brands, and Price-Value Brands

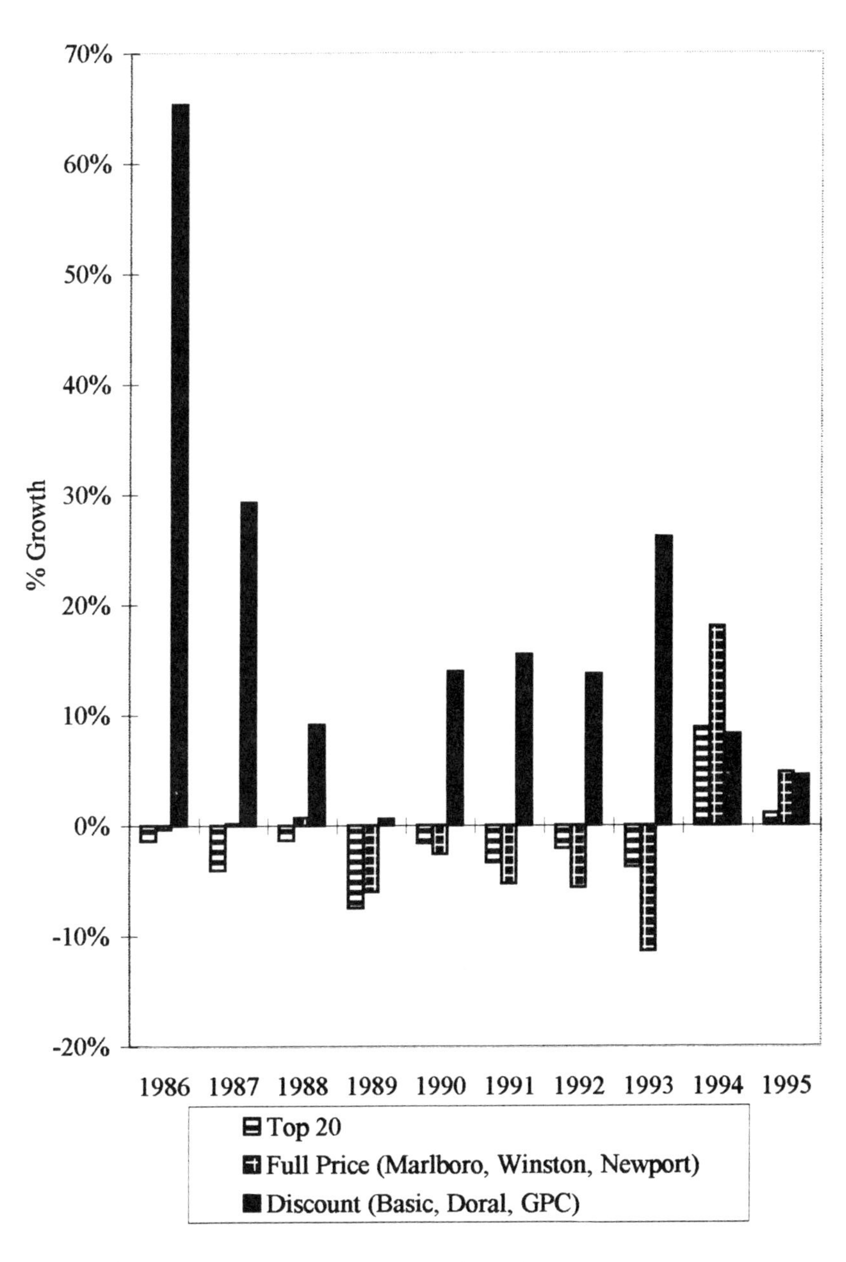

Source: Business Week, Annual Surveys, Tobacco International.

In summary, the industry has responded to declining unit sales brought about by the smoking and health issue with technological innovations (e.g., filter and low-tars) that aimed at a "safer" smoke. Traditional, pre-1950 mass-market approaches were replaced with niche marketing strategies. The dollar value of cigarette sales was more than maintained; sales were significantly increased by price increases that outpaced the rate of inflation. However, one central problem confronts the domestic cigarette industry: the growth of the price-value submarket introduced because of the demographic shift brought about by the anti-smoking movement. The growing popularity of cigarettes with a lower profit margin than full-price brands threatens the continuation of the unusual historic success of the cigarette industry. Marlboro Friday's pricing decrease is an attempt to return full-price brands to the fore—albeit at a "reduced full price."

Chapter 4

Theory and Hypotheses for Individual Firm's Strategic Choices

EVOLUTION OF STRATEGIC MANAGEMENT AND PORTER'S ROLE

Edward H. Bowman's (1990) assessment that the "academic field of policy/strategy went through...a birth in the 1960s" was one agreed upon by many other experts in the field including Hussey (1990), Hofer and Schendel (1978), and Rumelt, Schendel, and Teece (1991). Earlier historical antecedents such as Barnard's *The Functions of the Executive* (1938), Drucker's *The Practice of Management* (1954) and Selznick's *Leadership in Administration* (1957) played an important role in the development of the business policy/strategic management field. However, prior to the 1960s, the field's focus was on the general manager's role in ensuring that the narrow individual functional area viewpoints of the firm's constituents were integrated into a broader, more cohesive, and holistic corporate perspective. In the 1960s, academicians began to treat the strategy field not only as an amalgamation of the functions but rather as a field of study within itself. Strategy, qua strategy, concerned itself with the collective decisions, actions, and implementations of product/market choices, mission and goal definition, distinctive competencies, and resource allocations. The firm was seen to need not only to balance its environmental threats and opportunities with its internal strengths and weaknesses but to search for synergies or reinforcing fits between these elements. The midwives to this strategic birth, in the eyes of the experts, were A. D. Chandler's *Strategy and Structure* (1962), Andrew's *Business Policy: Text and Cases* (1965), and Ansoff's *Corporate Strategy* (1965).

Rumelt et al. (1991) viewed the 1970s as an era when the constructs of the 1960s were placed into practice by such leading-edge strategic consulting firms as McKinsey and Boston Consulting Group. Simultaneously, strategic management academicians formed scholarly societies such as the Academy of Management's Division of Business Policy and Planning and The Planning College of The Institute of Management Science (TIMS). They published their strategic research in newly established and exclusively strategic journals such as the *Strategic Management Journal* and the *Journal of Business Strategy* (both of which had their inaugural issues in 1980).

The 1980s were seen by Columbia's Donald Hambrick (1990) as substantially different from the 1960s and 1970s. He argued that nearly twice as much strategy research was conducted in the first five years of the 1980s as had been done in the prior twenty years. When he compared a list of the fifty-eight most heavily cited authors of the 1980–1985 time frame to a similar 1976 list of 105 authors, Hambrick found an overlap of just 7 authors. Based on this comparison, Hambrick stated that "this signal[d] a radical demarcation" between the research of the 1980s and the 1960s and 1970s. While the question of whether or not the 1980s marked a radical demarcation from prior research is not important to this work, one of the reasons that Hambrick picked 1980 as the beginning of a transition is significant for this study. In addition to the start of new strategic management research journals, Hambrick cited the "publication of Mike Porter's (1980) immensely important book" as a reason for choosing 1980 as the starting point of his study. Porter's book *Competitive Strategy* (1980) was found by Hambrick to have been cited 1,563 times during the 1980–1985 period. This compared to Gupta and Govindarajan's co-authored 1984 article, which placed second on Hambrick's most-noted strategic works with 875 citations.

Porter's 1980 book was far and away the single most important strategy publication of the 1980s. The importance of Porter's work was echoed by other experts in addition to Hambrick:

> Credit, for starting this movement must go to Porter (1980) whose approach to industry analysis has been one of the strongest influences on the development of strategic management. (Hussey, 1990, p. 10)

> The five-forces model of Michael Porter is perhaps the most widely known exposition of the Harvard School [model of corporate strategy]. (Thomas, 1986, p. 16)

> Porter's book...is the exemplar for the external industry focus. (Bowman, 1990, p. 12)

> Economic thinking moved closer to center stage in strategic management.... The most influential contribution of the decade from economics was undoubtedly Porter's *Competitive Strategy* (1980). In a remarkably short time, Porter's application of mobility barriers, industry analysis, and generic strategies became broadly accepted and used in teaching, consultation and many research projects.... Throughout the 1970s, it appeared that organization theory was the discipline of choice for strategy groups [within business school faculties]. However, this balance was reversed in the 1980s,

largely due to the success of Porter's approach to strategy. (Rumelt, Schendel and Teece, 1991, p. 14)

PORTER'S FRAMEWORK

Porter's approach to theory building has been through the use of a framework rather than models. Porter (1991) has discussed these alternative approaches to theory as follows:

> One might approach the task of developing strategy by creating a wide range of situation-specific, but rigorous (read mathematical), models of limited complexity...models abstract the complexity of competition to isolate a few key variables whose interactions are examined in depth. The normative significance of each model depends on the fit between its assumptions and reality. No one model embodies or even approaches embodying all the variables of interest, and hence the applicability of any model's findings are almost inevitably restricted. [whereas frameworks]...encompass many variables and seek to capture much of the complexity of actual competition...The theory embodied in framework is contained in the choice of included variables, the way variables are organized, the interaction among the variables and the way in which alternative patterns of variables and company choices affect outcome...there is a continually evolving environment in which a perpetual competitive interaction between rivals takes place.

Building on the Mason/Bain branch of industrial organizational economics, Porter turned the structure-conduct-performance paradigm from its traditional industry focus to that of the firm. The conduct variable had been relatively ignored in the earlier literature. In effect, the paradigm was viewed deterministically, that is, once the industry structure was known, the conduct and performance followed.

Structure → Conduct → Performance

Porter, by emphasizing the role of the firm (e.g., research and development, decisions to invest in preemptive capacity assets, and acquisitions) in its ability to affect industry structure, competitors, and performance, gave the paradigm a dynamic focus such that it is now viewed as:

Structure ↔ Conduct ↔ Performance

The foundation of the Porter approach is industry analysis. The industry was viewed as the most relevant environment for the study of the firm. Porter took such traditional structural variables as costs, concentration, product differentiation, and entry barriers, and added the concept of mobility barriers–entry barriers between strategic groups in the same industry and arranged them into his famous five competitive forces of industry analysis. The five forces are:

1. Bargaining power of suppliers.
2. Bargaining power of buyers.
3. Threats of new entrants.
4. Threats of substitutes.
5. Rivalry among existing competition.

An analysis of these industry forces allows us to determine a firm's relative competitive position. Porter tailored his industry analysis to specific generic industry environments reflecting an industry's stage of evolution (i.e., fragmented, emerging, mature, and decline). The mature and decline industry environments will be discussed in greater detail below.

After we determine a firm's competitive advantage vis-à-vis its industry rivals, this advantage is exploited by utilizing either a lower-cost or a differentiation strategy. Its competitive advantage is also influenced by its choice of scope; choosing to compete in a broad array of related product/markets or to focus on a specific niche. The ability of a firm to exploit its competitive strategy is viewed as the configuring and linking of a firm's activities (its human resources, technology, procurement, and infrastructure) into an effective "value chain" that creates customer satisfaction superior to that of a firm's rivals. The framework also dictates that we view the firm's value chain in a broader framework of a "value system." The value system encompasses both the firm's supplier value chain and its channels' value chains in evaluating the effect on the end user's value chain (Porter, 1996). With this base framework as background, Porter's specific concepts on maturing and declining businesses, diversification, new business entry, and industry histories are addressed.

Mature Industries

Industry maturity often brings fundamental changes into a firm's environment. Difficult strategic responses are called for. Firms have trouble perceiving these environmental changes. Even when the changes are recognized, "responding to them can require changes in strategy that firms balk at making" (Porter, 1980, p. 238). Industry change during transition is often marked by some of the following events.

1. Competition for market share increases due to reduction in demand growth.
2. Cost often becomes a more critical success factor.
3. Functional areas such as marketing, manufacturing, and distribution have to be reoriented.
4. International competition increases.

Transition to maturity often brings changes in the basic structure of the industry that have some strategic implications. For example, the strategic dilemma of choosing a generic strategy of either low-cost, differentiation, or focus is accentuated by the transition. During the growth phase, growth itself may have allowed all in the industry to prosper. "Strategic sloppiness is generally exposed by industry maturity, however" (Porter, 1980, p. 241).

Maturing industries develop particular needs such as sophisticated cost analysis, product mix rationalization, and price-level consciousness. Innovations in the manufacturing process and in the design of the product should be encouraged. There is a need to consider the potential of decreasing the cost of assets through their purchase from firms exiting the business. Different cost curves for a niche versus a leadership strategy should be addressed. The idea of competing internationally should be considered since industry conditions may be more favorable overseas.

Industries in transition risk certain strategic pitfalls. For instance, a firm with years of experience develops images of both itself and the industry. As the industry transitions to maturity, there is a risk that these perceptions are no longer valid. However, those very years of experience can cloud the fact that the industry is maturing. There is the danger of the cash trap where investments are needed to build share in a mature market where they may thought to be avoided. On the other hand, if the firm fails to recognize maturity, it may over-invest. Companies may be tempted to give up market share too easily in favor of short-run profits. Companies may resent and react irrationally to price competition ("We will not compete on price") or to changes in industry practices ("They are hurting the industry"). Clinging to "higher quality" may be used as an excuse for not meeting aggressive pricing and marketing moves of competitors.

Throughout his writings on maturity, Porter (1980) consistently emphasized the danger of denial, that is, that the firm will fail to recognize that the industry has commenced the transition to maturity. The strategic adjustments often call for "a new way of life." Given this potential unwillingness to change, combined with the likelihood that a new set of managerial skills to manage in maturity is required, a change in management is often appropriate.

Declining Industries

Declining industries are defined as those industries that have experienced an absolute decline in unit sales over a sustained period (Porter, 1980). There are three major causes of decline. One cause is product substitution whereby substitutions through either technological innovation or prominent shifts in relative costs and quality can reduce profits at the same time they negatively affect sales. A second cause is a change in demographics whereby a reduction occurs in the size of the firm's customer group. The third cause is a shift in the buyers' need for the product due to sociological or other reasons. These three causes of decline create indications for evaluating both the uncertainty of the future demand and the potential profitability of meeting that changing demand.

Exit Barriers. The flip side of an entry barrier is an exit barrier. Exit barriers can keep firms competing in a declining industry even though returns do not meet a firm's hurdle rate. For example, if the assets of a business are highly specific to that particular business, an exit barrier is created by the reduction of the liquidation value of the asset value, possibly even to salvage value. It is the equivalent of owning a building in a bad location suitable only to serve as a restaurant, versus owning a general-purpose building similarly situated. The market for restaurant-specific buildings would be "thin," and the liquidation value would be low. If the liquidation value is low, it could still be economically optimal for the firm to remain in business even if the expected discounted cash flows are low.

Another exit barrier involves the fixed costs associated with leaving the industry. Examples of obvious costs include labor settlements, skilled professionals required for divestiture, spare parts maintenance, employee resettlement costs, and long-term contract cancellation costs. Hidden costs, such as a reduction in employee productivity and an early loss of customer and supplier support, also exist.

Some of the strategic exit barriers include interrelatedness (the business of the strategic business unit (SBU) is part of a total corporate strategy), access to financial markets (reduction in the confidence of the capital markets), and vertical integration (an exit can affect an entire vertical chain versus just the one link). Then there are barriers created by management's emotional attachment or commitment to the business.

Alternative Strategies. Companies that remain in a declining industry can adopt alternative strategies. One strategy is to become an industry leader in terms of market share by taking advantage of the decline. The tactical steps to take in order to achieve this goal include: taking aggressive competitive actions in pricing and marketing; purchasing market share through acquisitions or retiring others' capacity; reducing competitors' exit barriers by manufacturing spare parts for their products or by the takeover of their long-term contracts; and demonstrating strong commitment and superior strengths through competitive moves and re-investment in new products and processes.

Another strategy involves targeting a niche—identifying a demand pocket that will be more stable than the market at large. Ultimately, companies pursuing this strategy switch to a harvest or divestment strategy. In a harvest situation, a firm seeks to optimize cash flow through curtailing investment and other spending while maintaining some historic strengths. Common tactics include the reduction of the number of product models, of the distribution channels, and of small customer accounts. Harvesting places great demands on administrative skills, given the need to placate or even motivate suppliers and employees when the ultimate endgame is sale or liquidation.

In a quick divestment situation, a firm maximizes its net percent value by selling early, sometimes even at the maturity stage. Early selling maximizes divestment income because potential buyers will not have the opportunity to see a clear decline. On the other hand, if a firm's forecast of decline in demand was pessimistic, the net present value of its divestment decision will suffer.

Choosing a Strategy for Decline. To determine the firm's position in a declining industry, a complete analysis should occur. Some questions a firm should consider include:

1. Is the structure of the industry compatible with a profitable decline?
2. What exit barriers do competitors face? What decline strategies will they likely follow? What are their capabilities with respect to executing a potential strategy?
3. What exit barriers does the firm face? What are the firm's strengths regarding the remaining demand pockets? What strategies can the firm choose and implement?

Framework for Choosing a Strategy

	Firm Has a Competitive Advantage	**Firm Lacks A Competitive Advantage**
Industry Has Favorable Structure	Leadership or Niche	Harvest or Divest Quickly
Industry Has Unfavorable Structure	Niche or Harvest	Divest Quickly

Diversification

Porter (1987) analyzed the diversification records of thirty-three large companies over the 1950–1986 period. Conclusions were based on this analysis. The corporate diversification strategies were found to have reduced rather than enhanced shareholder value overall.

A diversified company has two possible levels of strategy: competitive strategy at the business unit level and a corporate strategy at the company-wide level. Corporate strategy involves two areas: (1) what businesses the company should be in and, (2) how the corporation should manage these businesses.

Premises of Corporate Strategy. A company's corporate strategy operates under the following assumptions: (1) Competition takes place at the level of the business unit, (2) diversification adds costs and constraints to the individual business units, and (3) shareholders can easily diversify their own portfolios. Corporate strategy must add real value to the individual business units to offset the inherent costs of a corporate parent. Likewise, it must add true value to the shareholders by diversifying in a manner that they could not do for themselves.

Essential Tests. There are three essential tests for diversification. The first is the attractiveness test, which determines if the new unit's industry is structurally attractive or can be made to be such. The second is the cost-of-entry test— the new unit must return a stream of cash that exceeds the cost of capital. The last test is the better-off test—the enhancement of the competitive advantage of either the new unit or the firm because of the new unit's link to the corporation.

Concepts of Corporate Strategy. Porter states that there are four concepts of corporate strategy: (1) portfolio management, (2) restructuring, (3) transferring skills, and (4) sharing activities. In utilizing the concept of portfolio management, a company acquires units that remain autonomous while the corporation supplies capital and an infusion of management techniques. This was the most widely used concept in the past, but today its benefits have eroded. Large companies are no longer the only source of management techniques. Portfolio managers have also been overwhelmed by the sheer complexity of attempting to supervise a vast array of different types of businesses. Deconglomeration is today's response to the firms created by the historic use of portfolio management.

Under the concept of restructuring, companies actively transform sick or underdeveloped businesses through management changes, shifts in strategy, or the infusion of new technology. After a company has turned the business around, the business unit should be sold. This is often not done, and it is the Achilles' heel of this approach.

The transferring skills concept is an active process that can significantly change the strategy or operations of the receiving units. Competitive advantage is achieved only if the following criteria are met:

1. SBU activities are similar enough so that experience sharing is meaningful
2. Skills in the activities transferred must be important to competitive advantage
3. The receiving unit must obtain significant competitive advantage with the skills transferred. If the skills transfer is a one-off versus on going, the unit should be sold, as there will be no further creation of shareholder value.

With the sharing activities concept, the competitive advantage of the value chain should be enhanced by lowering costs or raising differentiation. Synergy of shared activities must be achieved, and a cost-benefit analysis can determine if this is possible. Sharing must involve activities significant to competitive advantage (e.g., distribution channels or sales forces).

In choosing a corporate strategy for either transferring skills, or sharing activities companies can follow these action steps:

1. Identify potential shared activities and skill transfers among already existing business units.
2. Select the core businesses that will be the foundation of the corporate strategy. The core businesses should be structurally attractive and capable of sustaining a competitive advantage. They should possess the capability for mutual interrelationships and provide a base of skills and activities for further diversification.
3. Create within the organization horizontal mechanisms to accommodate interrelationships between the core businesses.
4. Pursue diversification opportunities that allow first for shared activities and then for skill transfer. The goal is to build a cluster of related and mutually reinforcing business units.

Porter concludes, "The failure of corporate strategy reflects the fact that most diversified companies have failed to think in terms of how they really add value" (1987, p. 58).

Entry into New Business

According to perfect market theory, if market forces are working perfectly in the economic sense, no entry decision can yield an above-average return. Therefore, the key is to identify those industries where market forces are not working perfectly. Entry to an industry can be either by internal development or via acquisition.

Entry through Internal Development. If attempting entry through internal development, two potential entry barriers must be faced—structural entry barriers, especially excess capacity, and expected retaliation from incumbent firms.

An industry that is in disequilibrium is a prime target for entry. It may be a new industry that is developing, with rising entry barriers, and one can be an early mover. Or it may be a backwater industry where poor information exists with respect to potential entrants.

Another prime target for entry is an industry whose incumbents are expected to retaliate slowly or ineffectually because the cost of retaliation outweighs the benefits or the dominant incumbents are prone to protect the industry and not themselves.

From an internal viewpoint, a firm may have lower entry costs if either economies of scope exist or there are potential spillover effects on the entrant's already existing businesses.

Entry through Acquisition. The price of an acquisition is determined by the market. An efficient market works to eliminate any above-average profits. Acquisitions often do not meet managers' profit expectations because of this efficient market concept. Acquisitions have the best opportunity to be profitable if a low floor price is created by a seller's poor perception of the alternative of keeping the business or if the buyer, through either superior information or unique synergies, has potentially greater cash flows from the acquisition than does the rest of the bidding market.

Industry Histories

Porter (1981) has characterized the distinct elements of an in-depth industry study as follows:

> First, its emphasis is longitudinal, built around a careful re-creation of competitive moves and other events in the sequence in which they occurred. Second, it is broad and quite detailed in coverage of firm behavior and industry events rather than focusing on one or few elements of competitive behavior such as investment or pricing. Third, it emphasizes the uncertainties present in predicting the future that bear on the decisions facing firms. Fourth, it places great emphasis on a full and complete description of each major competitor, including its full range of activities in all markets in which it competes. (p. 454)

Porter defines the concept of strategy as the "playing out of strategies over time through investment decisions and tactical moves and counter moves." The end result of a successful strategic interaction, or a series thereof, is the creation of sustainable mobility barriers. Mobility barriers are entry barriers peculiar to a particular firm's strategic domain.

Dynamic cost reduction is vitally important in strategic interaction and has two components. The components are static economics of scale and dynamic learning (product and process technological changes). Learning is a function of cumulative volume, which implies that greater market percentage leads to lower costs through technical efficiency and innovative product/process improvements. The learning effect caused by cumulative volume can be reduced or nullified by the following occurrences. Learning may not go on indefinitely as it often stops on a percentage basis early in an industry's history. Second, it may not be possible to keep learning proprietary. To the extent that low-cost copying occurs and that learning is costly (high) research and development (R & D expenditures) the leader has a reduced incentive to innovate. Third, a new innovation may be so quantumly different that a "new" learning curve may be created.

Learning can also be a function of time in the industry ("how long" one has been looking versus a volume effect). This creates an incentive for first-movers advantage and for the acquisition of early-entry firms. The interaction of both volume- and time-based learning, combined with potential static scale economics, can produce a dominant market leader.

The Firm as an Interrelated Portfolio of Activities. Optimal diversification, if properly managed, can create tangible relationships (e.g., shared brand names, distribution channels, logistical network) and intangible relationships (e.g., similar generic strategies, same type of buyer) that reduce costs and create entry barriers relative to firms not so positioned. The possible implications for strategic interaction within an industry because of interrelated activities are:

1. Capital, managerial time and pursuit of learning curves may be allocated in a portfolio matrix approach;
2. Strategies and tactics amongst interrelated SBU's will be impacted; and
3. Strong pressures will be created for offensive or defensive related diversification or vertical integration.

Since related diversification has supplanted conglomerate diversification, strategic interaction often involves multiple industries because of horizontal strategies.

Global Competition. Global industries arise when there are opportunities for strategic advantage by coordinating a firm's activities across national markets, such as large scale economics in manufacturing or research or internationally cumulative learning (Porter, 1986, 1990). It may be, in certain industries, that a firm must be both global in scope and optimally diversified. This would not be true where industry structure was found to encourage multidomestic competition.

Factors that encourage an industry to evolve globally are (1) decreased transportation and communication costs, (2) a convergence of social and economic factors among countries, and (3) reduced government constraints. Sources of global advantage can be had from traditional comparative advantages, economies of scale, and learning.

Entry/Mobility Deterrence. Entry/mobility deterring tactics, such as commitment signaling, capacity expansion, advertising increases, price cutting, new product introduction, and raising exit barriers, often take time and occur in sequential fashion. The tactics can affect the relative costs of the dominant firm significantly less than its competitors (or potential entrants). Tactics can also vary in their specificity to a particular potential entrant or competitor versus the industry as a whole. Paradoxically, a dominant firm may encourage a weak firm to enter (or preserve an existing weak competitor) in order to discourage other, more powerful entrants.

Difference Among Firm's Objectives and Abilities. An industry's firm's objectives will differ because of (1) different patterns of related diversification; (2) different risk/reward utility functions among firms' management; and (3) different principal-agency design mechanisms to cope with the shareholder ownership versus management control issue.

Firms will also differ in functional and strategic abilities (Porter, 1996). Their differences, with respect to both choice of objectives and ability to accomplish, will affect strategic interactions between firms.

The Determinants of Market Structure. A "striking point," Porter (1981) states, is that "history and chance play an important role in interacting with economic variables to determine the structural outcome in an industry" (p. 458). The net effect to this historical and random viewpoint is that market structure is determined not only by the traditional industrial organizational factors plus the previously discussed dynamic cost effects of learning. Rather, it is the interaction of these economic variables with elements of history and chance that determine market structure.

The first determinant is chance decisions. Early strategic choices made by incumbents in an industry are usually made under great uncertainty, and chance plays a significant role. Porter uses Procter & Gamble's (P&G) choice of a one-piece diaper versus the competition's two-piece diaper choice in the disposable diaper industry and the growth of the Canadian whiskey industry due to U.S. prohibition as examples of the role of chance.

The second historical determinant of market structure is the "identity of the particular firms that happen to be participants in the industry during its infancy" (p. 460). Porter points out that this identity has a "high random component" in itself. Mature industries often undergo structural change because of the entry of new firms at that stage. History, rather than logic, often dictates which firms enter at this mature stage.

The third determinant concerns the level of uncertainty with respect to the early industry's technology and potential demand. Porter states, "Certainty encourages attempt at preemptive behavior during the industry's developmental period to reap first-mover advantages and deter subsequent entry" (and vice versa with respect to uncertainty) (p. 462). Preemptive behavior increases competition in the long run but is found to increase concentration as the industry matures.

METHODOLOGY

This study is a comparative case study. Porter (1981, 1991) has stressed the value of in-depth case studies that include industry histories in understanding industry environments and identifying firm's strategic interactions. Porter (1981) has characterized the distinct elements as follows:

> First, its emphasis is longitudinal, built around a careful re-creation of competitive moves and other events in the sequence in which they occurred. Second, it is broad and quite detailed in coverage of firm behavior and industry events rather than focusing on one or few elements of competitive behavior such as investment or pricing. Third, it emphasizes the uncertainties present in predicting the future that bear on the decisions facing firms. Fourth, it places great emphasis on a full and complete description of each major competitor, including its full range of activities in all markets in which it competes. (p. 450)

McGee and Thomas (1988) in their study of the office reprographics industry state that such "rich" studies allow for problem complexity and firm-level decision processes to be examined in the light of the industry evolution. Specifically, they state that such studies "can treat the major sources of complexity and high-light the dynamic nature of industry evolution, the range of strategies and positions occupied by firms over time and the sometimes temporary nature of market leadership by 'first-movers' or pioneers in markets" (p. 74).

Harrigan (1980b) has succinctly stated the weaknesses of such studies: "The confidence with which conclusions could be stated...will necessarily be reduced by the strong elements of judgment which will be needed in evaluating the findings as well as in describing a complex factual situation" (pp. 56–57). In other words, richness is gained by accepting dependence on the writer's judgment. However, since this study is one of theory verification of Porter versus theory generation, the writer's scope for judgment is reduced. As Post and Andrews (1982) have pointed out, theory empirification is a much more familiar process than theory generation. Despite this reassurance, the caveat must remain that, as with all case studies, the risk exists that, unconsciously, the case writer may distort the case facts.

In summary, the task requires the richness of an in-depth industry study that, by its nature, necessitates a degree of judgment. However, this judgmental dependency is lessened somewhat by the theory verification nature of the study. The study can be conceptualized as, first, the effect of the anti-smoking movement on the industry's overall demand and on the specific demand for particular product types (e.g., "safer"). Second, based on Porter's frameworks, hypotheses are developed with respect to both domestic market and diversification strategies. Third, these strategies are then tested against the firms' actual choices, which are contained in each firm's case history. Analysis of results and conclusions are the final element. Porter's framework was based on case studies dealing with industries declining, essentially because of substitute products. The purpose of his case studies was to generate theory. The methodology in this study is the use of multiple case studies to attempt to replicate, in a quasi-experimental sense, Porter's research in an industry whose maturity and decline have been brought about by hostile social factors concerning the industry's product. The analysis is intended to test theory and is an explanatory and predictive multiple case analysis.

Secondary information was gathered on (1) the smoking and health issue, (2) the industry, and (3) the individual firms. Main sources for a historical (1950 and prior) perspective were R. B. Tennant's *The American Cigarette Industry* (1950) and W. H. Nicholl's *Price Policies in the Cigarette Industry* (1951). Among more recent treatises, two were of particular usefulness. They were R. H. Miles's *Coffin Nails and Corporate Strategies* (1982) and R. A. McGowan's *Business, Politics and Cigarettes: An Analysis of Public Policy Interventions on Cigarette Sales* (1988, 1995). Archival information was garnered from Industrial Surveys and Company Analyses by both Moody's and Standard and Poor's, as well as company Annual Reports and Securities and

Exchange Commission (SEC) 10K filings. Investment banking reports, company histories, and industry publications such as *Tobacco International, Tobacco Reporter*, and The Tobacco Institute publications were utilized.

Forbes Annual Industry Surveys as well as *Business Week's* Annual Cigarette Industry Surveys also provided insight. This information was collected and sorted by both time chronology and the subject areas of the (1) smoking and health issue, (2) the industry, and (3) the individual firm's strategies. The material was further subdivided by the matrixing of the industry's evolution (growth rates, product types, etc.) with the Porter-generated hypotheses.

Although I do not believe it would in any way change the analysis or conclusions, a word about the numerical data is in order. The only single-source, absolutely reliable number set for this period is the total number of cigarettes consumed. Individual firms report sales or unit numbers, rarely both, and they change reporting formats periodically. One is thus forced to go to multiple sources, and at times one has to rely on one's own calculations and/or estimates. Trends and multiple-source triangulation do, however, lessen the likelihood of any significant error.

Financial numbers create difficulty for two reasons. First, line of business reporting is rarely consistent either across firms or within a firm. Second, excise taxes are sometimes reported as sales and other times as an expense item. Finally, because of the financial community's concerns with valuing the future with a firm's on-going operations, past results are always restated to reflect solely the on going operations. With this study's concern for historical evolution, year-by-year data as they unfold are required. Consequently, it is not always straightforward to compare the study-generated data with trend lines found in the financial community's standard references. I hasten to add that no significant aberrations were discovered when checking the study's data.

RESEARCH QUESTIONS AND HYPOTHESES

While the above description of Porter's framework is brief Porter took approximately 1,000 pages to explain, it does allow us to address the strategic management issues of the cigarette industry. From the 1953 publication of the Sloan-Kettering Report, linking smoking and cancer, to the 1990 proposed Congressional ban on print advertising, the cigarette industry has operated in an increasingly hostile environment. The major research questions are, What strategies have the industry's firms developed to cope with this hostile environment? and Why have specific firms chosen specific strategies and with what results?

It is hypothesized that the firms will follow the tenets prescribed by Porter in his work on competitive strategies. Hypotheses have been developed from his work on (1) industries in transition to maturity and (2) industries in decline.

Porter noted that as industries evolved through their maturity/decline phases, diversification occurred (see Figure 4.1). Hypotheses have been developed from his work on diversification.

There have been three major studies of the cigarette industry. Nicholls (1951) and Tennant (1950) both wrote major works on the industry as it had developed through the year 1950. Robert H. Miles (1982) studied the industry from 1950 through the mid-1970s. Miles's study was:

> intended to provide a rich account of the political economy of the modern business corporation, which would in turn provide some insights into the ways in which politics and economics interact to influence large, complex organizations and their embedding society.... [T]his investigation falls into the domain of exploratory research [because] there were no comprehensive theories to subject to rigorous testing (p. 26).

The present study is neither exploratory nor descriptive. Rather, it is a structured test of linked hypotheses developed from Porter's work on strategy, conducted in an industry-specific context. A review of 403 overwhelmingly supportive studies shows a dominating concern with a single particular feature of Porter's work, e.g., mobility barriers (Lieberman, 1989), strategic groups (Mascarenhas & Aaker, 1989), and generic strategies (Hill, 1988). Some of the studies modify Porter's model with such features as market segmentation strategies (Kim & Lim, 1988) or manufacturing strategies (Kotha & Orne, 1989). The different studies explored individual aspects of Porter's work and, in some situations, modified his concept. This study responds to Porter's (1991) call for "detailed longitudinal case studies, covering long periods of time" and utilizes the disciplined prism of single-industry case study to test more than one aspect of his strategic tenets. This focus on multiple aspects of Porter over a forty-five year interval of industry life is the unique and original feature of this research.

Figure 4.1
Evolution in the Cigarette Industry

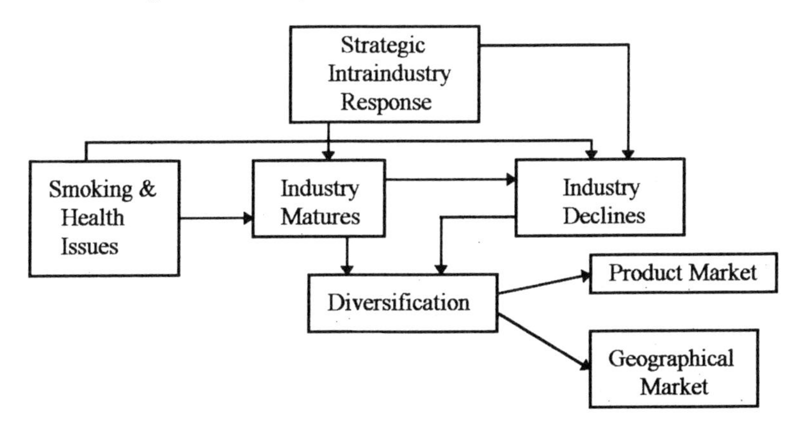

MATURE INDUSTRY HYPOTHESIS

According to Porter, maturity exposes strategic sloppiness. Growth allows strategic errors to go undetected to the point that an industry's collective firms may not only survive but jointly prosper. Maturity slows the firms' historical growth rates, absent the obtaining of market share from a competitor. Thus, as an industry matures, strategy becomes critical.

However, the transition to maturity is often not recognized by firms. The maturation process may be subtle and slow and hence hard to perceive. A firm may also balk, consciously or unconsciously, at the thought of changing a heretofore successful strategy. Industry leaders, tied to such a successful strategy, can be replaced during the maturity phase by rivals, whose flexibility is not heavily weighed by historical success. Followers can thus become leaders.

In the maturing cigarette industry, historic success (Tennant has pointed out in Chapters 2 and 3 that the status quo of the 1950s was established in the 1920s) will cause industry leaders to resist strategy changes. This failure to respond to maturing market conditions by industry leaders will cause a change in the ranking of the constituent firm's market shares.

Hypothesis 1: As the cigarette industry moves into the maturity/decline phase due to the smoking and health issue, there will be substantial change in the market share ranking of its participant firms.

Strategic Intraindustry Responses to Decline Hypotheses

As the industry growth rates slow to the point of decline, Porter hypothesizes four alternative strategies that a firm may follow, either individually or sequentially. The strategies are leadership, niche, harvest, and divest. Leadership is defined by Porter in terms of market share. In the face of decline, a leadership strategy is one where a firm demonstrates a strong commitment to the industry through its aggressive competitive actions in marketing and its reinvestment in products and processes. A leadership strategy states that a firm chooses to go after the number-one position in share of market. It is attempting to be the only (or one of the only) firms to remain in the industry. A niche strategy seeks to create or defend a strong position in a particular segment. Harvesting is defined as a strategy that seeks to optimize cash flow through the curtailment of investment and other spending. A divestment strategy attempts to maximize net investment recovery by selling early, sometimes even at maturity before decline sets in.

Porter further states that strategy selection is a function of matching the relative attractiveness of the industry with the firm's relative position in that industry. Given a high historical industry profitability, one would not expect to see firms adopt an initial harvest or divest strategy, although eventual decline will cause such a strategy to be adopted sequentially. Additionally, Porter points out that if the assets of the business are highly specialized, exit barriers are created because the liquidation value of such assets is diminished. Potential lawsuits likewise serve to diminish the value of the enterprise. In the cigarette industry, the historic profitability, the potential legal exposure from smoking liability lawsuits, and the highly specialized assets serve as an effective exit barrier to a harvest or divest quickly strategy. The logic of inertia, profitability, and high exit barriers dictate that firms that have successfully followed a niche strategy will continue to do so. The first hypothesis states that new industry leaders will emerge during the cigarette industry's transition to maturity. It will be these firms that adopt Porter's leadership strategy in the decline phase.

In summary, Porter states that as an industry declines, its firms will adopt one of the following strategies: leadership, niche, harvest, or exit.

Hypothesis 2: In the cigarette industry firms other than previous leaders will assume the leadership strategy during the industry's maturitydecline phase.

Hypothesis 3: Firms that have historically followed a successful niche strategy will continue to do so during the cigarette industry's maturity/decline phase.

Hypothesis 4: Due to historically high cigarette profits and to the existence of more favorable alternatives (leadership/niche) under Hypotheses 2 and 3, firms in the cigarette industry will not initially adopt a harvest strategy. They will, however, be forced to adopt such a strategy in the long run.

Hypothesis 5: Because (1) of historic profitability and (2) of high exit barriers due to substantial industry-specific assets and potential legal liability, firms in the cigarette industry will not seek to adopt an exit strategy.

Diversification Strategies Hypotheses

Porter states that as an industry matures, firms in that industry will search for new markets (new geographical or product markets) in order to "escape maturity."

Hypothesis 6: Firms in the cigarette industry will adopt diversification strategies during the maturity/decline phase of the industry.

Geographical Market Diversification. Porter (1980) states that firms in maturing industries will search for new markets in order to postpone or avoid decline. Geographical market diversification abroad presents to a domestic industry's firms an opportunity to continue to grow (albeit only temporarily) because of an increase in the size of the market. The same industry in a foreign country may be more attractive if the environmental forces contributing to maturity/decline in the domestic market are not yet present (or to the same degree) in the foreign market. The ability to follow a geographically diversified strategy is affected by a firm's domestic industry position and overall resources (Porter, 1986). It should be noted that this study is concerned with whether or not the industry will diversify geographically and with which firms in the industry will do so. It does not concern itself with such issues as whether or not a multidomestic or global strategy should be followed. Such an inquiry would require another study equivalent to the one found here and as such is not treated.

The anti-smoking movement, over the vast majority of this study's time frame, has been a significantly stronger force in the U.S. market than it has been in other countries' markets. These non-U.S. markets, by not sharing this experience either at all or to a lesser degree, have remained relatively attractive. The preferred lighter tobacco of American-type cigarettes combined with superior marketing skills (especially vis-à-vis the many state-owned cigarette enterprises found abroad) gives the U.S. firms a competitive edge in those markets. Geographical expansion appears viable for the industry. However, firms that have not adopted a leadership strategy in the U.S. marketplace would not be prone to make the necessary commitment to overseas expansion. Even if they did, they would most likely encounter a resources mismatch in facing the firms who have adopted a leadership strategy in the U.S. market. Firms who have chosen a leadership strategy have both the necessary resources and the commitment to expand internationally.

Hypothesis 7: Firms that undertake a leadership strategy under Hypothesis 2 will diversify into international markets.

Hypothesis 8: Firms that adopt other strategies (niche, harvest, exit) will not expand internationally.

Product Market Diversification. According to Porter (1985, 1987), product market diversification can be based on either a market-related strategy or a manufacturing/technology platform. Since cigarette manufacturing is sui generis, a manufacturing or technology-based strategy is not relevant. Diversification into new product markets based on a related market strategy (where knowledge could be shared and experience transferred) could be either by acquisition or new entry.

The cigarette industry is part of the broader consumer packaged goods sector. This sector is mature with some firms exercising leadership for over a century (Porter, 1990). Given this maturity and given the size requirement (the amount of sales, profits, and cash flow) for a new product area to actually diversify a cigarette firm, internal development of a related new product area is not feasible.

Acquisitions will be related to the firm's core competencies since Porter's diversification literature emphasizes the need for horizontal management between related business in order to achieve competitive advantage by exploiting appropriate horizontal relationships between business units. Porter emphasizes that it is the ability to exploit horizontal relationships that allows firms to achieve a future value in an acquisition rather than see such value consumed in the bidding process for an acquisition. When we reverse the lens to determine if such a perfect market theory logic applies to the industry firms as acquisition targets by others outside the industry, our vision becomes clouded.

An assumption of perfect market theory is perfect information. For an efficient market to function, all pertinent information regarding the firm must be readily available and of high quality to buyers and sellers alike so that each can make well-informed decisions. Information asymmetry exists with respect to this industry. The industry's collective legal, political, and research institutions inhibit the free flow of pertinent potential liability information to potential buyers. Such information inhibition not only distorts the market price but also, because of uncertainty over an item like addiction, clouds the ability to evaluate the marketing capabilities of the industry. The issue itself causes concerns that the industry management capabilities may be consumed in addressing the situation. Inability to evaluate management capabilities hinders the ability to envision horizontal management interrelationships. Hence, the only potential buyers will be those who believe the market has discounted the value of a cigarette firm too heavily. Such purchasers will acquire firms in the industry for investment portfolio or financial restructuring reasons.

Hypothesis 9: Due to (1) the cigarette firms' unique production/technology specificity (hence their lack of transferability), (2) the maturity of closely related industries in the consumer packaged goods sector), and (3) the absolute size requirement of a new product area for effective diversification, companies in the cigarette industry will choose an acquisition rather than an internal development strategy to achieve product market diversification.

Hypothesis 10: Cigarette firms will acquire businesses that will be related to their core competencies (i.e., consumer packaged goods marketing).

Hypothesis 11: Because uncertainties over legal liabilities and industry viability impair the perfect market assumption of perfect information which also impairs any acquiring firm's visualization of future horizontal management capabilities, cigarette firms that will be acquired by firms from outside the industry will be acquired for investment portfolio or financial restructuring reasons.

Chapter 5

Hypotheses Tested by Individual Firm's Actual Strategic Choices

The forty-five year evolution of the smoking and health issue was described in Chapter 2. The industry's reactions to these issues, in terms of product types, market segmentation, and brand proliferation, were outlined in Chapter 3. In this chapter, the strategies of the individual firms within the previously described industry environment are elaborated. Individual firm's responses to the intraindustry strategic interactions, along with product and market diversification efforts, are chronicled. The firm's actions are then tested against the Porter-generated hypotheses that were developed in Chapter 4.

PHILIP MORRIS

One of the most spectacular successes in recent corporate history, Philip Morris has grown over the past four decades from a minor player in the cigarette industry to a major international company. As recently as 1961, Philip Morris—based in Richmond, Virginia—was the smallest of the "Big Six" cigarette companies, holding only a 9.6% market share (compared with R.J. Reynolds's 33.6% share). By 1995, the company had grabbed 46.1% of the domestic market. It was propelled to that position largely by its flagship brand, Marlboro, which the company boasts as "the world's best-selling consumer packaged product" (Philip Morris, *Annual Report*, 1990). In addition, Philip Morris's food and beverage subsidies, Kraft General Foods, Inc. and Miller Brewing Company, have demonstrated continued profit-making abilities since their acquisition by Philip Morris in the mid-1980s and late 1960s, respectively.

Philip Morris & Co. was incorporated in 1902 in New York City by Gustav Eckmeyer, the sole U.S. distributor for the British-based Philip Morris firm (established in 1847). Initially, Eckmeyer's company simply imported and sold the English-made cigarettes. In 1918, however, Philip Morris & Co. devised and distributed a domestic cigarette, English Ovals, a brand containing a domestic blend similar to the highly successful Camel brand produced by R.J. Reynolds. Throughout the 1920s, Philip Morris existed solely as a distributor of other companies' cigarettes, especially, Stephans Brothers. In 1924, Philip Morris began to distribute its own Marlboro brand, which was originally and unsuccessfully promoted as a women's brand. In 1929, Stephans Brothers. ceased manufacture of Philip Morris brands, forcing Philip Morris to take up cigarette production itself. In 1933, the company made a bid for a share of the national cigarette market with the reformulation of its Philip Morris English Blend brand. By 1938, the brand had exceeded Lorillard's Old Gold brand in sales and ranked fourth among the leading brands. The Philip Morris brand, with Johnny the page boy "calling for Philip Morris," achieved an 11.1% share of the domestic market in 1950, but sales began to decline thereafter (its market share fell to 1.9% in 1961, and by 1995, it was Philip Morris's only nonfilter product and constituted less than one-tenth of 1% of its sales).

1950–1995

Despite the decline of Philip Morris's eponymous brand in the 1950s due to the smoking and health issue, that decade saw the company's first indications of future success. The anti-smoking movement had created a consumer demand for a perceived safer cigarette—a filter tip. Philip Morris had to respond, and respond they did. Supported by a marketing campaign that created one of the most recognized cultural icons of postwar America, the Marlboro brand with filter tip was relaunched in 1954 as a full-flavored man's cigarette. The rugged masculine image of the Marlboro Man, accompanied by the theme music of the popular western *The Magnificent Seven*, would come to saturate television screens by the 1960s. After the 1971 ban on cigarette advertising on television and radio, the Marlboro Man became just as ubiquitous in magazines and on billboards. This marketing campaign, which included Marlboro's distinctive red-and-white flip-top cardboard box, imitated R.J. Reynolds's Winston brand claims to being a "full-flavored" filter cigarette. By 1956, Marlboro was the tenth best-selling brand in the domestic market, with a market share of 3.4%; in 1966, it joined the ranks of the top five brands, with a market share of 6.0%. Nine years later, in 1975, Marlboro became the country's best-selling brand, a position it held through 1990, in which year it claimed a 26.3% market share. By mid-1993, the growth of generics had reduced Marlboro to a 23.5% share of market. The company had projected Marlboro's share to go below 20% if events continued unabated. However, Marlboro Friday and subsequent marketing support have resulted in a 1995 market share of 30.1%.

Although not quite a single-brand cigarette company, Philip Morris's fortunes throughout the 1950s and 1960s remained tied largely to Marlboro. The 1954 acquisition of the Benson & Hedges cigarette company had provided Philip Morris with two successful king-size brands, Parliament and Benson & Hedges (in 1989, both brands, having been reformulated, were among the twenty best-selling brands). Its menthol brand, Alpine, was introduced into an already overcrowded submarket in 1959 and failed to attract consumer attention, never achieving even a 1% market share. Not until 1968 did Philip Morris introduce another successful brand. In that year, the company unveiled the Virginia Slims brand, in effect creating a cigarette submarket of brands designed exclusively for women. Content to expand its Marlboro product line through brand extensions such as Marlboro Lights, unveiled in 1971, Philip Morris introduced no major new brands until 1976, when it followed Lorillard's True and R.J. Reynolds's Vantage into the low-tar submarket with its Merit brand, which by 1979 surpassed both early entry brands in sales and ranked eighth among the top brands with a 3.7% market share. Philip Morris flawlessly executed a coordinated marketing, production, and logistics campaign for Merit, which *Business Week* characterized as the most successful in cigarette history. In 1990, Merit remained in the eighth berth among the top brands. In the generics battlefield of the 1990s, Merit had slipped to as low as number sixteen among the top twenty in 1993. However, as premium brands did generally after Marlboro Friday, it climbed to number eleven by 1995.

The growth of the price-value submarket after 1980 had also forced Philip Morris in 1985 to introduce the Cambridge brand, which by 1990 claimed a 2.9% market share. With the introduction of Bristol and Bucks, Philip Morris's overall share of the price-value segment grew to 26.6% overall in 1995.

Simultaneously in the 1980s, Philip Morris, which historically had pushed price increases, was able to fully exercise price leadership in the full-price segment (Ostroff, 1990). The effect of such price leadership can be seen in Figure 5.1 when comparing taxes as a percentage of the retail sales price: 1960 (49.8%), 1970 (48.4%), 1980 (33.3%), and 1990 (25.6%). In 1992, the ratio reached a nadir of 24.9%; by 1995, it climbed back to 31.6% because of Marlboro Friday's pricing policies, a 20% increase in federal excise tax (to $.24 pack) and a 28% increase in the average state tax (to $.33 pack).

Figure 5.1
Average State and Federal Cigarette Taxes as a Percentage of Average Retain Prices, 1954–1995

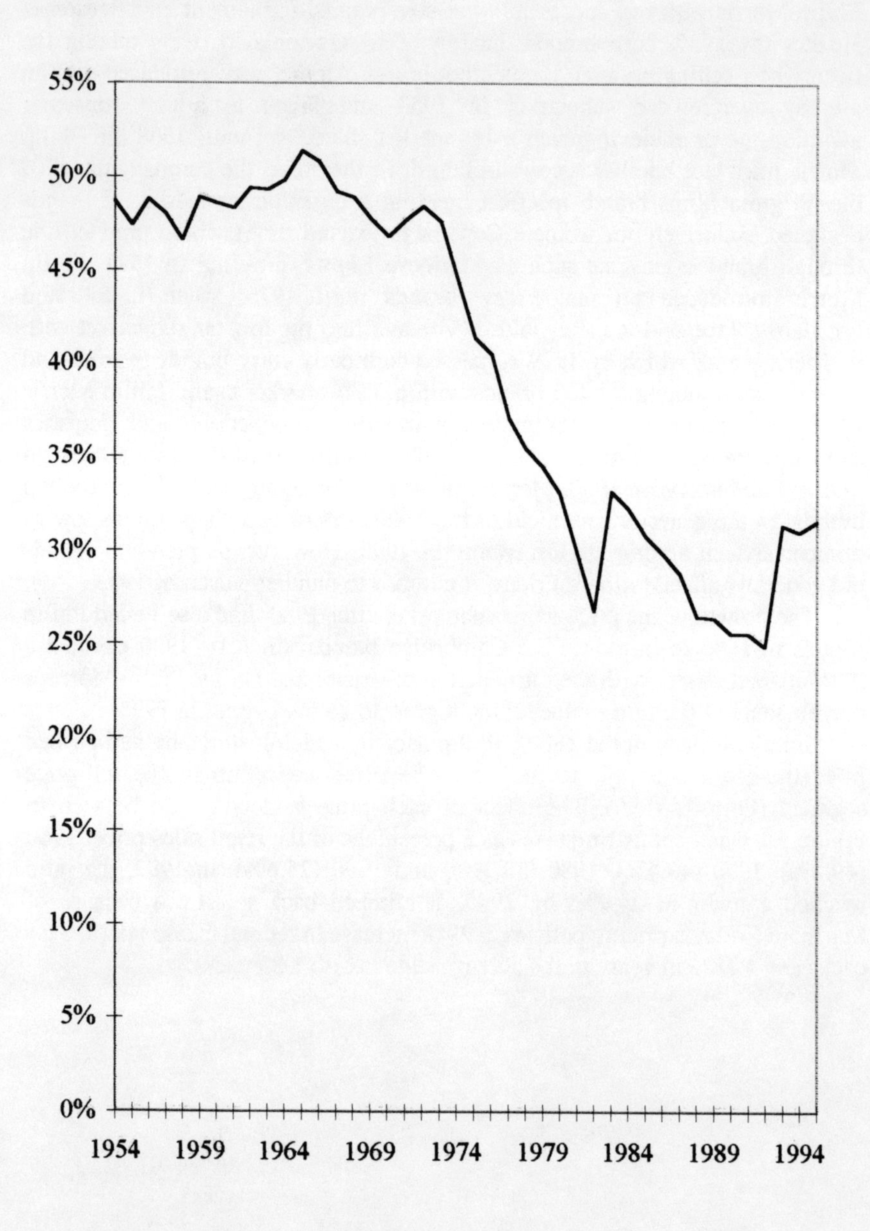

Sources: Tax Burden on Tobacco, 1995.

Figure 5.2
Weighted Average (Median) Price per Package, 1954–1995

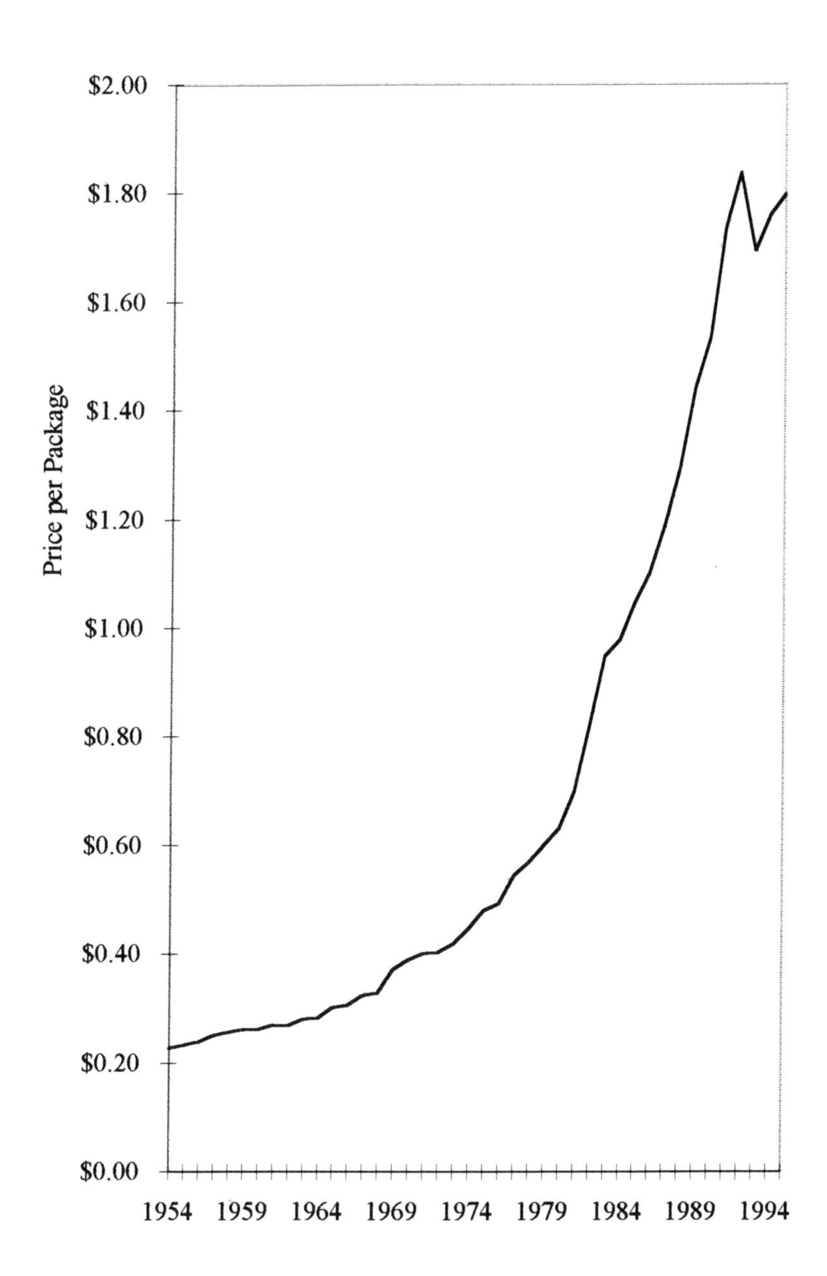

Sources: Tax Burden on Tobacco, 1995.

Figure 5.3
Average State and Federal Cigarette Taxes per Package, 1954–1995

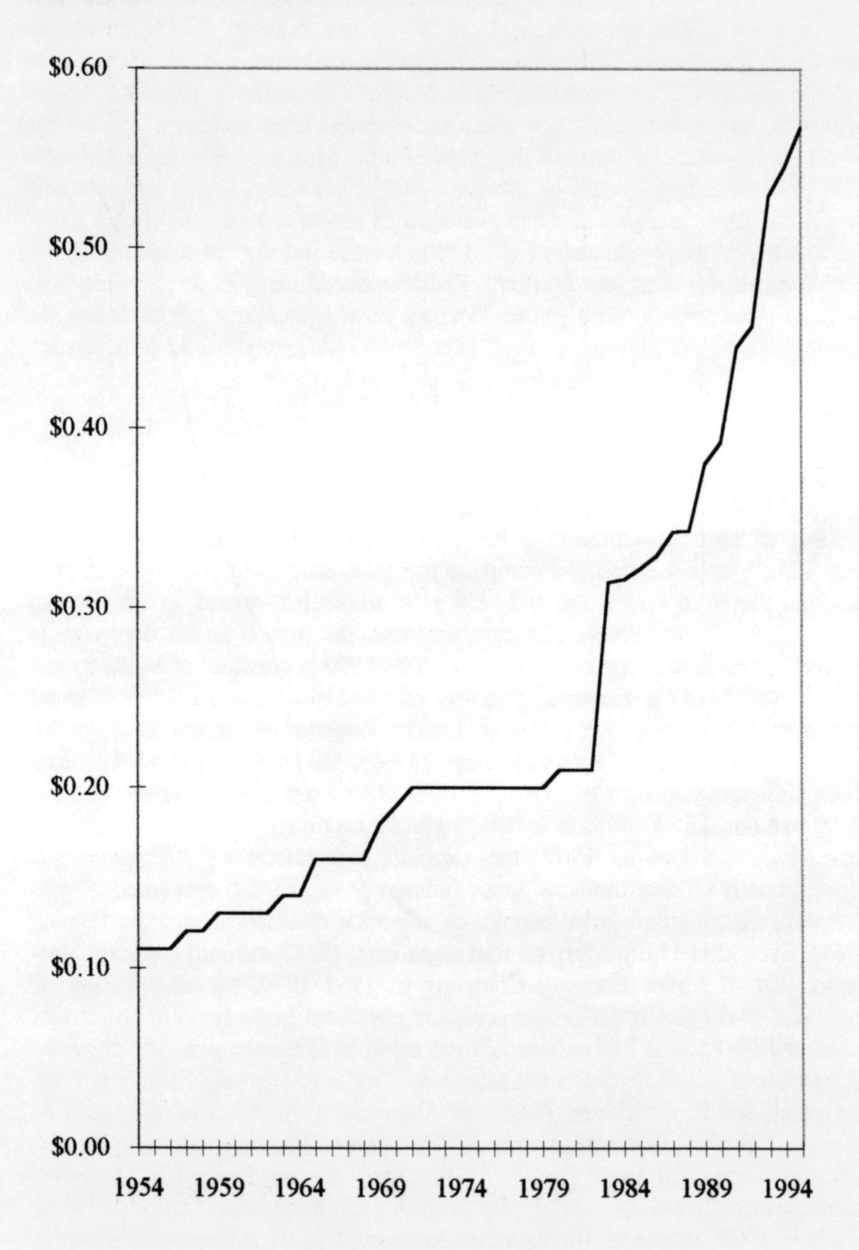

Sources: Tax Burden on Tobacco, 1995.

It was actually taxes that made Philip Morris realize how lucrative this cigarette business could be. During the 1960s, the average retail price increased from $.261 per pack to $.389 as shown in Figure 5.2. Average federal and state taxes (Figure 5.3), which went from $0.13 per pack to $0.19, drove this increase. Despite this 50% price increase over ten years, consumption overall also increased 435 billion units. Philip Morris's chairman at the time, Joseph Cullman, has stated that it was these tax-inspired price increases without the expected downturn in demand that made Philip Morris realize how profitable the cigarette industry could be (Davis, 1989). That was a lesson well learned. Operating profit margins that had averaged 18 to 20% in the 1970s grew to the 32 to 40% range by the end of the 1980s for the industry as a whole. In the 1990s, generic brands and Marlboro Friday reduced margins to less than 30% but had subsequently (with Philip Morris's price leadership) rebounded to the 37 to 39% range. Philip Morris has exercised brand, market, and price leadership.

Product Diversification

If Philip Morris's success in the cigarette business has been due to a strategy of cautious imitation rather than innovation (*Business Week*, 1976) excluding Virginia Slims, the company proved equally cautious in the diversification efforts to which the industry as a whole has turned in the face of declining per capita sales. The company was the first cigarette company to diversify outside the tobacco business with its 1957 acquisition of Milpint, Inc. and Nicolet Paper Co. However, this was followed by a limited number of small company acquisitions over the next decade: Polymer Industries, Inc. (1958), American Safety Razor Products Corp. (1960), Burma-Vita Co. (1963), and Koch Convestographic Co. (1968). Philip Morris felt that its 1960s balance sheet size (e.g., $500 million in 1965) and its relatively low price-to-earnings ratio (P/E) (as late as 1969, the cigarette manufacturer's P/E ratio was approximately 60% of the Dow Jones Industrials in general) prevented it from making an acquisition large enough to affect its diversification ratio (Davis, 1989). Even after Philip Morris's first significant ($227 million) company purchase, that of Miller Brewing Company in 1969–1970, the contribution of cigarettes to the total sales of the company remained high. In 1970, cigarettes accounted for 85% of Philip Morris's net sales; in the same year, the cigarette component of R.J. Reynolds's net sales was 73.1%; of Loews's (which in 1968 had purchased P. Lorillard), 72.8%; of American's, 76.9%; and of Liggett & Myers's, 55.0%. Throughout the 1970s, Philip Morris remained largely dependent on cigarettes. The 1978 purchase of the Seven-Up Company (subsequently divested) took Philip Morris's diversification ratio down to 64.4% in 1979. However, the cigarette component of its net income remained the highest in the industry: Philip Morris, 82%; R.J. Reynolds, 77%; Loews, 22%; American, 58.6%; and Liggett & Myers, 15%.

Only in the mid-1980s did Philip Morris begin to diversify in earnest. In 1985, it purchased General Foods Corp. for $6 billion, which dropped its diversification ratio to 49.9%. Looking to expand its food business further, in 1988 Philip Morris acquired Kraft, Inc. for $13 billion. By 1989, cigarettes contributed only 40.5% toward Philip Morris's net sales (in 1990, 41.2%). In 1990, the Swiss-based coffee and confectionery Jacobs Suchard was acquired for $4.1 billion. Essentially, a significant ($23 billion in acquisitions) diversification effort in the mid-1980s redefined Philip Morris as a consumer packaged products company, although in 1990, the core cigarette business still contributed a disproportionate share—67.6%—toward the company's total profits. By 1995, the diversification ratio had climbed back to 48.9%. This increase in the ratio essentially resulted from the sale of the bakery and food service operations, which were not seen as having the capability to reach desired growth and/or profitability goals.

Market Diversification

In the international cigarette industry, Philip Morris pursued a much more vigorous strategy of expansion. Beginning with the 1954 organization of Philip Morris (Australia) Ltd., the company set up affiliate companies and signed licensing agreements in various countries around the world: Panama (1956), Switzerland (1957), West Germany (1960), Hong Kong (1961), Italy (1962), Guatemala (1962), France (1965), Nigeria (1967), Sweden (1969), Belgium (1971), Japan (1972), Brazil (1974), Bulgaria (1975), Czechoslovakia (1978), Malaysia (1982), and Eastern Europe and Russia (1990). Aggressive export marketing and international brand name recognition of the Marlboro Man trademark drove international sales spiraling upward to the point now where they operate in 170 countries with 140 brands. Philip Morris's 1978 purchase of the Liggett & Myers international cigarette business gave the company access to a number of internationally recognizable brand names, chief among them Chesterfield, which for a time was the world's best-selling international brand. In 1972, they passed R.J. Reynolds as the leading U.S. company in internationals sales. In 1995, they were more than five times larger. This international growth has resulted in Philip Morris surpassing BAT Industries PLC (a British-based conglomerate) as the largest producer outside the United States for the first time in 1994.

The economics of non-U.S. cigarette sales are not as attractive as domestic sales. Analysts estimate profitability per pack to be $.30 in the United States, $.20 in Asia/Pacific, $.15 in Western Europe, $.06 in Latin America and $.04 in Eastern Europe (Cohen & Reidinger, 1995). While the volume is significantly greater (e.g., in 1995, Philip Morris sold 593.2 billion units overseas versus 221.8 billion units in the U.S.), the operating profits remain slightly higher in the U.S. ($3.45 billion overseas versus $3.74 billion in the U.S.). The single biggest factor is excise taxes. In 1995, Philip Morris's federal excise tax bill was $3.4 billion compared to $9.5 billion in foreign excise taxes. Excise taxes restrain the operating profit margins. Overseas cigarette margins were 29.9%, contrasted to 38.9% in the U.S. However, the 29.9% overseas cigarette margins compare favorably to Philip Morris's food operating margins of 14.4%.

Another factor of importance to Philip Morris's international cigarette operations is growth. The U.S. market is in decline, as previously discussed. The European Community (EC) is expected to decline 1 to 2% per year. Worldwide consumption had been growing at a 2.1% rate between 1960 and 1985 (Taylor, 1989), whereas in the late 1980s, growth in consumption had decreased to 1.2% per year (Nomura Securities, 1989). A 1% growth per year for the next several years appears to be the consensus forecast. Despite this worldwide slowdown in consumption, growth comes about for Philip Morris because of a trend toward "lighter" cigarettes (à la the U.S. market in the 1920s and 1930s) and toward a loosening of government controls worldwide. Figure 5.4 shows the torrid growth of the East Asian markets. The effect of East Asian exports on previously declining U.S. export growth is shown in Figure 5.5.

Figure 5.4
U.S. Cigarette Industry Exports to East Asia, 1985–1995

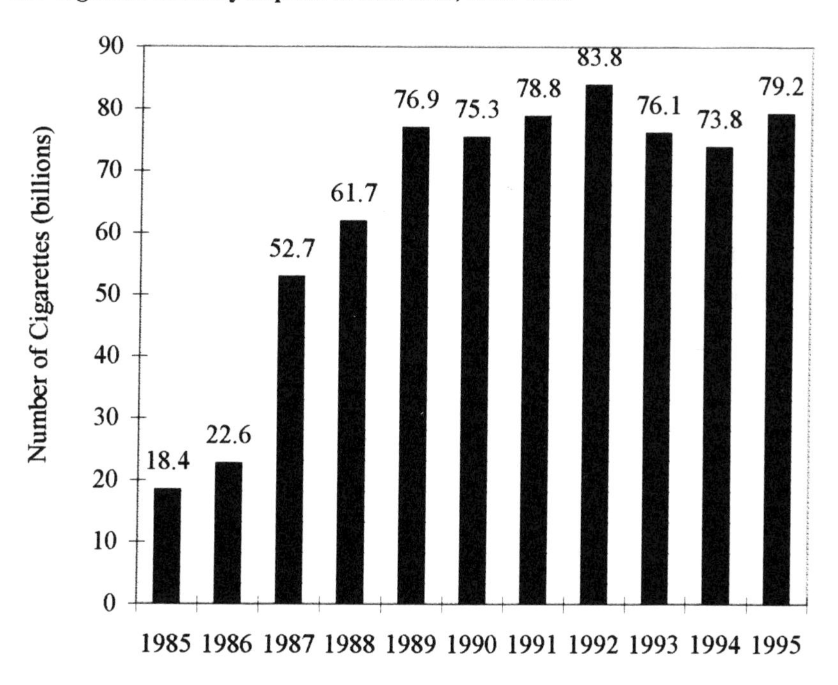

Note: Includes Brunei, China, Hong Kong, Indonesia, Japan, Malaysia, Philippines, South Korea, Taiwan, and Thailand.
Source: USDA 1985-95, Standard and Poor's *Industry Reports*, 1985-95.

Figure 5.5
U.S. Tobacco Industry Export of Cigarettes, 1950–1995

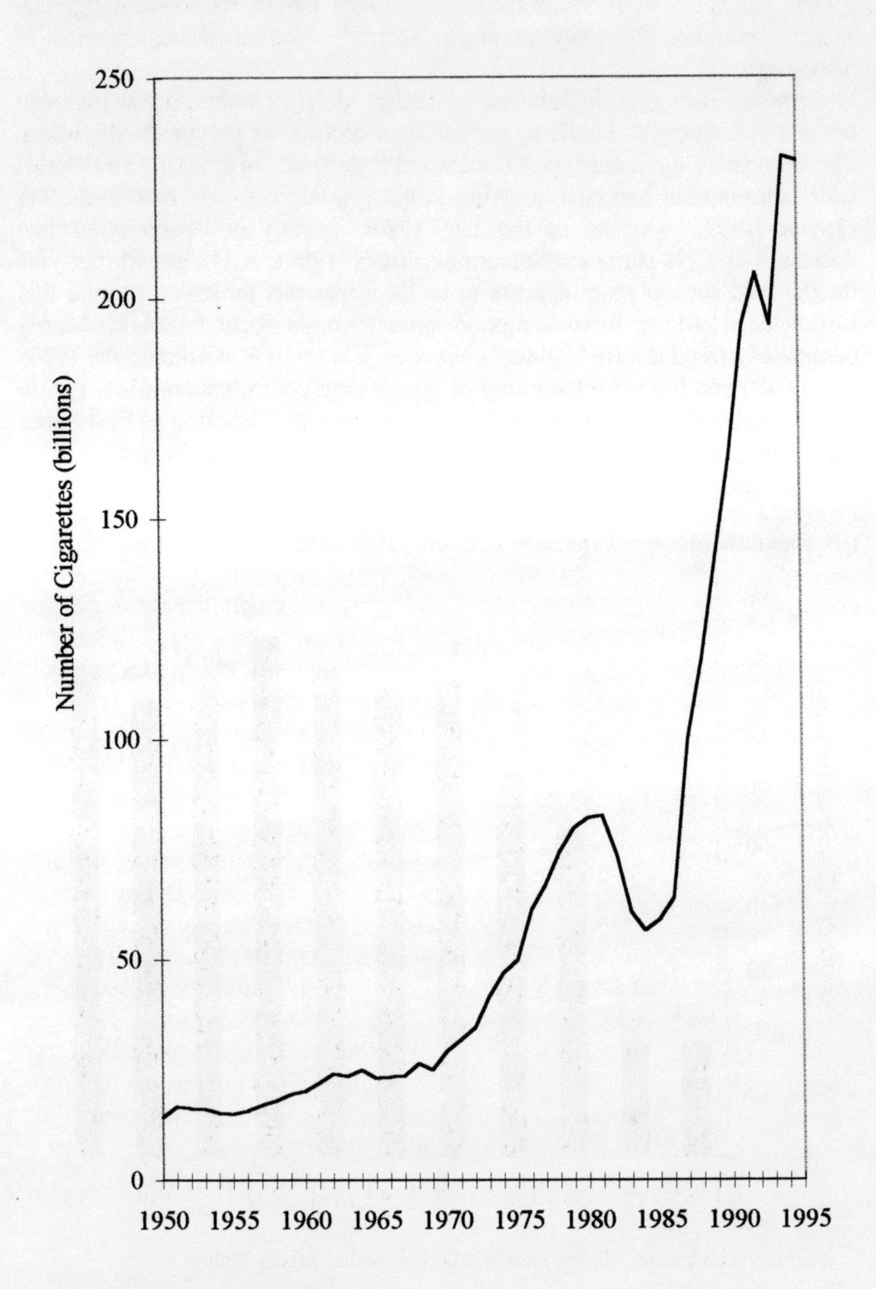

Sources: Maxwell, 1983, USDA.

In the late 1930s, dark tobacco constituted 53.3% of the world's tobacco crop; in 1959, it was 37.1%, and in 1991, 14.6% (*Economist Intelligence Unit*, 1991). These figures document the trend toward lighter American blend cigarettes. It has been this trend toward lighter cigarettes that has provided Philip Morris with the possibility to grow from a nonexistent international sales presence in 1950 to the point, in 1990, where for the first time international dollar sales surpassed domestic sales (unit volume had done so previously, as discussed earlier). As to the future, *The Economist* (1992) has pointed out that in 1980 Western cigarette sales had access to only 25% of the worldwide market as opposed to 90% of the 1990 market because of the opening of the COMECON (Council for Mutual Economic Assistance) countries and the important Asian markets of Japan, South Korea, Taiwan, and Thailand. The former were opened by the fall of communism, whereas the latter were pried open by the effective use of Section 301 of the 1974 Trade Act. The bottom line is that the international market that is now opened to Philip Morris is nine to ten times larger than the U.S. market. American blend cigarettes constituted approximately 31% of the 5.4 trillion cigarette worldwide market (Maxwell, 1995).

Philip Morris has been sensitive to its international operating environment. Historically, Philip Morris has exported, licensed, joint ventured, and manufactured as the respective markets and governments dictated. For example, in Venezuela, sales commenced when an import license agreement was signed in 1956. In 1959, a partial ownership was taken in the licensee by Philip Morris, and local production commenced in 1960. Philip Morris would license state-owned enterprises that held a national monopoly—e.g., France in 1961 and Japan in 1971. If the state-owned enterprise loosened (or was forced to loosen, the 301 action) its controls over marketing and distribution, Philip Morris responded—e.g., it established marketing operations in France in 1971 and television advertising in Japan in 1987. The evolution of Philip Morris's international activities has resulted in Asian and Arab markets being supplied by exports (22% of international unit volume), the European Union (EU) by wholly owned indigenous subsidiaries (48% of international volume) and Central and South America, Canada and Great Britain through unconsolidated subsidiaries (18% of volume). Twelve percent of the international volume is conducted through licensees (Ostroff, 1990). In 1994, Philip Morris surpassed British American Tobacco as the largest cigarette producer outside of the United States. In their 1995 *Annual Report*, Philip Morris pointed out that their share of world demand had reached 15%, a 50% increase over their 1989 position of 10%.

Philip Morris holds a 30% (1994) market share in the EU, where it is the market leader. Germany (38.7% market share in 1994) and Italy (56.1%) represented 40% of Philip Morris's international earnings in 1989 (Ostroff, 1990). In both these markets, Philip Morris is the leader. Philip Morris has exercised leadership in Japan. In 1990, Philip Morris at 9% market share had more of the Japanese market than all other U.S. companies combined. Ability to advertise on television has allowed the American companies to exploit the recently 301-opened Japanese market (cigarettes have gone from the fortieth most televised advertised product to the second since the market was opened). Their sales are especially lucrative to Philip Morris since they represent export sales that due to U.S. operations' economy of scale, are especially profitable. Exports from the U.S. have a 6.79% operating profits to sales per 1,000 units margin (versus 1.92% for consolidated subsidiaries). Overall exports account for 53% of international operating earnings, with Japan alone making a 15% contribution (Ostroff, 1990). By 1994, Philip Morris had increased its share of the Japanese market to 14% (Cohen & Reidinger, 1995). Operating profits from the Pacific region continued to exceed those of all other international regions (E. Goldman, 1995). Philip Morris exercises leadership in the worldwide growing American blend–type cigarette market.

Summary

The history of Philip Morris since 1950 has been a commercially enviable one in industry, both tobacco oriented and otherwise. Philip Morris awaits the development by competition of a new category (filters, low-tar, price-value) that has a mass-market appeal (not a niche) and then implements its brand plan extremely well. Its focus on its flagship brand Marlboro repeated the strategy of the successful firms of the 1920s to the 1950s. Whereas the early firms combined the innovation of lighter blends of tobacco with a twenty cigarette package and single-brand national advertising, Philip Morris combined the "perceived safer" but "full-flavored" cigarette with a masculine red-and-white flip-top box and the national advertising of the Marlboro-man. Marlboro constituted 65% of Philip Morris's domestic sales in 1995. This contrasts with the second-place domestic brand Winston, which accounts for 22% of the number-two market share firm R.J. Reynolds. The value of the Marlboro brand has been ranked highest in the world (even over that of Coke) by the publication *Financial World* (Ourusoff, 1992).

Philip Morris repeated this approach with Benson & Hedges (100 mm), Merit (low-tar), Virginia Slims (women), and Cambridge (price-value)—all large non-niche market segments, with a well-supported brand name and a goal of being number one or two. Figure 5.6 shows the results of Philip Morris's following its strategy in the price-value market. The market was initiated by L&M, expanded by RJR and Brown & Williamson, and finally entered by Philip Morris, which, five years later, had a second-place market share. It then exercised market leadership with its Marlboro Friday actions.

Figure 5.6
Company Shares in Price-Value Market, 1980–1995

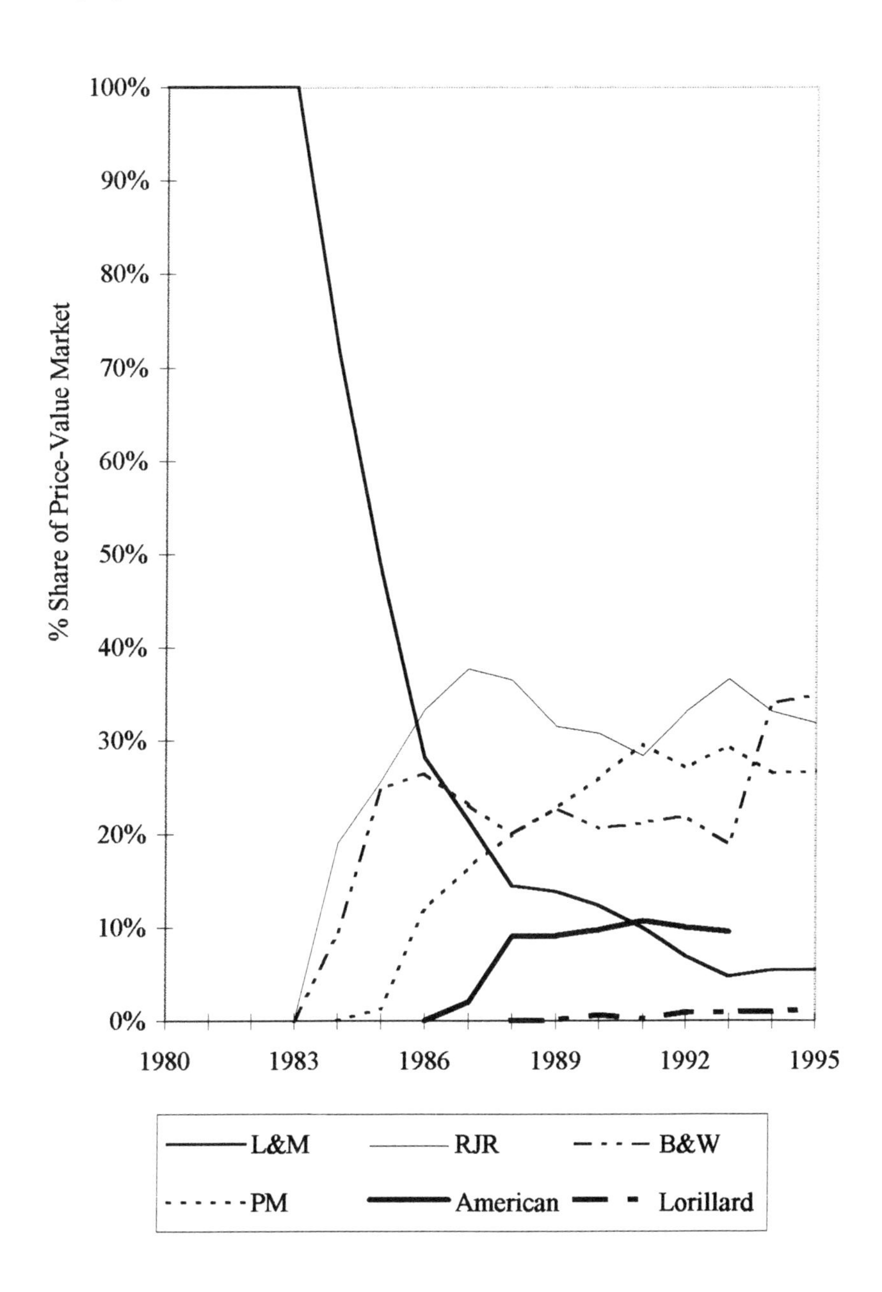

Source: Maxwell; Tobacco Reporter, Corporate Reports, Bernstein Estimates.

In beer, Philip Morris through a technological innovation (reduced calorie but flavorful; similar to Marlboro) and a transfer of marketing skills (from "Champagne of Beers" to "Miller Time") drove the Miller Company to second spot in the beer industry. Four Miller brands ranked in the top ten beer brands in 1990; Lite (light premium segment); Genuine Draft (premium); Milwaukee's Best (price/value); and Sharp's (nonalcoholic). By 1995 Miller, like its sister cigarette division, was focusing on the premium segment of the market and on international expansion. Internationally there had been a 78% increase in shipments between 1991 and 1995. A refocusing on core brands, the acquisition of the Molson brand in the U.S., and the introduction of specialty brands (e.g., Red Dog, Ice House, Leinenkugel) resulted in premium priced beers representing 81.7% of 1995 sales versus a 70% figure in 1991.

In its food diversification, Philip Morris again followed R.J. Reynolds, which had entered that industry in the mid-1960s with a series of small acquisitions. It even acquired General Foods six months after R.J. Reynolds had purchased Nabisco. But with General Foods, Kraft, and Jacobs Suchard, it vaulted to the position of largest food company in the United States and second only to Nestle worldwide. Philip Morris estimates that 72% of its food revenues come from brands that are ranked either number one or two in their respective market segments. By 1995, they had forty-one brands that exceeded $100 million in sales.

All three major industries that Philip Morris competes in are either mature or declining. In 1973, *Business Week* heralded Philip Morris as "a growth company in a mature industry." In 1995, it was still a growth company, now in three mature industries. From 1975 through 1990, its net earnings compounded annually at a 20% rate. This superior earnings growth has resulted in Philip Morris's outperforming the S&P (Standard & Poor's) 500 by a ratio of 10:1 over the decade of the 1980s. Philip Morris, between 1980 and 1995, gave a total return to shareholders (stock appreciation and dividends) of 25.5% annually versus approximately 15% annually for the S&P 500.

Philip Morris has accomplished this by exercising a leadership strategy both in its core tobacco business and in its related diversified operations of food and beer. It focuses on major market segments and attempts to be number one or two in market share. If it needs a brand name to do that, it buys it whether it be cigarettes (Benson & Hedges for 100 mm; Parliament King-size; L&M's overseas rights for the international markets), beer (Miller), or food (Kraft and General Foods and Jacobs Suchard). Philip Morris then actively pursues a program to integrate its acquisition with existing businesses. To implement the potential synergies of Kraft and General Food's, Philip Morris undertook a $179 million restructuring effort in 1989. The words shared, pooled, and synergies appear repetitiously over the years in the firm's own publications and in the investment analysts' reports from Wall Street. Philip Morris actively works to transfer knowledge and share experience in all of its business areas. Such efforts are helping it to achieve its stated goal of being "the world's most successful consumer packaged products company" (Philip Morris, *Annual Report*, 1990). It will accomplish this through "powerful premium brands...in new and established markets...building on an extensive global infrastructure" (Philip Morris, *Annual Report*, 1995).

If Philip Morris cannot exercise leadership, it abandons the area (Seven-Up; industrial products). Philip Morris maintains its leadership positions with aggressive advertising (e.g., Marlboro outspent Winston $114 to $38 million in 1990) and significant capital expenditures (e.g., it has allocated $1.57 billion to its cigarette business over the last three years and anticipates spending $3.5 billion more over the next five years). In the crucial 1970s when Philip Morris almost doubled its market share and rose from fourth to second in the industry, it demonstrated its commitment and money to the core cigarette business by maintaining a ten year average ratio of dividends as a percentage of earnings of only 27% (versus 50% for American and 43% for RJR). In the 1970s, U.S. consumption increased 84 billion units—Philip Morris increased 89 billion units. During the 1980s, U.S. consumption fell by 107 billion units—Philip Morris increased 32 billion units. From 1990 to 1995, U.S. consumption dropped by 42.4 billion cigarettes, while Philip Morris increased 2.3 billion units, the only firm not to have suffered a drop in U.S. unit volume. Philip Morris has demonstrated sustained commitment to a leadership strategy. The results in terms of cigarette market share and segment sales are shown in Figures 5.7 and 5.8.

Figure 5.7
Philip Morris's Market Share: Domestic Cigarettes, 1950–1995

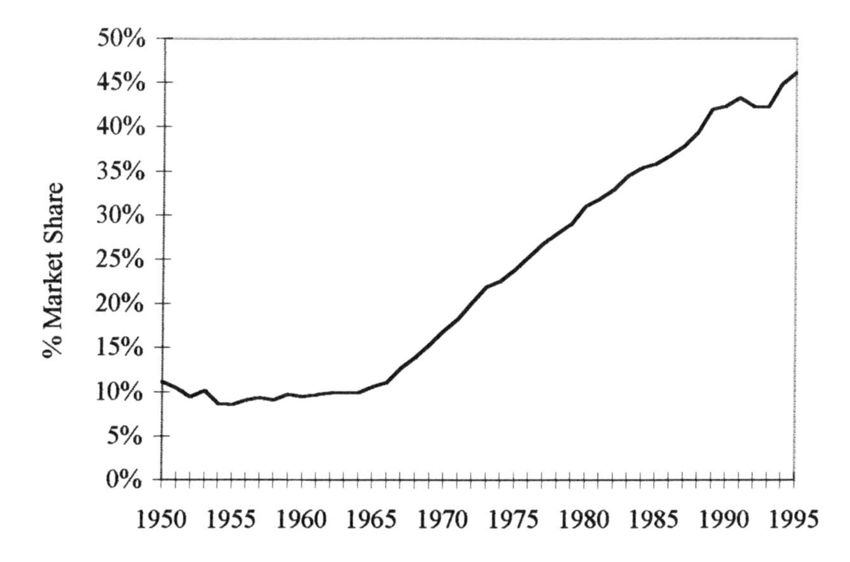

Sources: Business Week, 1950-1990; Maxwell; *Tobacco Reporter*, 1991-1995.

Figure 5.8
Philip Morris's Net Sales by Industry Segment, 1970–1995

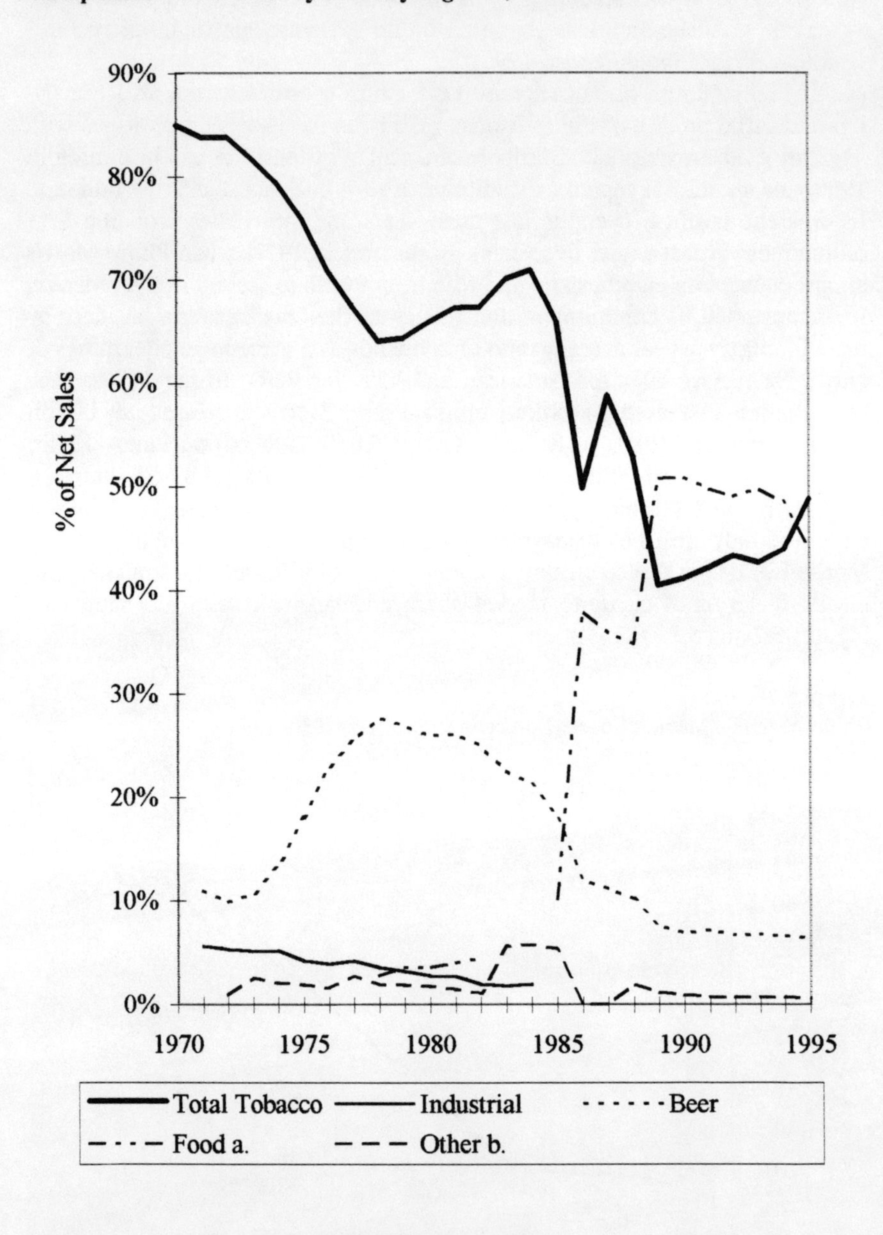

Notes: a. Includes 7-Up, 1978-1982, sold in 1985.
b. Primarily real estate from Mission Viejo; includes 7-Up, 1983-1985.
Sources: Moody's Industrial Manuals; Company Reports.

Hypotheses Testing

In the final chapter, all the hypotheses will be listed, and the findings from all the firms will be summarized under each. Here (and after each firm's historical description of choices) a brief summary of pertinent hypotheses will be presented.

Philip Morris, who was not a previous market leader, adopted a leadership strategy as the market matured/declined owing to the smoking and health issue. Its activities were consistent with Hypothesis 2. As an industry leader, it did pursue market diversification with its aggressive overseas expansion; thus, it was consistent with Hypothesis 7. At no time did Philip Morris attempt product diversification by internal development, as predicted by Hypothesis 9. After a period of learning, Philip Morris's market diversification efforts were restricted to the related consumer packaged goods industry; thus, it showed consistency with Hypothesis 10.

R.J. REYNOLDS

In 1875, Richard Joshua Reynolds left his father's tobacco farming concern in Virginia to set up a factory in Winston-Salem, North Carolina, where he manufactured a number of plug tobaccos that he then sold around the country through wholesalers. By the end of the nineteenth century, the R.J. Reynolds company was enjoying considerable commercial success; the Winston-Salem factory was turning out over 5 million pounds of plug every year, and several R.J. Reynolds brands, among them Red Apple, Hill Billy, and Brown's Mule, had become extremely popular. The success of R.J. Reynolds inevitably attracted the "covetous" attention (Corina, 1975) of the self-styled tobacco monopolist James Buchanan "Buck" Duke, whose American Tobacco Company had acquired a number of smaller tobacco concerns, largely cigarette and small cigar companies, and formed a virtual monopoly over U.S. cigarette production. Despite the protests of his lieutenants, Duke had decided to move beyond the highly profitable cigarette business into, at that time, the more lucrative plug tobacco market. Having acquired both Liggett & Myers and P. Lorillard, two of the largest plug producers near the turn of the century, Duke turned to R.J. Reynolds and offered a generous merger deal that Reynolds accepted in 1899. Under the umbrella of the Continental Tobacco Company, Duke's plug concern, Richard Reynolds set about both to expand his chewing tobacco production and to obtain a "solid foothold" in the smoking tobacco business (Tilley, 1985).

Nonetheless, at the time of the dissolution of Duke's American Tobacco Combination on November 16, 1911, the R.J. Reynolds company trailed the "Big Three"—American, Liggett & Myers, and P. Lorillard—in both smoking tobacco and cigarette production and was ahead of only P. Lorillard in chewing tobacco. A year later, Reynolds first expressed interest in expanding into the increasingly lucrative cigarette market. By 1915, the R.J. Reynolds company had introduced Camel, the cigarette brand that revolutionalized the tobacco industry, and in that year shipped 2.26 billion Camel brand cigarettes, up from 1.15 million in 1913; in 1924, Camel shipments totaled 31.4 billion cigarettes. The success of the Camel brand was a combination of a novel blending of traditional Turkish tobacco with lighter American blend tobaccos, which produced a milder smoke; new packaging ideas, including moderately priced, $.10 (rather than premium-priced, $.15) twenty cigarette packs as well as cartons; and memorable national advertising campaigns ("The CAMELS are coming!"; "I'd walk a mile for a Camel"). Largely due to the phenomenal success of Camel, the *Wall Street Journal* was able to declare in 1922 that R.J. Reynolds's net earnings were "the highest ever recorded by any company in the tobacco industry" (Tilley, 1985). Camel remained the best-selling brand in the national market until American's Lucky Strike, boosted by a strong advertising campaign, became the industry leader in 1930. Between 1930 and 1959, Camel and Lucky Strike alternated as market leaders. R.J. Reynolds settled into second place among the cigarette companies in overall market share, behind American Tobacco.

1950–1995

With the emergence of the smoking and health issue and the dramatic rise in demand for both king-size and filter brands, R.J. Reynolds's flagship brand (the regular-sized and unfiltered Camel) proved ill-suited to survive in the new market conditions. Between 1952 and 1959, when American's king-size brand Pall Mall replaced it as market leader, Camel's sales dropped an average of 6.6% every year, from 104.5 billion cigarettes sold in 1952 to 64.0 billion in 1959. However, as Camel's sales declined throughout the 1950s and 1960s, R.J. Reynolds launched a new cigarette brand in 1953 to compete in the booming filter segment. The Winston brand was advertised as a "good-tasting" filter cigarette, contrasting it with flavorless early entry brands such as Viceroy and Kent. In 1960, Winston entered the ranks of the three best-selling brands, popularized by the successful broadcast media advertising jingle "Winston tastes good like a cigarette should." In 1965, Winston's advertising and filter catapulted it above unfiltered king-size Pall Mall to capture the top spot in the brand race. With the success of Winston, the continued (albeit declining) fortunes of Camel, and the increasing popularity of the menthol brand Salem (introduced in 1956), R.J. Reynolds in 1958 pushed ahead of American in overall market share, a position it maintained until 1983.

However, the 1971 ban on broadcast advertising for cigarettes deprived its Winston brand of the trademark broadcast-oriented jingle "Winston tastes good like a cigarette should," which had for so long defined it. The jingle could not be utilized effectively in the print media. By 1975, the brand had fallen into decline, allowing Philip Morris's Marlboro brand, the strong, silent Marlboro Man image of which proved as effective in print as in broadcast media, to become the top-selling brand. Similarly, RJR's menthol brand, Salem, experienced some aging, allowing Brown & Williamson's Kool to briefly (1972–1980) take a lead in market share. A revamped advertising campaign helped to propel R.J. Reynolds's menthol back above Kool (*Business Week*, 1980). Another brand success for R.J. Reynolds has been its most venerable brand, Camel, which was given a filter in 1965, a low-tar expansion in 1978, and a new advertising image in 1988. The late 1980s advertising campaign for this septuagenarian brand, although controversial, has successfully redefined Camel's image using brand mascot Joe Camel, a hip, cartoon dromedary, the brand recognition of which is extremely high among youths. This youth recognition is crucial to RJR's future since presently Philip Morris holds a 68% share of entry-level smokers (Ostroff, 1990). Joe Camel is an attempt to "age" the Marlboro Man ("My father smoked Marlboro" kiss-of-death-type comment) in the eyes of today's youth. While Joe Camel did not tame the Marlboro Man, it was the only other premium-priced non-menthol brand besides Marlboro whose market share had increased by 1995. So successful has Joe Camel been that the FTC, in May 1997, charged RJR with illegally targeting minors with this ad campaign. RJR is contesting the FTC action. However, from the time of the buyout to 1995, RJR's overall market share slid from 31.8% to 25.7%, while Philip Morris's increased from 41.9% to 46.1%.

R.J. Reynolds's readaptation of its older brands, Camel and Salem, has proved more adept than its attempts to launch new brands. Its early entry low-tar brand, Vantage, while successful, has been out-performed by Philip Morris's low-tar Merit, which, like the Winston brand in the early 1950s, beat out early-entry brands by appealing to taste and flavor, qualities lacking in the first-generation low-tars. R.J. Reynolds' two most resounding failures stemmed from misjudgments in niche marketing. In 1978, hoping to capitalize on the "natural ingredients" marketing fad, RJR introduced the Real brand, the advertising of which boasted the cigarette's "100% natural" composition. The brand failed to attract consumers and cost the company between $50 million and $60 million. In 1990, RJR began test-marketing a brand aimed at black smokers, Uptown, but community opposition forced the company to withdraw the brand after spending $10 million.

A third new brand introduction that met with failure was Premier. Test-marketed in 1987, Premier burned charcoal, contained a flavor capsule and had a tobacco filter, allegedly eliminated tar, reduced nicotine, and virtually eliminated ash and secondary smoke. This product could have been a significant weapon against the anti-smoking movement since it was alleged both to be safer to smokers and to eliminate sidestream smoke. However, test-market results were disappointing, and the product was withdrawn at an estimated $.5 billion R&D investment loss to RJR (Gladwell, 1989). Some industry observers felt that RJR made a hasty withdrawal decision due to the cash flow crunch created by the KKR (Kohlberg Kravis and Roberts) buyout (discussed below).

By 1996, with debt from the KKR leveraged buyout having been reduced to $10 billion from 1989 levels of $29 billion, RJR was test-marketing Eclipse, a nearly smokeless cigarette, in Chattanooga, Tennessee. With the 1996 *Science* article (D. Stout, 1996) that found the first cellular evidence demonstrating a direct link between smoking and lung cancer, perhaps it was Eclipse that prompted RJR's Chief Executive Officer (CEO) Steven Goldstone to remark that if the *Science* article was valid, a "major business opportunity" had possibly been created (Hwang, 1996). It so happens that Eclipse has a significantly reduced amount of the chemical found in the *Science* study to have caused lung cancer from cigarette smoke.

Product Diversification

The company began its long association with the packaged food industry with the acquisition of Pacific Hawaiian Products in 1963. Other food concerns acquired by R.J. Reynolds included Chun King Corp. (1966), Patio Foods, Inc. (1967), Del Monte Corp. (1979), Heublein, Inc. (1982), and Nabisco Brands, Inc. (1985), which brought about the change in the company's name to RJR Nabisco, Inc. At the same time, the company did attempt significant diversification beyond related industries such as food. In 1969, R.J. Reynolds merged with McLean Industries, parent company of Sea-Land Corporation, the international shipping concern. In the next year, American Independent Oil Co. was purchased; further energy operations, Burmah Oil Company's principal U.S. subsidiaries and Signal Petroleum, were acquired in 1967 and 1979, respectively. R.J. Reynolds's unrelated diversification efforts proved disappointing; despite large capital outlays (e.g., $522 million was paid for Burmah and over $1.2 billion in capital expenditures was allocated for American Oil and Sea-Land in the late 1970s), profits from these subsidiaries remained elusive (4% return on assets in their 1979 transportation business). Thus, in 1984, R.J. Reynolds divested itself of both its transportation and energy operations. The 1985 merger with Nabisco, which included Planters and Lifesavers, confirmed a new policy of solely related diversification, that is, the consumer packaged food industry. Therefore, in 1986 and 1987, the company sold off the Kentucky Fried Company and the spirits and wine business, both of which had come within the Heublein acquisition. After the KKR buy out (discussed below), the firm sold off $8.1 billion of its European and Asian food business and its Del Monte and Chun King operations. The net result was a consumer packaged food diversification (Nabisco, Planters, and Lifesavers) that was concentrated in the Americas. This Americas emphasis remained in 1995 when Canada and Latin America accounted for 84% of Nabisco's non-U.S. sales. However, as food has gone from 42% of RJR's sales in 1990 to 52% in

1995, international sales fueled $1.5 billion of that sales increase versus $600 million domestically.

Market Diversification

R.J. Reynolds had held the leadership role in overseas cigarette sales among U.S. domestic producers through 1972. Its Salem brand had become in the late 1980s the world's largest-selling menthol. Further, RJR has been a leader in the Soviet-Sino sphere: In China, there was a 1980 marketing agreement and, in 1988, a joint venture manufacturing pact, while in the Soviet Union in 1990, a 14.1 billion per year cigarette supply contract was signed. Since 1990, RJR has invested over $300 million in the former Soviet block of countries. RJR estimates that it now has the largest production capability (and is continuing to expand) and market share (12%) in this area of the world (RJR Nabisco, Annual Reports, 1994, 1995). In China, RJR has a manufacturing license under a joint venture agreement in the Xiamen province. Overall, RJR operates in 170 overseas markets with over ninety brand names, of which Winston, Camel, and Salem are its international leaders. However, RJR's market share outside the U.S. has stayed flat during the 1990s, while BAT's has increased significantly and Philip Morris's has doubled.

By 1972 Philip Morris had surpassed RJR as the leader in international cigarette sales among U.S. domestic cigarette producers. This occurred despite RJR's 1972 leadership in overall cigarette sales (21.4% greater than Philip Morris) and RJR's overall corporate revenue stream being 39% larger than that of Philip Morris's. This switch in overall leadership roles occurred for two reasons. First, RJR concentrated on exporting its domestic brands, and as a consequence, in the words of 1979 chairman Paul Sticht, "the acceptance of our brands among international smokers was limited" (Overton, 1981, p. 175). In contrast, Philip Morris, although utilizing its milder Marlboro brand, also continued to push the harsher-tasting nonfilter Philip Morris brand overseas (which had been de-emphasized domestically in the late 1950s, as discussed above) as well as leading with such local brands as Target in Nigeria and Lido in Venezuela (Corina, 1975). In 1976, despite Marlboro, 60% of Philip Morris's international sales came from regional and national brands (Shepherd, 1989). Although cognizant of and contributing to the worldwide trend toward lighter American blend cigarettes, Philip Morris, on initial market entry, often maintained the existing national brand (Shepherd, 1989) or altered the tar and nicotine content of its own international brands (Taylor, 1989) to suit the local mass-market characteristics. Then it slowly, through gradual tar and nicotine reformulation, evolved the product to its international standard. RJR, self-admittedly, initially attempted to sell its standard American formulated Camels and Winstons to its foreign markets. It was unsuccessful, as Sticht stated.

Second, RJR was not as aggressive or as attentive as Philip Morris was with respect to overseas operations. RJR consolidated and focused its international operations in 1976, whereas Philip Morris had done so in 1955. In 1968, it was Philip Morris that acquired Godfrey Philips, a British firm with mainly European interests. In 1978, it was Philip Morris again that acquired the rights to Liggett & Myers's overseas business. In 1981, an awakened RJR courted Rothmans International (a European consortium of four nonmajor cigarette companies), but again it was Philip Morris that acquired a 25% interest. RJR's product sales diversification ratio went from 27% to 47% in the 1970s, as opposed to Philip Morris's going from 15% to 34%. This greater diversification effort, intensified by the operating problems of these same diversified businesses (*Business Week*, 1978), resulted in RJR's loss of focus on international cigarette operations. Philip Morris, more focused on its cigarette operations, had been more attentive to the international market needs and overall more aggressive in obtaining entry thereto. Philip Morris closed 1995 with a 3:1 sales advantage over RJR in the international cigarette arena.

The KKR Buyout

Kohlberg Kravis and Roberts (KKR) is a leveraged buyout (LBO) firm that had acquired Houdaille Industries (1979), Amstar (1984), Safeway and Beatrice Foods (1986), and Owens-Illinois (1987), among others, before it acquired RJR Nabisco in 1989. During the 1980s, it was estimated that KKR raised close to $60 billion for the purpose of LBO takeovers (Anders, 1991b). The takeover of RJR Nabisco took $28 billion of that KKR money pool. KKR's goal was to achieve the same 46% return on equity that it stated it had achieved on its equity investments through 1986 (Anders, 1990c).

Essentially, KKR purchases a public firm at a market premium with mainly debt that is secured either by undervalued or unleveraged real assets or by the value of a brand name (unrecognized by the accounting profession but potentially significant as shown by our prior discussion of the value of the Marlboro brand) and junk bonds. After the acquisition, assets not related to the core businesses (and even those, if necessary) are sold to reduce the debt to a level that the firm's cash flow can cover. The cash flow will not likely be reduced by income tax since the interest on the debt is both significant and tax deductible. Management (existing or new) is required to pledge a significant portion of their net worth to purchase stock and will receive further stock for performance. The increased focus on efficiency caused by the need to cover debt service and management's ownership should theoretically act as incentives for a superior corporate financial performance. After a three-to seven-year time frame of such operations, during which time debt is reduced, the goal is to bail out in the public market with significant returns (40% plus) on equity investments. KKR has been in the financial engineering business of taking firms private with leverage, deleveraging, and selling out in the public market since 1976. This strategy of getting in and out of LBO within seven years is known as "flipping companies" on Wall Street. KKR added RJR Nabisco to its portfolio of firms that have been taken public. KKR was not an operating company; rather, its strategy was financial restructuring.

Because of their cash flows, both Philip Morris and RJR had been rumored as possible takeovers in 1988 (Davis, 1989). However, as we have seen, Philip Morris utilized its cash flows to purchase Kraft, while RJR's cash flows were in effect capitalized by KKR to self-buy itself. By the end of 1990, post-LBO, RJR's revenues had decreased 17.6% (mainly because of the asset sales previously discussed), 5,300 employees were let go (exclusive of those employees at divested units), and operating profit had increased 15.5% with tobacco's contribution also increasing 15% (Anders & Lowenstein, 1991). As previously mentioned, asset sales had eliminated European food operations for Nabisco. KKR had stated that it desired to continue in the cigarette and food business, although the food business had been expected to be diminished to raise capital to pay debt. The failed management buyout of RJR, which had encouraged KKR's action, had proposed to restrict RJR to cigarette operations only. It was the battle between KKR and management, led by then-CEO Ross Johnson, that was immortalized in the book *Barbarians at the Gate*. In 1995, this issue, cigarettes versus cigarettes and food, remained a focal point for RJR. Figures 5.9 and 5.10 show cigarette market share and segment sales. The LBO required cash to pay down the debt of $29 billion at the same time that the growth of generic cigarettes (from 15% of the market in 1989 to 36.8% in 1993, see Figure 3.10) reduced domestic tobacco contributions from $2.3 billion in 1990 to $1.2 billion in 1993, a 48% drop (Ferst, 1995). This cash limitation restricted international cigarette expansion, whose sales and profits grew only 9% and 12%, respectively, between 1990 and 1993. Since the occurrence of Marlboro Friday in 1993, RJR's market share in the U.S. has declined from 30.5% in 1993 to 25.7% in 1995 (see Figure 5.9). Both Winston and Salem have seen declines in market share. Only Camel, with its controversial Joe Camel advertising and promotion campaign, has increased its market share, as shown in Table 3.2. Internationally, cigarette sales increased from $2.25 billion in 1990 to $3.23 billion in 1995. Contrast that with Philip Morris's gain from $5.86 billion to $20.8 billion over the same period. RJR was weakened operationally by the LBO, and Philip Morris seized on this weakness both internationally and domestically.

Figure 5.9
R.J. Reynolds's Market Share: Domestic Cigarettes, 1950–1995

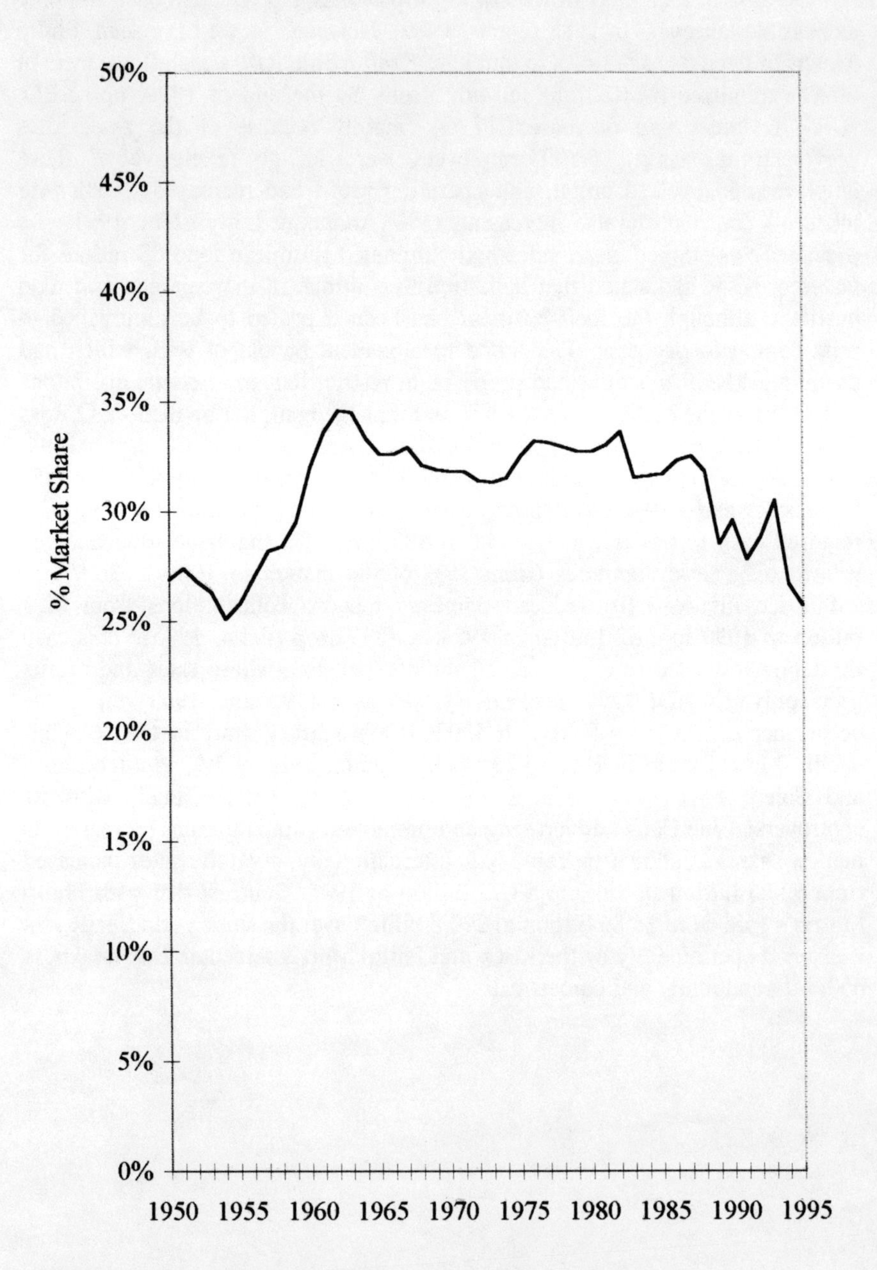

Source: *Business Week*, 1950-1990; Maxwell, 1983, 1996, *Tobacco Reporter*, 1991-1995.

Figure 5.10
R.J. Reynolds's Net Sales by Industry Segment, 1970–1995

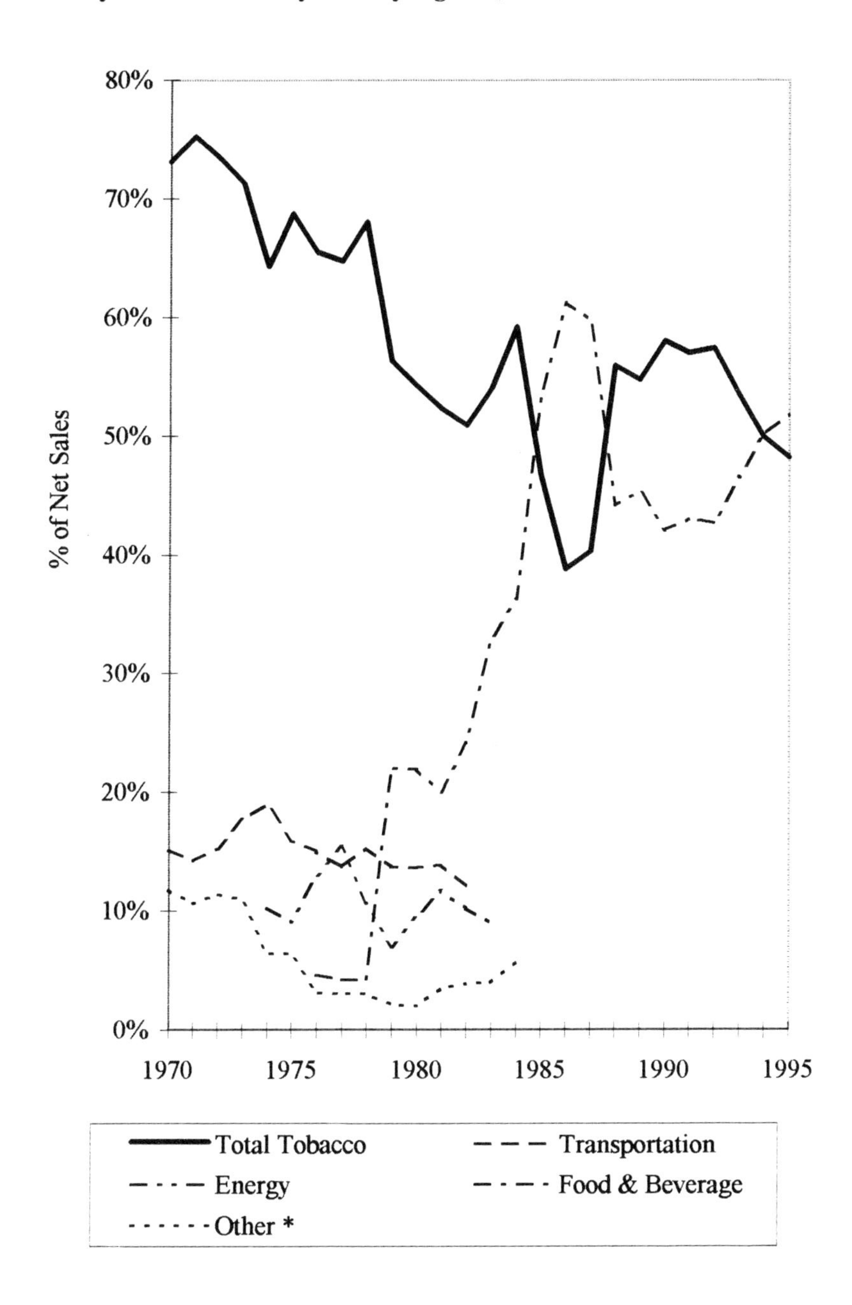

Source: Moody's Industrial Manuals, Company Reports.

KKR's shareholders obtained, at best, an S&P 500 index return in 1993, versus their normal bail-out in the public market returns (Smith & Shapiro, 1993). Having gone public with RJR in 1991 at $11.25 per share, RJR had a $5.625 per share value in September 1994, when KKR announced it was swapping $2 billion of RJR stock for stock of the struggling Borden, a chemical and food concern. Borden had diversified into too many unrelated fields in the 1980s and suffered accordingly. Analysts computed that the average fund investor with KKR had obtained a 17% return on their investment compared to an S&P 500 index return of 51% over the same time frame (Steinmetz, 1994). Subsequently, in March 1995, KKR disposed of its final shares in RJR for $5.73 per share versus an adjusted $5.62 per share that it paid for RJR. A KKR spokesperson stated that KKR "did preserve their investors' equity" (Lesly, 1995).

Having been weakened by the LBO, RJR then faced a financial market takeover attempt by corporate raider Carl Ichan, who had allied himself with Brooke Group's Bennett LeBow in 1994. In April 1995, their proposed board of directors failed to garner the necessary votes in a proxy fight. Ichan, who owned approximately 7.5% of the shares of RJR, desires to separate the food and cigarette businesses, which Figure 5.10 shows have evolved to a roughly 50-50 split in sales. His belief was that Nabisco's food operations were being significantly undervalued by being tied to the tobacco operations. RJR agreed with the concept of a Nabisco spin-off; however, its board of directors believed that debt must be further reduced and any remaining debt must be investment grade to ensure that any spin-off would be legally valid to protect Nabisco against any future tobacco liabilities. LeBow, on the other hand, wanted to combine Brooke's Liggett operations with RJR's tobacco business. However, it was LeBow's settlement with plaintiffs' lawyers suing the industry (to be discussed below in the Liggett & Myers section) that scuttled any hopes of an Ichan/LeBow victory. Subsequently, LeBow and Ichan have separated and could possibly be antagonists in any future RJR proxy fight.

Summary

RJR and American battled for industry leadership between 1930 and 1960. After 1960, Philip Morris was RJR's antagonist. RJR at the end of 1995 found itself a distinct number two to Philip Morris in domestic and international cigarette sales and in market diversification. The KKR LBO ensured, due to financial exigencies, that RJR attempted a leadership strategy domestically (Joe Camel) and internationally in the former COMECON countries. Simultaneously, the LBO restrained the necessary use of resources. Philip Morris exploited this weakness. The only additional point is the focal question of whether cigarette and food operations should be combined or separate, the same question they faced at the time of the 1988 LBO.

Hypotheses Testing

RJR, although a distinct second to Philip Morris, is exercising a leadership strategy. Since it had the same strategy prior to the time of the anti-smoking movement, its actions were not consistent with Hypothesis 2. As a market leader, it did expand overseas (over 40% of unit sales are to international markets), thus being consistent with Hypothesis 7. It did not attempt internal product diversification, and like Philip Morris, did learn to diversify into related businesses. Thus, its activities were consistent with Hypotheses 9 and 10. It was acquired for financial engineering purposes in accordance with Hypothesis 11.

AMERICAN BRANDS

American Brands, previously known as American Tobacco, was the corporate parent of the powerful cigarette trust assembled by James B. Duke at the turn of the century. The company was one of the four successor firms that were structured out of the 1911 dissolution of the trust. In direct response to the success of RJR's Camel brand introduction (light tobacco, twenty pack, reasonable price, and national advertising), American introduced a similar product, Lucky Strike, in 1916. Heavily advertised from 1918 onward, Lucky Strike was battling Camel for the number-one brand ranking throughout the 1920s, a position it did achieve in 1930. Between 1930 and 1950 these two brands, Camel and Lucky Strike, as did their parents RJR and American, dueled for the position of market leader.

With American's 1936 introduction of a reformulated (from dark to a light tobacco blend) Pall Mall brand, which was converted to king-size in 1939, American slowly pulled ahead of RJR for company market share leadership from 1940 onward. By 1950, it enjoyed a four-point lead with a 30.9% share. It was the king-size Pall Mall with a sales volume of 23.5 billion units that enabled American to top RJR as the industry's leading firm since RJR's Camel brand with 98.5 billion units was leading Lucky Strike, which had sold 82.5 billion units in 1950.

1950–1995

With the advent of the 1950s anti-smoking movement, American began a steady decline in the domestic cigarette market. In 1958, RJR passed American as the leading cigarette firm in sales. In the 1950s, nonfilter Lucky Strike commenced a stagnation that took its market share to single digits in the 1960s and to 0.3% in 1995. Pall Mall faced a similar fate (1.1% in 1995), except for a temporary rise in the mid 1950s at the time that king-size cigarettes were viewed as a safer cigarette. American had failed to respond to the filter tip revolution caused by the anti-smoking movement. As late as 1962, over 90% of

American's cigarette sales were of the nonfilter types, whereas the market composition at that time was over 50% in filter cigarette sales. Despite the introduction of such filter brands as Montclair, Waterford, Sweet Caporals, and Bull Durham in the mid-1960s, American has never had a competitive filter cigarette brand. It likewise has failed to penetrate the menthol market. American's Tareyton brand, which was introduced as a king-size brand in the 1940s and converted to a charcoal filter in 1958, remained as a top ten selling brand through 1976 because of the perceived safety of king-size and filters. However, by 1995, its market share was 0.4%. Carlton, the first low-tar cigarette introduced in 1964, rose to the eleventh-ranked brand due to a National Institute of Health Report that was misinterpreted to say that Carlton was a safer smoke than other cigarettes. By 1995, it had slipped to less than 2% market share. This failure to capture a significant portion of the mainstream filter market or the menthol segment resulted in a 10.7% market share in 1980—a far cry from its 1957 market leadership or even from its 19.3% market share second-place finish in 1970.

American was able to maintain its overall market share at the 6 to 7% range in the late 1980s through 1994 because of its 1987 entry into the price-value market with such brands as Malibu, American Filter Montclair, Misty, and Bull Durham. Price-value brands constituted 24% of American's cigarette sales (versus a 19% share for price-value brands as a percentage of domestic consumption). Price-value brands were said to be the emphasis of American's domestic future (American Brands, *Annual Report*, 1990). However, American was late in entry and ranked fifth among its competitors in this market segment. It trailed the segment leader, RJR, by almost 20%. By 1993, its market share had still remained the same, while RJR's had increased by a 6% market share gain and Philip Morris's by 3%. American Brands did increase its market share of the price-value market by almost 50% between 1993 and 1994, but that was the result of the conscious decision by Philip Morris and RJR to concentrate on the premium segment of the overall market after Marlboro Friday. However, the fact that price-value brands constituted only 19% of Philip Morris's cigarette product mix in 1994 (versus 57% for American) helped to explain why American's domestic cigarette operating profit margins were in the 21% profit range versus Philip Morris's 34% range. The net effect of American's failure to recognize the effect of the anti-smoking movement in the U.S. has been that American went from the market leader to a so-so player in various market segments. Only in its traditional strong area, nonfilter cigarettes, which is less than 3% of the total market, did it have a dominant 45% market share. American's niches had turned out to be nonfilter sales (18% of its unit sales), ultra-low-tar (22%), and price-value (57%) (Maxwell, 1991). Thus, American had gone from a 1950s leadership position to a next-to-last spot in industry rankings. Given a recent American Brand's strategic dictate to be a "powerhouse" brand, American Tobacco's fate was sealed. American

Brands announced the sale of American Tobacco to the Brown & Williamson unit of BAT at the end of 1994.

Product Diversification

American Tobacco was the last cigarette firm to diversify in 1966. By 1969, it had changed its name to American Brands to reflect its purchase of Sunshine Biscuits (1966), Jim Beam distillers (1967), Duffy-Mott Foods Co. (1968), and Bell Brand Foods (1968). American reached a cigarette sales specialization ratio of 65% (versus 77% in 1970) by entering, in late 1977, the office supply business with the purchase of Acme Office Records and Swingline and also the hardware business through Master Lock. The hardware business was enhanced with the 1974 purchase of Marvel Lighting Company. The toiletry business had been entered with the 1970 purchase of the Andrew Jergens Company. With the 1976 purchase of Acushmet, American entered the golf field with the Titleist brand. Between 1977 and 1979, American entered the life insurance field with its purchase of the Franklin Life Insurance Company.

By 1980, American broke its sales down into eleven categories besides cigarettes (63.2%) and miscellaneous (1%). The company had sunk approximately $1.8 billion into diversification between 1965 and 1980—thus, in the words of *Baron's* "Kicking the Habit" (Grant, 1978). Tobacco's operating income contribution had been reduced to 58.6%, down from the 1975 level of 69%. It dipped to 55.7% in 1984. However, this contribution was back up to 69% in 1990, mainly due to Gallaher's success in the United Kingdom (discussed below) and price hikes in the U.S. market. The fact that cigarette sales as a percentage of total sales dropped another 5 to 58% in 1990 from 1980 while almost doubling in absolute sales terms indicates that American's diversification efforts had increased over six times in absolute sales terms, a $5 billion increase. This occurred despite the disposal of over $.5 billion in food sales over the decade of the 1980s. Tobacco as a percentage of total sales was still at 59% in 1994 just before American Tobacco was sold. Profit contribution was at the 58% level.

The distilled spirits business increased fivefold due to the acquisitions of U.S.-based National Distillers and the United Kingdom's Whyte and MacKay Distillers. Here American appears to have learned from its lesson in the domestic cigarette business and is attempting (Jim Beam number-one Bourbon; DeKuyper, number-one selling cordial line) to gain brand leadership in the various market segments. The same approach appears to have been taken in office products (Swingline, number-one in Staplers; Day-Timers, number-one in time management products), in hardware (Master Lock, number-one security lock; Moen, number-one in single-handle faucets), and in life insurance (Franklin, number-three in return on assets). These businesses (tobacco, distilled spirits, office products, hardware, and life insurance) were considered "core businesses" by American, whereas all other products ($2.3 billion in sales with a return on sales of $61 million, or 2.6%) are lumped into specialty products and are not considered core businesses, which had an average 13.5% return on sales in 1990. Noncore businesses such as Jergens (1988) and Regal China Co. (1989) have been continuously sold throughout the 1980s, as were the core businesses of insurance (1994), domestic tobacco (1994), and international tobacco (1997).

The divestitures of the food operations and the specialty products operations were spurred by the attempted LBO takeover of American by the conglomerate E-II Holdings, Inc. in January 1988. Utilizing the so-called Pac-Man defense (named after the video game where players eat their opponents before they are eaten), American purchased E-II for $1.2 billion one month later. Five months later, retaining pertinent hardware and office products supplies divisions, American sold off the remainder of E-II. At about the time of the E-II divestiture, Bennett LeBow, the controlling shareholder of the Liggett Group (Liggett & Myers cigarettes) made hostile gestures toward American, spurring speculation that LeBow hoped a Pac-Man fate awaited his Liggett holdings (Smith & Freedman, 1988). To ward off these acquisition threats, American stated it was divesting noncore businesses and purchasing back 20% of its shares on the open market. While more widely diversified than either Philip Morris or RJR, who have only food and cigarettes, American has narrowed its focus from thirteen lines of business to five core businesses: cigarettes, distilled spirits, life insurance, office products, and hardware/home improvement products. American defines a core business as one where operations are large enough to substantially contribute to its overall results and in which their scale is sufficient for them to compete as major players (American Brands, *Annual Report*, 1988). The question for American is whether or not the leadership strategy of having a major brand in its respective fields is sufficient glue to hold across such a diversity of industries. American believes that its future success lies with the eighteen "powerhouse" brands (brands with sales of over $100 million) it possessed at the end of 1995.

Market Diversification

American's nondomestic cigarette operations, both historically and currently, are intertwined with the British Isles. Historically, American's founder, James Duke, attempted to divide the cigarette world into three segments: the U.S. market to American Tobacco, the British market to Imperial Tobacco, and the rest of the world to British American Tobacco, a joint venture between American and Imperial. The dissolution of the American trust laid these plans asunder. However, an ongoing legacy of that plan was the retention of worldwide (outside the U.S.) rights to existing American's brand names by British American Tobacco. Since American held fast with its nonfiltered brands after 1950, it did not have any new brands to play a significant role overseas, except for a historical investment. In 1927, American had purchased a British coupon discounting cigarette firm called J. Wix & Sons. Wix, with a 1959 3% market share in the United Kingdom, was sought by Gallaher Ltd., which was the number-two competitor in the British market behind the Imperial Tobacco Co. By 1961, Gallaher had persuaded American to swap its Wix ownership for a 13% interest in Gallaher. Ironically, the other large shareholder in Gallaher was Imperial, whose 42.5% ownership had been purchased in 1932 because it feared that American, through Wix, was about to purchase Gallaher. In 1968, Imperial announced that it wanted to sell its shares in order to utilize the proceeds to diversify into the food industry (Corina, 1975). Ever alert, Philip Morris, who had recently purchased Gallaher's Australian operations, immediately offered to purchase the shares. Gallaher rebuffed Philip Morris's offer and sought out American as the "White Knight." American raised the bid price and simultaneously, in questionable legal circumstances, obtained a controlling block of stock on the open market (Corina, 1975). Philip Morris retreated but did purchase Godfrey Philips at that time, as previously mentioned. American subsequently, in 1973 and 1975, purchased the remaining 24% of Gallaher that it did not own.

Immediately in terms of sales, American was slightly more of an international cigarette company (albeit restricted to the British Isles) than a U.S. one. Moreover, as American's U.S. market share declined, its United Kingdom market share increased—to a 46% market share leading position in 1990. By 1995, this share had fallen to 39.2%, essentially because the price-value market had grown to a 50% market position. Mayfair was American's leading brand in this segment with only a 5.6% market share. Imperial, the former leader and formerly part of Branson, is the leading competitor. Gallaher's Benson & Hedges filter tip brand (Philip Morris in 1954 only purchased the U.S. rights to this brand) dominates the premium market with a 28% market share. To exploit Gallaher's Benson & Hedges position in the United Kingdom, American Brands exchanged the overseas trademarks of American Tobacco's Lucky Strike and Pall Mall brands plus present and future contingent cash payments with BAT for their Benson & Hedges trademark in Europe. Its low-tar brand entry, Silk Cut, holds second place with a 10% market share. It would appear that American has been successful in translating its gaffes in the U.S. market into success in the United Kingdom market. American exercises a leadership strategy in Britain. The foreign excise taxes are higher (76% of retail price in 1994 versus 26.7% in the U.S.), and the market is smaller (87 billion units versus 490 billion units in the U.S.) than the United States. However, with its focus on the premium segment and its growth in exports, Gallaher was, as of 1995, the largest contributor (50.6%) of operating income to American Brands. It has been Gallaher that has driven tobacco and cigarette operating income as a percentage of total income (58.3%) to mirror the sales diversification ratio, which had dropped from 64.5% cigarette related in 1975 to 56.6% in 1995. Gallaher contributed 24% of the cigarette earnings in 1975, whereas the 1994 figure was 67.6%. American, facing Imperial rather than a Philip Morris in the United Kingdom and having learned its lessons in the U.S. market, exercised leadership in the filter, low-tar and price-value market segments. Figures 5.11 and 5.12 show the historical evolution of the domestic market and line-of-business sales.

Figure 5.11
American Tobacco Market Share: Domestic Cigarettes, 1950–1995

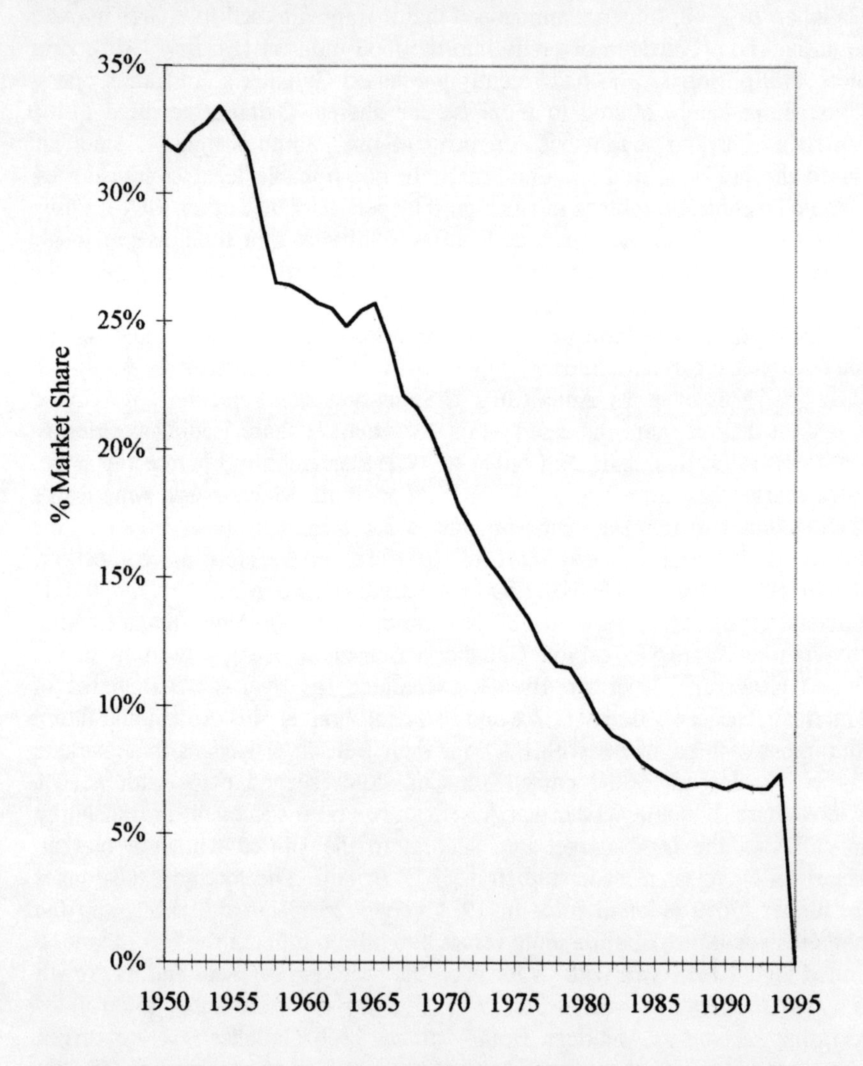

Sources: Business Week, 1950-1990; Maxwell, 1983, 1996, *Tobacco Reporter*, 1991-1995.

Figure 5.12
American's Net Sales by Industry Segment, 1969–1995

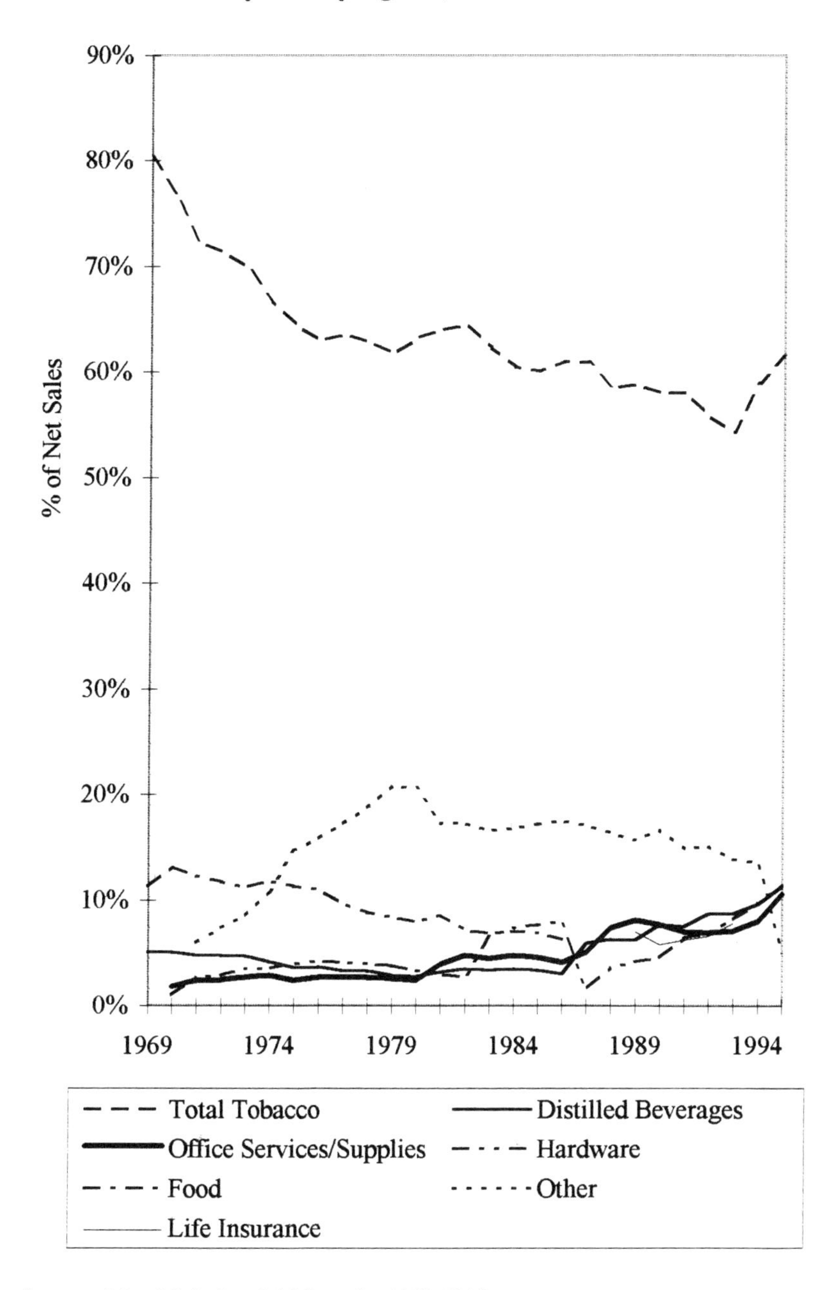

Source: Moody's Industrial Manuals, 1969-1995.

American Brands had stated that its stock price had been affected negatively and incorrectly because of its ownership of Gallaher. From American Brands' viewpoint, the stock market had failed to recognize that its tobacco exposure was different than other U.S. cigarette companies. First, with the sale of its U.S. American Tobacco subsidiary to Brown & Williamson, American Brands had been indemnified by both American Tobacco and Brown & Williamson against smoking, health and fire claims arising from the activities of American Tobacco. Thus, liability in the United States should be, in American Brands' mind, a nonissue. American Brands' second point was that the Gallaher United Kingdom home-based legal and regulatory environment was significantly different than that found in the United States (Hwang & Parker-Pope, 1996). However, when the adverse $750,000 Florida judgment (see Chapter 2) was announced, American Brands' stock did drop by 4.5%. A month later, in September 1996, a contingent class action suit was filed in Great Britain against Gallaher and Imperial by a group of British cancer victims. This was the first time tobacco firms had been sued in Great Britain.

Apparently, these two actions were the straw that broke the camel's back. American Brands announced in October 1996 that, subject to shareholder approval and favorable tax treatment, Gallaher would be spun off within in a year and American would change its name to Fortune Brands. Duke's American Tobacco had come to an end.

Hypothesis Testing

American missed the filter-tipped revolution caused by the anti-smoking movement in its domestic market (from number one to number five over the course of this forty-five year study); thus, it was consistent with Hypothesis 2. In fact, it further confirmed Hypothesis 2, by utilizing its costly lessons learned from the U.S. market in the United Kingdom market, where it powered its market share to a commanding 46% market share (from a 28% share in 1975) through the use of a brand leadership strategy in the filter, low-tar, and price-value segments. American's leading brand position in each of these United Kingdom cigarette segments is consistent with Hypothesis 2. Yet this international success cannot be said to not confirm Hypothesis 7, which states that nonleaders will not go overseas, since American's Gallaher's position had been established in 1927 by way of the Wix acquisition. In point of fact, if industry leader Philip Morris had not gone after Gallaher (supporting Hypothesis 6) it is highly likely that American's then-small passive Gallaher investment would have remained just that; that is, it was because of Philip Morris's leadership strategy that American's overseas operations became significant. The fact that no internal developments were undertaken was consistent with Hypothesis 9. Hypothesis 10 is in limbo. All product lines that were acquired were in consumer goods. Their breadth (four core business areas) clearly contrasts with Philip Morris's and RJR's concentration on food. Additionally, their four core businesses were five in 1990 and included cigarettes and insurance, which are no longer pertinent and did not include golf and leisure products, which it now does. This relatively larger and changing breadth argues for a lack of configuration. However, Porter (1985) does state that intangible marketing relationships, such as "product management, brand positioning and advertising concepts...[even if] performed separately...[are examples of the] transference of generic skills" (p. 324), can be the basis for a related diversification strategy for entry into new businesses. Hence, American's activities with respect to Hypothesis 10 are considered to be neither consistent nor inconsistent with Hypothesis 10, although American has clearly evolved to stating that it is now following a brand-driven consumer product strategy similar to Philip Morris's and RJR's, albeit with a broader focus of core areas and without cigarettes.

BROWN & WILLIAMSON

Brown & Williamson (B&W) is the U.S. subsidiary of the British-American Tobacco (BAT) Company. BAT, as previously discussed, was originally formed in 1902 as a joint venture between Imperial Tobacco of Great Britain and the United State's American Tobacco. Since the original concept was that BAT would not operate in the U.S., it had no cigarette operations there through 1926. However, in a tit-for-tat strategy in 1927, BAT purchased Brown & Williamson, a small snuff and plug firm, in response to American's purchase of United Kingdom-based J. Wix & Sons, which eventually evolved into American's ownership of Gallaher, as previously discussed (Corina, 1975).

In the United States, B&W was the latest entry into the market among the Big Six producers. By 1940, it was number four on the industry ladder with a 10.6% market share. It followed a niche strategy to accomplish this. In the price-value segment, it led with Wings and Avalon on a straight discounted basis, and with the Sir Walter Raleigh brand, it utilized a coupon that could be cumulated and exchanged, like Green Stamps, for other merchandise. Raleigh grew to a 2.1% market share and number nine brand position by 1950. The other niche segment pursued by B&W was the mentholated market, with its Kool brand. Kools grew throughout the 1940s (from 2.5 billion units in 1940 to 9.2 billion units in 1950), ending up with a 2.5% market share, and was the 1950s seventh-ranking brand.

Upon entering the domestic market, B&W did not attempt to go after the mass market with one heavily advertised brand. Rather, it went after these two niche segments, price-value and mentholated. An unexpected problem with its price-value strategy was World War II which eliminated the pure discount brands because of tobacco rationing, price control, and soaring wartime incomes. B&W's Avalon and Wings brands essentially disappeared from the market in the 1940s, causing B&W's market position to drop a notch to fifth place (Nicholls, 1951).

1950–1995

Another niche market cigarette introduced by B&W in 1937 was a filter-tipped (cork and cellulose paper) brand called Viceroy. Through 1950, it had never exceeded 3% of B&W's sales, let alone become a market factor. B&W's fortunes with Viceroy were to turn around after 1953 as a cancer-worried smoking population turned to its almost venerable filter brand Viceroy in their search for a "safer" cigarette. Sales of Viceroy increased in 1953 by 110%; in 1954, sales of the brand rose an even more impressive 148%. Although Viceroy's meteoric use calmed in the next few years, it did peak as the sixth-highest-selling brand in 1957, achieving a market share of 6.7%. Thereafter, the brand increasingly lost ground to the new generation of "full-flavor" filter brands (Winston and Marlboro), though Viceroy remained one of the top twenty cigarette brands until 1984, when it managed to hold on to a 1.1% market share.

As sales of Viceroy slowed in the mid-1950s, B&W was busy revamping its mentholated Kool brand, which, without a filter, suffered annual sales decreases. A filter was added in 1956, and the fortunes of the brand immediately turned around. In 1965, Kool surpassed the falling Viceroy brand and claimed the eighth spot among top-selling brands. Two years before, B&W itself had edged into third place among the Big Six with a 1963 market share of 10.5%. Since then, B&W has remained remarkably consistent, running third in overall market share, which between 1963 and 1990 had meant approximately 14% of the total market, peaking at 18.8% in 1977 and ending in 1993 at 10.9%. With the former American Brand products, B&W's 18% share of the market put them 7.7% behind second-place RJR in 1995.

Until 1985, B&W's success depended almost entirely on the fortunes of its Kool brand. Certainly the sales of other brands such as Viceroy, Raleigh, and Belair contributed. All these brands reached the ranks of the top twenty brands at some time from 1960, when Belair was first introduced, to 1980. However, Kool's consistently solid performance among the top five brands between 1969 and 1990 has guaranteed B&W's own consistent performance. From 1972 to 1981, Kool moved ahead of its longtime rival, RJR's Salem to become the best-selling menthol in the domestic market, due in large part to a redesigned marketing campaign. Since then, Salem has maintained market leadership over Kool, although only 0.1% separated them in 1995. However, since 1993, Lorillard's Newport has captured the number-one slot in the menthol market.

B&W's stability among the top brands does obscure the company's continued adherence to the strategy of innovation and specialty marketing that has defined it since 1927. In the early 1960s, B&W manufactured eight brands, more than any other manufacturer. Then-president of B&W, William Cutchins, explained the strategy behind his company's "restless innovation" as lying in the existence of a segmented market and the "need to catch the consumer's every change in taste and mood" (*Business Week*, 1962). However, few of B&W's innovations proved successful, except somewhat Belair—a coupon brand in the tradition of Raleigh. Other than the brands mentioned above, the only B&W brand able to break into the top twenty has been the company's low-tar entry, Barclay. The limited success of the Barclay—which never achieved even a 2% market share—was vastly overshadowed by the size and cost of the marketing campaign that launched it in 1980, perhaps the most expensive in cigarette history due to heavy advertising and the distribution of free *cartons* (rather than the traditional packs) during the first month of introduction (*Business Week*, 1980).

In the price-value segment, B&W converted Viceroy to a price-value brand and utilized a brand extension—Raleigh Extra—to complement its manufacture of black-and-white generic packs. GPC, a branded generic originally introduced deep discount in 1986, had risen to a 5.8% market share in 1995. This made GPC the number-two brand in volume behind Marlboro. Such positioning has led to B&W taking third place in the price-value market from 1986 to 1993, thus securing its overall third-place market position. Their acquisition of American Brands' products has placed them first in the price-value segment for 1994 and 1995. However, Lorillard is battling B&W for third place in the premium segment and did edge B&W into fourth place in 1995. In the future, focused marketing efforts by Philip Morris with Basic and RJR with Doral will intensify competition for GPC in the price-value segment, while RJR is expected to intensify its Salem campaign against Kool in the premium segment (Warburg, 1996). B&W's historical evolution of market share is shown in Figure 5.13.

Figure 5.13
B&W Market Share: Domestic Cigarettes, 1950–1995

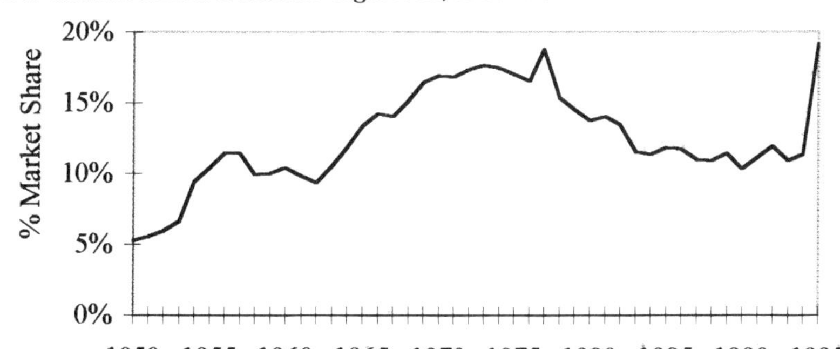

Note: B&W purchased American Tobacco in 1994.
Source: *Business Week*, 1950-1990; Maxwell, 1983, 1996, *Tobacco Reporter*, 1991-1995.

Diversification

B&W was from its inception a geographical diversification for British American Tobacco, which has cigarette operations in 160 countries worldwide and was the world's leading cigarette producer through 1990 (it was passed by Philip Morris in 1991). Therefore, it is not reasonable to speak of B&W diversifying its cigarette operations abroad. Nor is it appropriate to speak of B&W, a U.S. subsidiary of BAT, diversifying into other product markets. This is a BAT, not a B&W, decision. BAT did decide to diversify, in earnest and with size as a criterion, in 1970 due to the smoking and health issue (Covina, 1975). U.S. cigarette sales were approximately 21% of BAT's worldwide unit sales at that time.

Prior to 1960, BAT had been involved in paper manufacture, printing, and packaging as ancillary activities to its tobacco business. Beginning in 1962, however, BAT began a policy of "planned investment" in those industries irrespective of their relationship to tobacco. The policy was kicked off that year with the formation of Mardon Packaging International Limited. Mardon was jointly created by BAT and the Imperial Group, each of which invested over 20 million pounds (Corina, 1975). Mardon has a number of companies in the United Kingdom producing cartons, cases, tins, and plastic bottles and packs.

Shortly after this investment, in 1962, BAT acquired a 30.37% interest in Wiggins Teape Ltd. (since 1970 a wholly-owned subsidiary of BAT), which manufactures high-grade printing and writing papers in addition to a wide range of specialty industrial papers. Mills and factories are established in the United Kingdom, Belgium, Latin America, Africa, and Asia.

BAT's first major departure from tobacco (in an operating versus an investment mode) was its entry into the perfume industry where, beginning in 1965, it acquired a succession of famous houses, including Lentheric (1965), Morny (1966), Yardley (1967), Germaine Monteil (1968), Cyclay (1974), Juvena (1977), Carven (1982), and Gres (1983). The acquisitions established BAT as Britain's largest cosmetics company (Arbose & Burstein, 1984).

With annual sales of 200 million pounds and a spray of famous names, British-American Cosmetics was still only a footnote to BAT's worldwide turnover of 11.8 billion pounds in 1983. Because cosmetics did not provide the volume growth prospects that were originally projected, BAT's cosmetics business was sold to Beecham, the British pharmaceutical group, for $150 million in 1985.

As BAT entered the 1970s, its acquisition strategy focused on size. Richard P. Dobson, chairman of BAT at that time, articulated the firm's acquisition philosophy: "We are thinking all the time in very large dimensions—the big and powerful concerns. We are quite convinced it's no good buying any little companies; they take up just as much management time, and the rewards are too small" (Covina, 1975, p. 279). BAT's acquisition record during the 1970s reveals that Dobson was making no idle statement.

Early in the 1970s, BAT proceeded with major diversifications in the United States, beginning with the acquisition of Kohl's Food and Department Stores (1972), Gimbels, which owned Saks Fifth Avenue (1973), Mac Market Grocery Retail Business (1979), and Marshall Field & Co. (1982). Other interests in retailing acquired by BAT during this period included International Stores (1972), F.J. Wallis (1977), both supermarket chains, and Argos (1979), a large catalogue showroom chain, all located in Britain (Arbose & Burstein, 1984).

Finally, in June 1977, BAT purchased (for $141 million in cash) the international cigarette business of the Lorillard Corp., a division of Loews Corp., which includes the trademarks and goodwill of all brands sold by Lorillard outside of the United States.

BAT poured additional resources into the area of paper making, packaging, and printing when it purchased the remaining outstanding shares in the Wiggins Teape Group (1970), at the time Britain's third-largest paper firm and largest paper exporter (Corina, 1975). In addition, BAT purchased U.S.-based Appleton Papers (1978), which was the world's leading producer of carbonless papers. BAT also purchased the remaining 50% interest in Mardon Packaging Group (1979) from the Imperial Group. Mardon had by then become firmly established as a world market leader in flexible packaging (Moody's United Kingdom Industrials, 1987).

During the 1970s, a major BAT goal had been to expand into the U.S., which it successfully did with its retailing purchases. Upon entering the 1980s, another element to the diversification strategy was added when the company moved into financial services. BAT spent $2.1 billion to acquire Britain's Eagle Star Holdings (1984), primarily a property-casualty insurer, and Hambro Life Assurance (1985) (whose name was subsequently changed to Allied Dunbar Assurance), an insurance and pension management company (*The Economist*, 1984).

After establishing this base in the United Kingdom insurance sector, the priority was then to extend into the U.S. financial services market. Thus, BAT acquired the U.S.-based Farmers Group, Inc. (1988) for $5.2 billion. With over 11.5 million policyholders, Farmers' property and casualty interests rank as the eighth largest in the United States and the third largest automobile and homeowner insurer (BAT, *Annual Report*, 1988). Kevex, a leading U.S. manufacturer of instrumentation equipment for the materials analysis market, was also acquired that year.

BAT's objective, of course, was to further diversify BAT from its dependence on its tobacco business. Ultimately, BAT's strategy was to be composed of four equal parts—tobacco, retailing, paper, and financial services. Managing Director Patrick Sheehy says of BAT's 1980s strategy: "The leadership of our companies knows the four areas we want them to be in, and we expect them to seek opportunities in those areas. If they are in other businesses, they better be thinking of getting out. If it is part of an existing business that can't be grown, we will vacate it" (Melcher, Schedon, & Tarpey; 1985).

Toward that end, BAT sold its British supermarkets, International Stores Ltd. (1984) and F.J. Wallis Ltd. (1984). Additional businesses deemed to be outside of this strategy that were sold included Mardon Packaging (1985) and the company's stake in the cigarette machine manufacturer Molins (1985). Although most of these businesses were reasonably profitable, they held little promise of becoming a major BAT business (BAT, *Annual Report*, 1985).

In the United States, BAT's midlevel retailers (Gimbel Brothers, Kohl's, Frederick & Nelson, and The Crescent) were seen to be losing market share to higher-end competitors (like BAT's own Saks and Marshall Fields) and were consequently sold for a $175 million loss in 1986. A specialty shop for women, Thimbles, was likewise disposed of in early 1989.

In July 1989, a major narrowing of BAT's diversification focus was commenced. Sir James Goldsmith, the Anglo-French newspaperman and financier, launched a proposed $21.2 billion LBO takeover bid for BAT Goldsmith stated that he intended to sell off all BAT's operations except for the cigarette business (Forma, 1989). Goldsmith, in effect, argued that the day of the conglomerate was over and that the pieces were worth more than the whole. BAT accused Goldsmith of "no more than an ill-conceived attempt at destructive financial engineering." However, BAT was forced to go to the shareholders in October to receive approval for a plan to reduce its focus from cigarettes, financial services, retailing, and paper to just cigarettes and financial services. In April 1990, Goldsmith withdrew his bid owing to the failure of the investment banking firm Drexel Burnham Lambert, of Michael Milken fame, who was to provide the junk bonds and also because of the failure of the California State Insurance Board to approve his purchase of Farmer's Insurance due to overleverage concerns. Before and after this withdrawal, BAT was on a sales course to rid itself of its approximately 6 billion pound revenue retailing and paper businesses. By the end of 1992, discontinued operations had been disposed of and BAT was refocused on cigarettes and insurance only.

In 1996, its tobacco operations were reorganized into five regional teams. The purpose was to push decision-making responsibility as close to the regional consumers as possible. Simultaneously, seven functional areas were created on a global basis. BAT will attempt to integrate the firm's activities by matrixing the functional areas with the regional teams, with the strategic imperative of developing a focused segmented and differentiated brand portfolio that will exploit existing international brands while maintaining BAT's traditional strength in local and regional brands. BAT has consistently followed a niche strategy. Worldwide, BAT has nine brands with sales of over 20 billion units annually, whereas Philip Morris has five and RJR has four. However, Philip Morris's five brands account for 73% of shipments, and RJR's four brands constitute 65% of its total shipments, whereas BAT's nine brands represent only 37% of BAT's total shipments. While not abandoning a niche strategy approach, BAT, with its international brands emphasis, is attempting to obtain some economies of scale to raise its margins of 20.4% (earnings before interest and taxes) to RJR's 27.9% and Philip Morris's 35.9% levels (Warburg, 1996).

Complementing this brand strategic imperative was the imperative of supporting the customer's choice to smoke. One of the seven functional areas, and a new one, is the Consumer and Regulatory Affairs (CORA) function. CORA was created to counter the anti-smoking movement on a worldwide basis. BAT Industries' CEO Martin Broughton has stated that "CORA's creation shows a clear understanding of the nature of the challenge...In the future, end markets will have the support they need to argue our case effectively" (*Tobacco International*, 1996). BAT, with markets in more than one hundred countries and 170,000 employees, has declared global war.

Hypotheses Testing

B&W clearly entered the U.S. market as a niche operator and has steadfastly remained so, with mentholated Kool constituting 47% of B&W's premium sales, while GPC constituted 56% of the price-value brands. B&W's activities are consistent with Hypothesis 3 (niche marketers will remain so). All other hypotheses are not relevant given B&W's status as a BAT subsidiary, although the parent activities have the appearance of an American Brands' experience.

LORILLARD

The P. Lorillard Company began operations as a manufacturer of snuff and pipe tobacco in New York City in 1760. Over the next one hundred years, it also came to produce cigars and plug tobacco. It was acquired by James Duke in 1899. Upon the trust's dissolution in 1911, Lorillard, a successor company, was granted, by court degree, the largest number of the former trust's medium-price Turkish brands. This segment had the greatest growth between 1911 and 1915. As previously discussed, the Camel revolution occurred in 1915.

Lorillard continued to push its Turkish blend cigarettes versus the new lighter American blends until 1926. Between 1913 and 1925, Lorillard's volume had dropped by 50% despite a fivefold increase in the total market (Tennant, 1950). Lorillard simply missed one of the great shifts in the industry's history. Finally, in 1926 Lorillard introduced an American light blend cigarette—Old Gold. However, by 1925, RJR's Camels, American's Lucky Strikes, and Liggett & Myers's Chesterfield had already captured 82% of the national market. There was no place for Old Gold. In 1930, its fourth-place market share of 6.9% paled in comparison to Chesterfield's (21.3%), Camel's (28.5%) and Lucky Strike's (34.9%). During the 1930s, Lorillard introduced an economy brand called Sensation, which by 1939 accounted for 43% of its sales.

With wartime rationing of cigarettes, Lorillard ceased producing the economy brand in order to maximize production of its full-price Old Gold brand. By 1950, Old Gold had slipped to sixth place with a 5.4% market share, having now been passed by the Philip Morris's eponymous brand (11.1%) and American's king-size Pall Mall (6.4%). Such a performance placed Lorillard ahead of only late entrant Brown & Williamson in the firm's market share rankings as 1950 began.

1950–1995

With the smoking and health issue changing the rules of the game in the 1950s, Lorillard could potentially reverse its flagging fortunes. Lorillard was one of the leaders of the filter revolution with its Kent brand. Kent was successfully marketed with extensive health-oriented advertising, and its volume had reached 4.0 billion units in 1954. In 1954, however, Winston introduced the full-flavor Winston and contrasted its "satisfying taste" with that of Kent's. By 1956, Winston had reached ten times greater sales than Kent, which had slipped to a 3 billion units volume.

In 1957, Lorillard reformulated Kent as a high-filtration brand. Its promotion campaign was centered on its "micronite" filter. An article in a 1957 *Reader's Digest* issue, stating that Kent had the lowest tar and nicotine, gave a significant boost to the brand (Wootten, 1957). Kent went from the fourteenth most popular brand in 1956 to a fifth place ranking in 1960 on a 34 billion unit increase. However, that was the peak for the so-called hi-fi cigarettes and for Kent. By 1970, it was ranked the seventh most popular brand; by 1980, the tenth, and in 1990, the fourteenth. Lorillard's other health-oriented cigarette was True, a low-tar filter brand introduced in 1966. True turned out to be a rerun of Lorillard's situation with Kent. Two later entrants—RJR's Vantage (1970) and Philip Morris's Merit (1976)—were perceived to be more flavorful. They eclipsed True from the top twenty brands by 1990. Together, the Kent and True brands in 1995 accounted for 1.4% of the market, down from 2.9% in 1990. Harley-Davidson and Style are Lorillard's two other premium-priced, nonmenthol products, with a 0.3% market share apiece in 1995. Lorillard had refused to enter the price-value market segment until the summer of 1990 when it introduced its Heritage brand. In 1995, Old Gold was its only discount brand, with a 0.4% market share. Old Gold represented 5% of total Lorillard sales; Lorillard essentially sells only premium-priced products.

The remaining 70% of Lorillard's sales came from the Newport menthol brand, up from 60% in 1990. It was introduced in 1957 at a king-size length and with a filter. Given the attention paid to Kent and subsequently to True, the battle in the menthol segment was mainly between B&W's Kool and RJR's Salem. However, in the late 1970s with a campaign aimed specifically at young blacks (*Business Week*, 1986), Newport began to take off. From a 1977 market share of 1.21% (7.3 billion units), Newport grew to a 4.6% share (25.6 billion units) in 1990 and a 5.6% (27 billion units) share in 1995.

This success story has helped to push Newport ahead of Kool and Salem in the mentholated market share rankings. Overall, Lorillard finished 1995 with 38.6 billion units sold, which equated to an 8.0% market share overall. Historical market share is shown in Figure 5.14.

Figure 5.14
Lorillard Market Share: Domestic Cigarettes, 1950–1995

Sources: *Business Week*, 1950-1990; Maxwell, 1983, 1996, *Tobacco Reporter*, 1991-1995.

When we compare these 1995 figures to the 1960 volume of 49.8 billion units and a 10.6% market share, there has been a 22.5% drop in volume and a 24.5% decline in market share. However, due to aggressive price leadership in the 1980s and in 1993 by Philip Morris and because Lorillard's product mix had essentially zero price-value brand sales, Lorillard enjoyed 41.9% operating income margins in 1995 versus 13% margins in 1960. Such margins resulted in net cash flow from operations of $319 million for 1995. Such a cash flow was what the Tisch brothers had hoped for in 1969 when they had acquired Lorillard in an LBO before they were called LBOs.

Diversification

In 1968, the Loews Corporation with $120 million in sales from movie theaters and hotel operations acquired the $564 million Lorillard Corporation, essentially a cigarette company since its charter, until 1962, did not permit any operations but tobacco. In the Wall Street parlance of the day, "The minnow had swallowed the whale"—and it was done with paper debt. The purchase was for $402 million of debentures plus a warrant to purchase one share of Loews, which reflected a thirteen times P/E ratio valuation. Since Wall Street had sent the industry's P/E ratio down in the 1960s, reflecting the Street's viewpoint that the industry was about to cease growth due to the smoking and health issue, Lorillard's failure to diversify resulted in its status as Loews's cash cow. While American, Philip Morris, and RJR diversified into food and liquor to utilize their marketing and brand management skills, Loews diversified into the Lorillard net cash flow to initially make it pay for itself and subsequently to make other acquisitions for Loews. Loews purchased CNA Insurance Company in 1974, the Bulova Watch Company in 1979, and a controlling 25% interest in CBS in 1985, which was subsequently sold to Westinghouse at the end of 1995. Loew's also operates hotels and oil and gas drilling rigs. The rights to its cigarette brands outside the United States were sold to BAT in 1977.

Loews acts strictly as a financial holding company. Its 10K clearly states before each and every business segment that it "operates as a separate business entity." The Tisches are described by the business press as investors and portfolio managers. They are compared, favorably by the way, to such investment legends as Warren Buffett and John Templeton. They are not operators. *Financial World* has called Loews "a closed-end fund or a holding company" (Ozanian & Bicsada, 1990). It was, and is, clear that Loews acquired and utilized Lorillard for investment reasons, to wit, to act as a cash cow for its portfolio of investments. Loews's net sales by industry segment are shown historically in Figure 5.15.

Figure 5.15
Loews's Net Sales by Industry Segment, 1970–1995

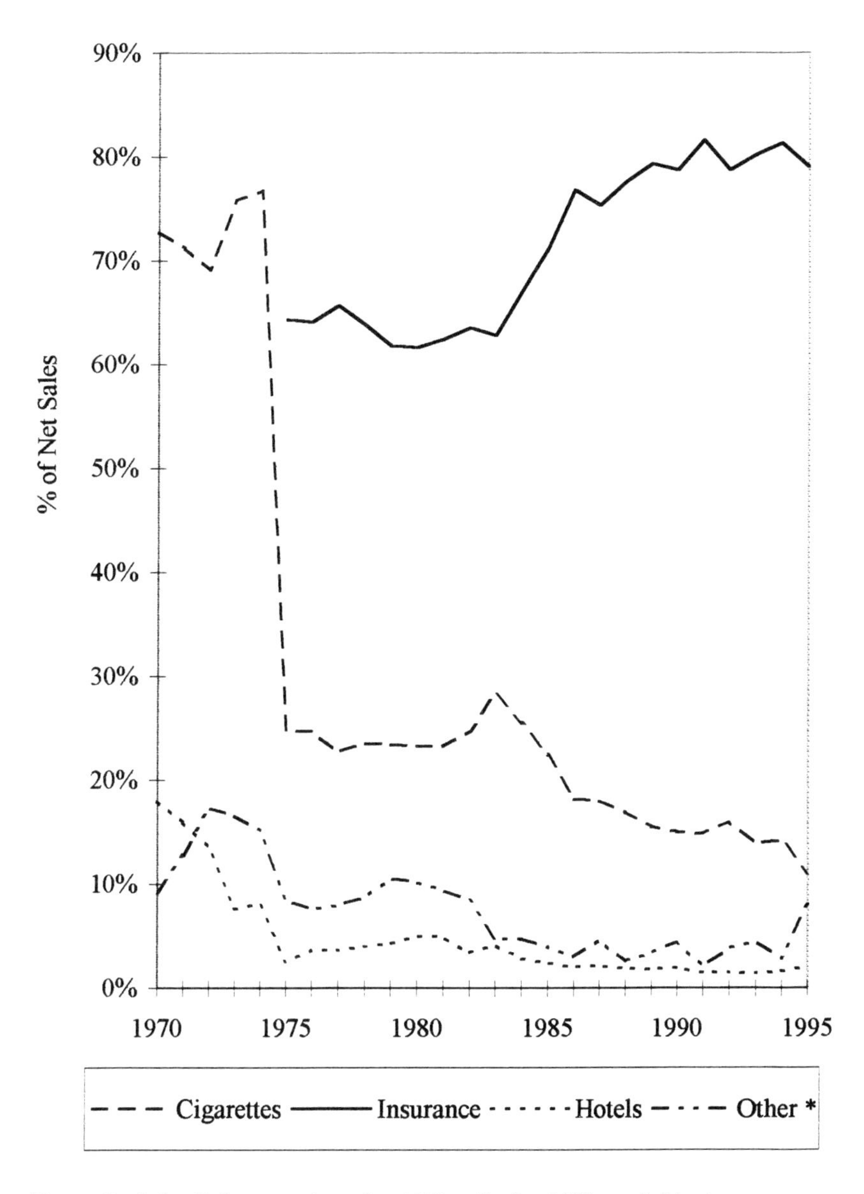

Note: *Includes Bulova watches after 1979; oil after 1988; and shipping, theatres, and residential development.
Sources: Moody's Industrial Manuals, ValueLine, 1970-1995.

Hypotheses Testing

Lorillard was late with its Old Gold, and it remained an also-ran among regular brands. Although the war had stopped production of its economy brand Sensation, the attempt by Lorillard to create a niche demonstrated that Lorillard knew it was a niche player, albeit by default and unsuccessful. After the smoking and health issue, Lorillard has created niches in the hi-fi segment (Kent) and the menthol niche (Newport). Newport's success did not come until after the Loews's acquisition. Lorillard's activities were neither consistent nor inconsistent with respect to Hypothesis 3 concerning niche actors. Lorillard did not exercise market leadership and sold its overseas operations to BAT thus, its actions were consistent with Hypothesis 8. Lorillard was acquired by Loews, a self-described holding company. This action is consistent with Hypothesis 11.

LIGGETT & MYERS

Liggett & Myers commenced operations in 1822 in Illinois. Although founded as a snuff manufacturer, L&M had become the largest plug chewing tobacco in the world by 1885. It succumbed to the Duke trust in 1899 and emerged from the trust dissolution with the leading brand Fatima. Fatima was a Turkish-Virginia blend cigarette, not the new lighter American blend–type product. However, it was still the fourth most popular brand in 1925, albeit with only a 2.7% market share.

Liggett & Myers's rank as one of the "Big Three" cigarette firms, however, was due to its Chesterfield brand, a Camel knockoff. Chesterfields were blended, packaged, priced, and marketed just the same as RJR's Camels and American's Lucky Strikes. Chesterfield put a lock on L&M's third-place industry rank through 1958.

1950–1995

Similar to another Big Three firm, American, L&M suffered a severe setback from the smoking and health issue. L&M was incapable of exercising any market leadership in filters, low-tar, or menthol or any market niche. While it had entries in most segments, it could not produce a market winner. Naturally, unfiltered Chesterfield declined.

Liggett entered the filter market in 1952 with the L&M brand. The best the brand could do was a number-eight brand ranking in the late 1950s and early 1960s. From there, it took a continuous slide and in 1980 was out of the top twenty brands. L&M's low-tar entry, the charcoal filtered Lark introduced in 1963, had a five-year interval at the bottom part of the top twenty brands and then suffered an L&M fate. It attempted to enter the menthol market in 1976 with the Decade brand. This was twenty years after the last successful brand,

Lorillard's Newport, had been introduced. The brand ceased to exist within six years. Eve, a cigarette introduced in 1970 for the women's segment, could never successfully compete against Philip Morris's Virginia Slims.

By 1980, Liggett's total market share had been reduced to 2.3%; this was less than 25% of fifth place Lorillard's position. Liggett's international rights were sold to Philip Morris in 1978. An attempted sale of the cigarette business by Liggett (it had diversified, as will be discussed below) in 1979 failed when the prospective buyer backed out after the proposed sale was announced (Overton, 1981). Liggett then began to make plans to close down its cigarette operations (Adler & Freedman, 1990). Enter Topco, a grocery store cooperative that distributed generic foods and paper goods to its co-op members.

In 1980, Topco approached Liggett with a proposal to manufacture black-and-white generic packages of cigarettes. Given the industry's historic emphasis on brand image and marketing, it is highly likely that no other cigarette firm would have seriously considered it. However, since Liggett was considering going out of business anyhow, it had nothing to lose. By 1985, Liggett's production of generic cigarettes commanded 70% of its production volume. By 1985, its sales of generic cigarettes allowed Liggett to more than double its 1980 market share to 4.97%. These products were appealing to that price-sensitive segment of lower-educated blue-collar workers who had, in effect, been forced on the industry by the smoking and health issue. As shown in Figure 5.16, this price-value segment grew to 36.8% in 1993. Subsequent to Marlboro Friday, price-value cigarettes had declined to the 30% level in 1995.

Figure 5.16
Price-Value Brands: Share of Total Cigarette Market, 1980–1995

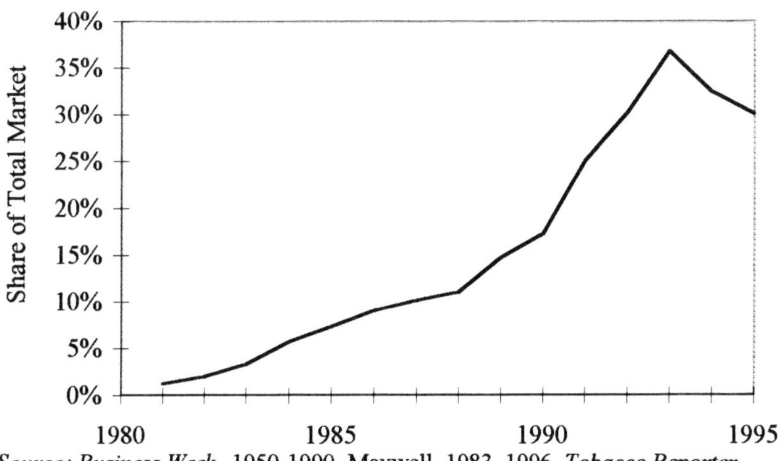

Source: *Business Week*, 1950-1990, Maxwell, 1983, 1996, *Tobacco Reporter*, 1990-1995.

Unfortunately, Liggett's 72% domination of the price-value segment in 1984 was not to last. Brown & Williamson aggressively pursued Liggett's customer base by offering a rebate significant enough that the industry's poor cousin sued B&W, unsuccessfully, on the grounds of predatory pricing (Adler & Freeman, 1990). Within three years, B&W had a slightly higher market share than did Liggett. However, this segment attracted the attention of the Big Two (Philip Morris and RJR who between them held 70% of the total market) in the mid-1980s. Albeit reluctantly, owing to their concern not to expand this less profitable segment, the Big Two did enter and quickly established dominance due to their use of branded generics and greater marketing support. This, as shown in Figures 5.6 and 5.17, had reduced Liggett's share of the price-value market to 4.7% in 1993 and to an overall market share of 2.4%, approximately the same share as their 1980 position before this price-value segment had been developed. Marlboro Friday resulted in a 7% decline in the price-value segment of the cigarette market. Within this declining market, B&W's aggressiveness resulted in an overall market share of 34.8% by 1995. Liggett's share had further declined to 5.5% in that market and to 2.2% in the total market. By default, Liggett's core competency in 1996 was its ability to turn around short production runs quickly, that is, compared to Marlboro's continuous production run, Liggett was a batch producer. Liggett does not have a top-thirty brand. It has 75.2% of its business in the discount segment where numerous private label brands are produced for different distributors. Liggett has evolved to batch producer status.

Figure 5.17
Liggett & Myers's Market Share: Domestic Cigarettes, 1979–1995

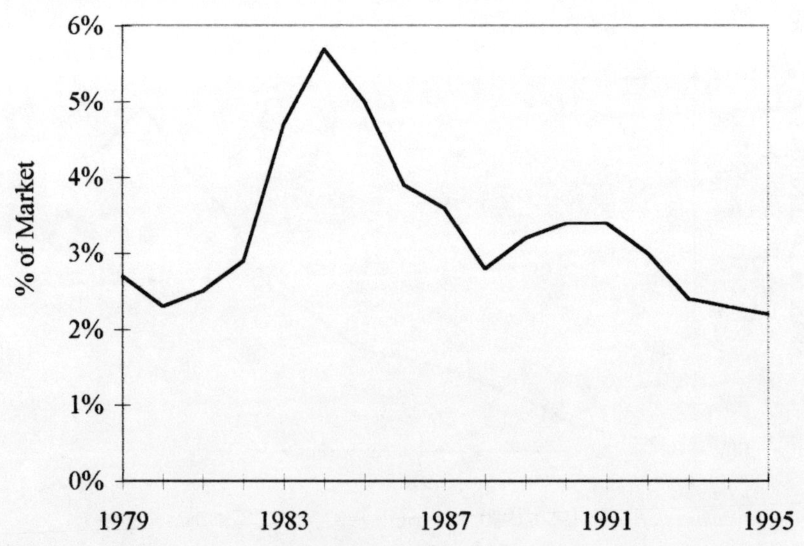

Sources: *Business Week*, 1950-1990; Maxwell, 1983, 1996, *Tobacco Reporter*, 1991-1995.

However, from 1980 to 1990, sales expanded 90% (from $278 million to $545 million), and operating profits exploded 299% (from $17.4 million to $69.4 million). The firm with the worst market share, the worst estimated operating profit margins (Ostroff, 1990), and the worst product mix of price-value brands to full-price brands (65%) produced a $69.4 million operating profit in 1990. Liggett's ability to initially develop and dominate the price-value segment, although its dominant share was subsequently diminished, gave it breathing space to be saved (the proposed close-down) by the price hikes initiated by Philip Morris. The average manufacturer's price for the cheapest generic type of price-value brands in 1990 was still 53% higher than the 1980 price of a standard brand. The average manufacturer price per 1,000 cigarettes increased from $23.75 in 1980 to $40.08 in 1990 (Ostroff, 1990). These increases outstripped retail prices and the consumer price index, thus allowing real profit increase for the cigarette firms. Over this ten-year time frame, Liggett's operating profit margins tripled. However, it was not thoughts of these future cigarette profits that British-based Grand Metropolitan Ltd (Grand Met) had in mind when it had acquired Liggett in mid-1980.

Diversification

Grand Met had acquired Liggett in order to acquire Liggett's liquor business to further expand its own liquor operations. Liggett had previously acquired a liquor importer, Paddington, in 1966 and a distiller and importer in 1969, the Austin, Nichols Company. Liquor contributed 24% to Liggett sales in 1979. Rebuffed in its efforts to buy Liggett's spirit operations (whose importing business imported Grand Met's own best-selling J&B scotch) separately, Grand Met felt compelled to purchase all of Liggett.

All of Liggett consisted not only of the cigarette and liquor businesses but also pet food, through Liggett's purchase of the Allen Company (Alpo) in 1964. By 1979, pet foods were contributing 19% of the sales, spirits were 24%, cigarettes were 27%, smoking and chewing tobaccos where another 6%, and others (cereal products, watch bands, and household cleaners) were 24%. Between 1964 and 1970, Liggett had reduced its cigarette sales specialization to 46%. Its further reduction to 27% by 1979 cemented its position as the most diversified cigarette firm. Cigarettes contributed only 15% of Liggett's operating profits in that year. Liggett had been accused of being "too late with too little" (Miles, 1982) in its cigarette operations. Its specialization, in terms of both sales and operating profits, was of a different ilk. The leadership role of a Chesterfield had been replaced by an Alpo in dog food and J&B and Grand Marnier in the spirits business. Similar to American, Liggett appeared to be putting the costly knowledge it acquired in the cigarette business to its diversified operations. Figure 5.18 shows the historical evolution of L&M's business segments until its acquisition by Grand Met. Since Grand Met had only acquired Liggett for its spirit operations, it was only a matter of time until the cigarette business would be divested from a Grand Met increasingly focused on the food and liquor industries.

Figure 5.18
Brooke Group's (L&M) Net Sales by Industry Segment, 1965–1978, 1989–1995

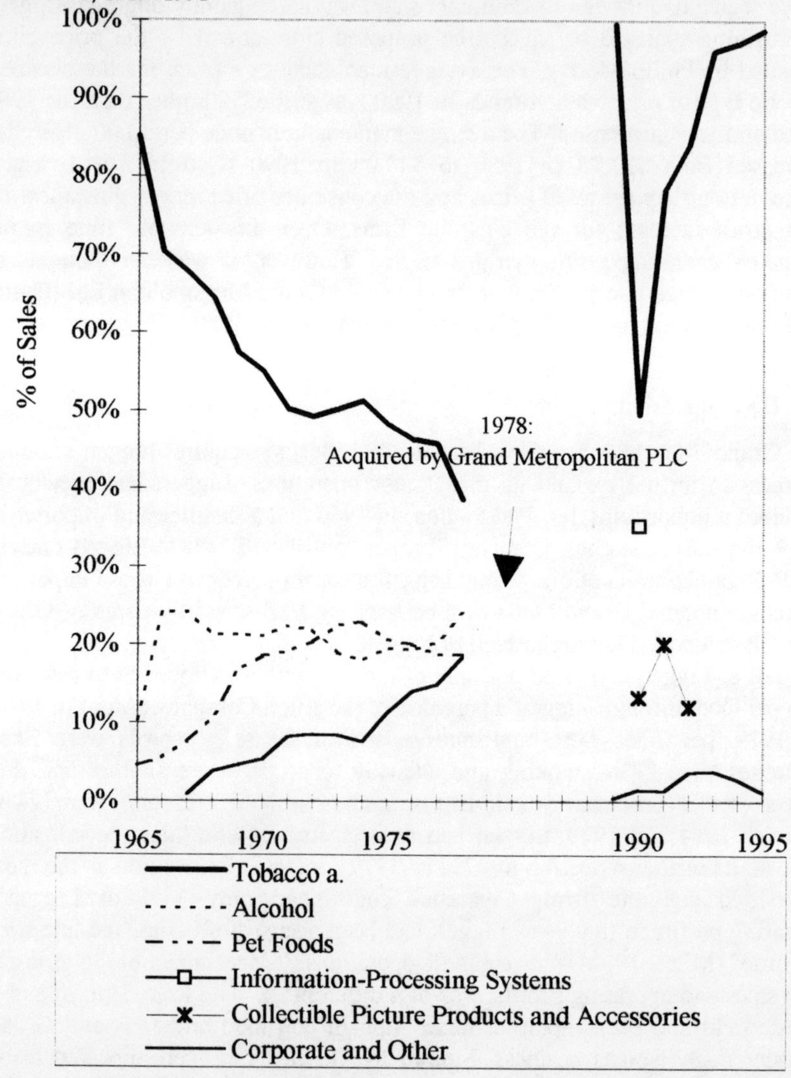

Notes: a. Includes chewing and smoking tobacco, which contributed an average of 6.1% of net sales between 1973 and 1979. b. Grand Met did not break out sales after their acquisition.

Source: Moody's Industrial Manuals; Corporate Reports.

This divestment occurred in 1986 via an LBO by investor Bennett LeBow. LeBow then spun off a 16% interest to the public in late 1987. In late 1990, LeBow merged two money-losing ($66 million) ventures (trading cards and applications software) into the Liggett operations. At that time, Liggett sales were $545 million, and operating profits were $69.4 million. In 1995, sales were reduced to $456 million, and operating profits were down to $16.7 million.

Diminutive industry size and Marlboro Friday actions disproportionately affected Liggett's heavily weighted price-value product sales ratio. However, LeBow's financial engineering removed the focus from the cigarette business's 1980s extraordinary turnaround from probable extinction to salvation through price increases. Suffice it to say that the Brooke Group no longer has interest in trading cards or applications software or Western Union but has had two of these three subsidiaries go through bankruptcy proceedings. Presently, the Brooke Group has interest in Liggett, real estate, and cigarette manufacturing in the former Soviet Union and, through its New Valley operation, a stake in RJR Nabisco. The Ichan-LeBow stake in RJR was discussed earlier in the RJR section.

Not discussed was the March 1996 settlement by Liggett whereby it agreed to a payment schedule of between 2% and 7% of its pre-tax operating income for twenty-four years for smoking-related health care expenditures with five (and potentially all states) states suing for same. Additionally, it covered lawsuits based on the addiction theory with the Castano class-action plaintiffs in return for the payment of up to $50 million over twenty-five years for smoking cessation programs. The settlement allowed RJR to come under the Liggett umbrella. Critics from the industry were quick to point out that the settlement, which hurt the share price of all firms, was merely an attempt by LeBow to strengthen his position vis-à-vis RJR. Critics further pointed out that the agreement still allowed all of the lawsuits not based on the theory of addiction. Subsequently, they crowed when the Castano lawsuit was decertified as a class-action. Liggett, accordingly, still has a problem: what does the settlement still cover? The intensity of the question is only magnified by the recently signed tobacco accord which is discussed in the next chapter. Given its size, one major judgment against Liggett could put them out of business. According to its 1995 10K report, Liggett continues to receive unspecified "financial assistance from others in the industry in defraying the costs incurred in defense of smoking and health litigation and related proceedings" (Liggett Group; *10K Reports*, 1995).

Hypotheses Testing

Liggett, a pre-1950 leader, did not remain so after the smoking and health issue surfaced. Thus, its actions were consistent with Hypothesis 2. As the industry matured, it did diversify. This action was consistent with Hypothesis 6.

Since it was not a leader, it did not diversify internationally, thus being consistent with Hypothesis 8. It did not do any internal development for new businesses, showing consistency with Hypothesis 9. And it acquired related businesses but itself was acquired for financial engineering purposes; so its activities were consistent with both Hypotheses 10 and 11.

Chapter 6

Analysis and Conclusions

The domestic consequences of the strategic interactions between the six firms are shown in Figure 6.1. Philip Morris's leadership strategy has resulted in its dominant position. With respect to product diversification, Figure 6.2 shows that the industry, in aggregate, has had greater sales in nontobacco products than in cigarettes since 1985. Figure 6.3 shows that, also since 1985, international cigarette sales have surpassed domestic sales. Three factors—the growth of the Far East market, the expansion of the price-value segment, and the acquisitions of Nabisco, Kraft, and General Foods—help to explain why these aggregate numbers changed from 1985 onward. Before discussing the successes and failures of the individual firms, a review of Porter's hypotheses vis-à-vis the firms' actions described in Chapter 5 should give an indication of whom we should expect to be successful.

Figure 6.1
Market Share by Company, 1950–1995

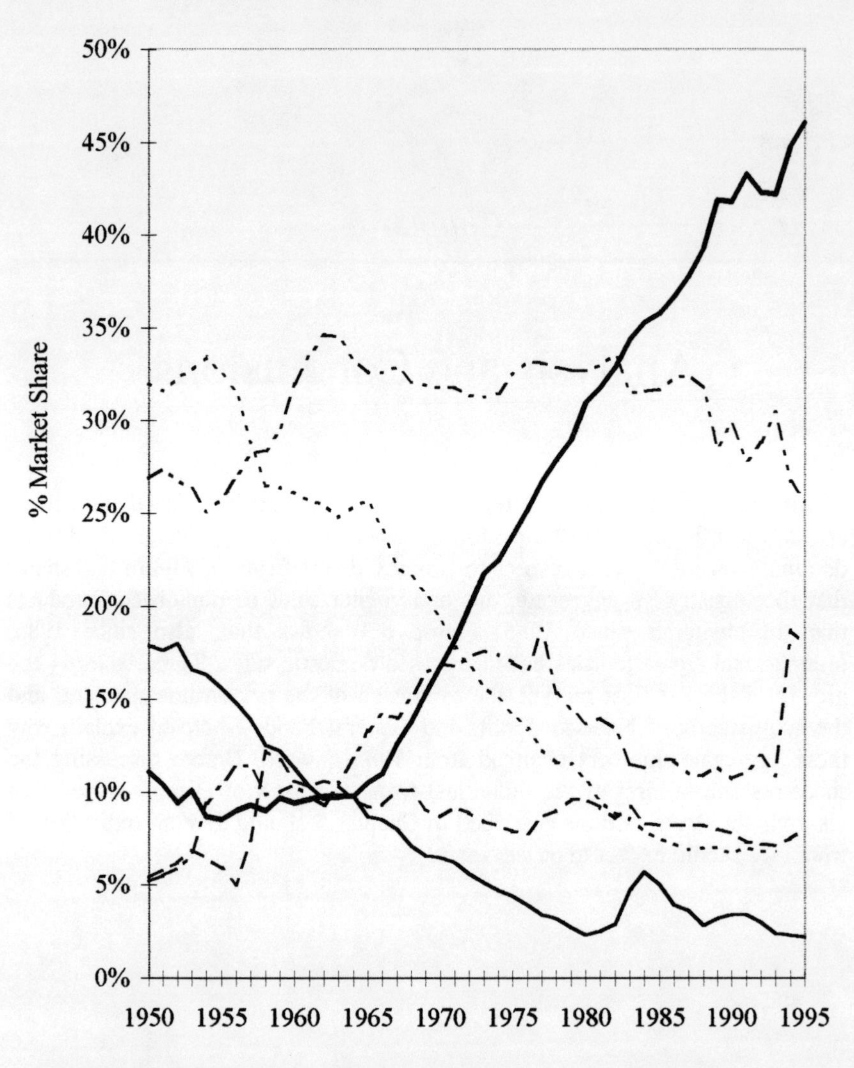

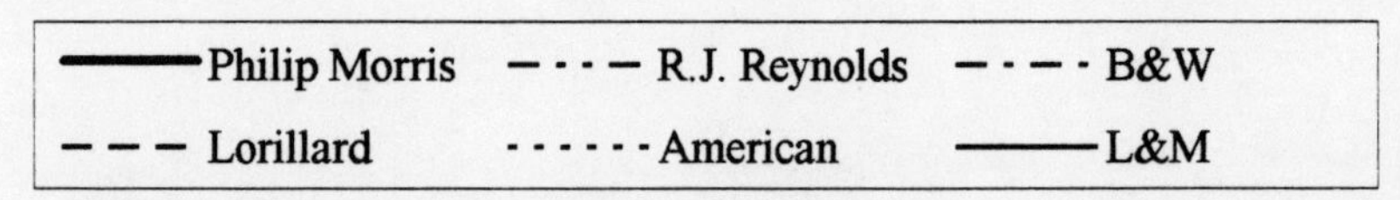

Sources: *Business Week*, 1950-1990, Maxwell,1983, 1996, *Tobacco Reporter*, 1991-1995.

Figure 6.2
Total Tobacco versus Other Sales, 1967–1995

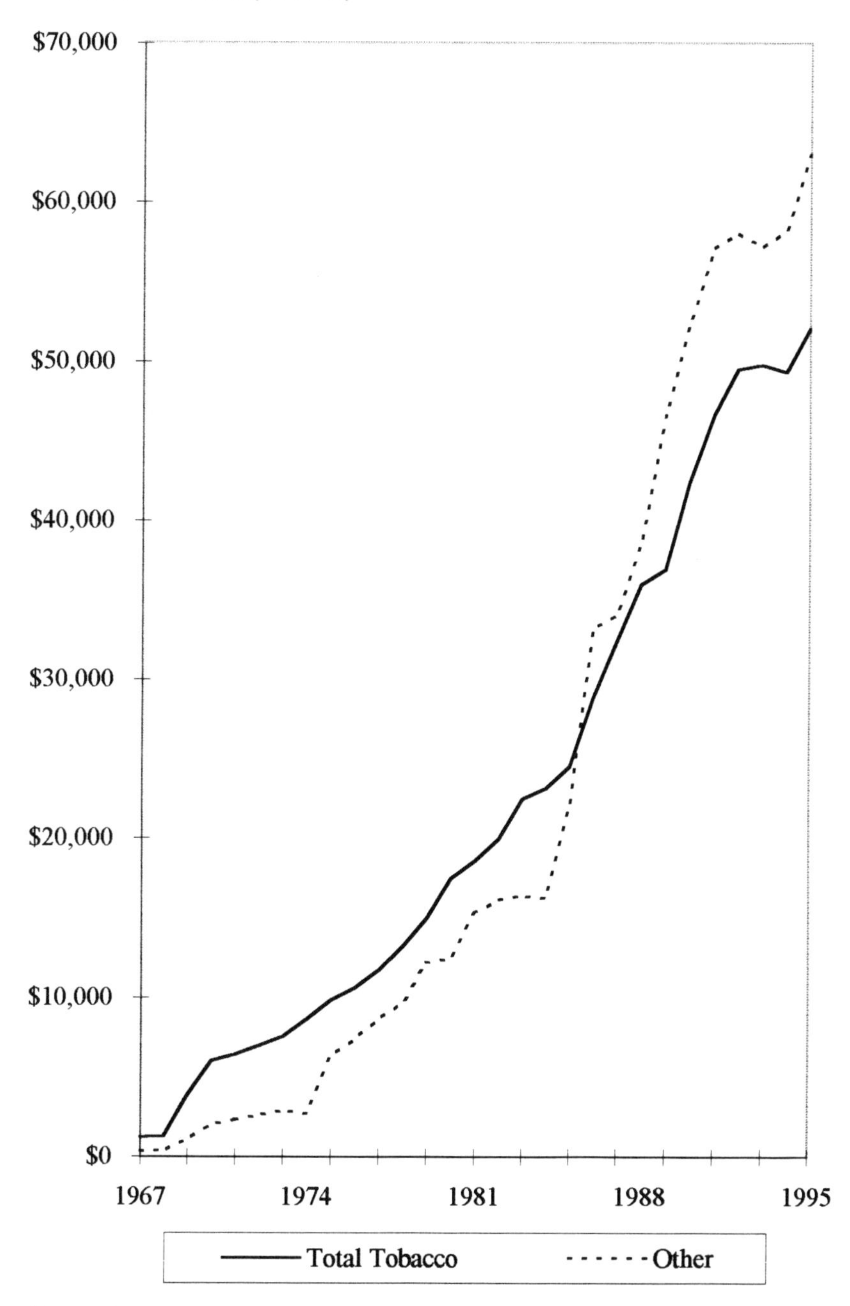

Source: Corporate Reports; author's calculations.

Figure 6.3
Percentage of Sales: International Cigarettes, 1975–1995

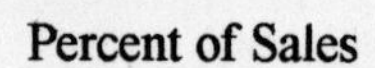

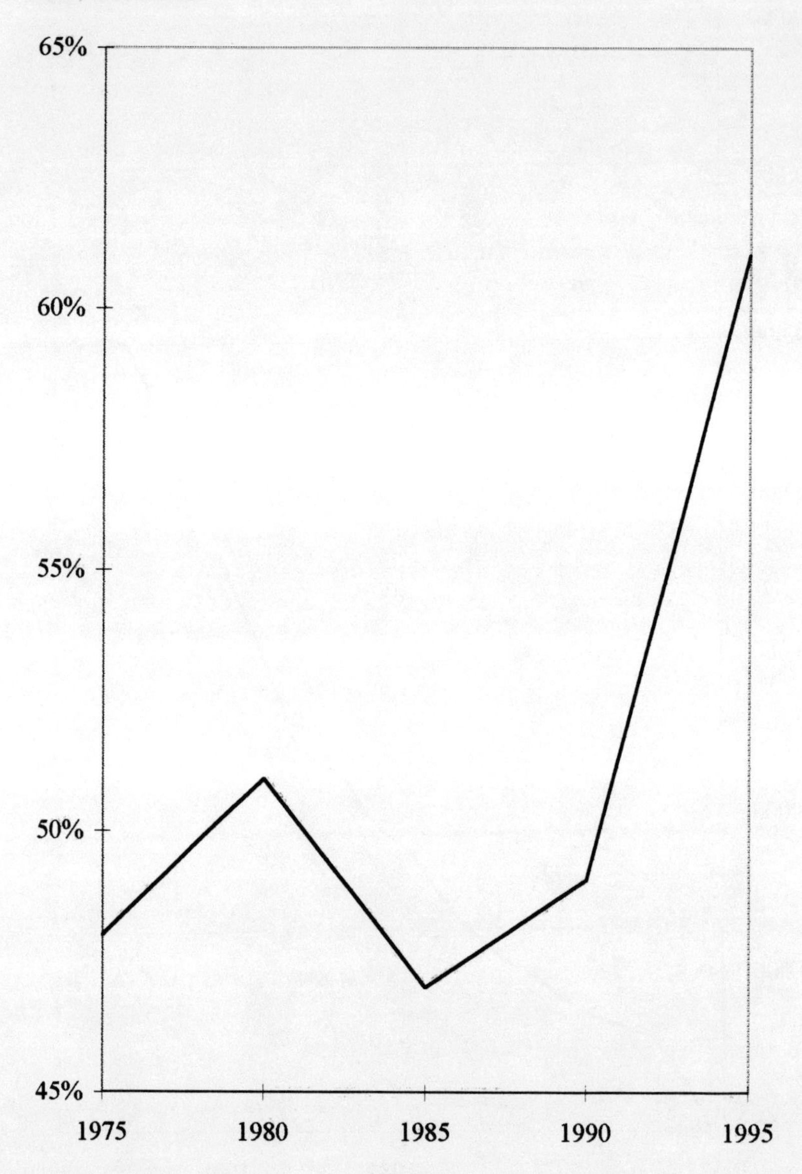

Sources : Corporate Reports; author's calculations.

THE HYPOTHESES REVISITED

Hypothesis 1: As the cigarette industry moves into the maturity/decline phase due to the smoking and health issue, there will be substantial change in the market share ranking of its participant firms.

Figure 6.1 is consistent with this hypothesis. RJR was the only firm to maintain a bookend position, second, during this study's time frame. Even that is misleading, given RJR's position as number one during most of this time. The 1950 leader, American, exited the industry. Philip Morris moved from fourth to first. B&W moved from fifth to third, while Lorillard moved from sixth to fourth, and Liggett went from third to fifth position.

Hypothesis 2: Industry leaders often exhibit substantial inertia in adjusting their strategies to new circumstances; therefore, in the cigarette industry firms, other than previous leaders will assume leadership positions during the industry's maturing/decline phase.

The Big Three of 1950 became the Big Two of 1995. Number-one American exited the industry, and number-three Liggett came to occupy fifth place. Philip Morris moved from fourth to first. Only RJR's activities, with its maintenance of second place, were not consistent with this hypothesis.

Hypothesis 3: Firms that have historically followed a successful niche strategy will continue to do so during the cigarette industry's maturity/decline phase.

B&W, a clear niche player, continued to do so throughout this study's time frame; thus, it was consistent with this hypothesis. Lorillard was unsuccessful with its price-value brand, Sensation, immediately prior to 1950. Its niche attempts in hi-fi (Kent) and low-tar (True) have been mediocre. Only Newport, a menthol, has experienced success, and that came under Loews's leadership. Hypothesis 3 is neither consistent nor inconsistent with Lorillard since it was not following a successful niche strategy before industry maturity/decline but did so during that phase but under Loew's direction.

Hypothesis 4: Due to historically high cigarette profits and to the existence of more favorable alternative (leadership/niche) under Hypotheses 2 and 3, firms in the cigarette industry will not initially adopt a harvest strategy; they will, however, be forced to adopt such a strategy in the long run.

None of the firms initially adopted a harvest strategy. As of 1995, all firms' domestic operations were being analyzed, solely, in terms of free cash flow. All the firms' activities were consistent with the hypothesis.

Hypothesis 5: Because (1) of historic profitability and (2) of high exit barriers due to substantial industry-specific assets and potential legal liability, firms in the cigarette industry will not seek to adopt an exit strategy.

Liggett was the first firm that attempted to exit the business. Its potential buyer reneged and no sale occurred. But it did attempt exit; thus, Liggett's activities were not consistent with Hypothesis 5. American has effectively exited the business, albeit nine months after the close of the study. The other four firms did not seek exit and thus were consistent with this hypothesis.

Hypothesis 6: Firms in the cigarette industry will adopt diversification strategies during the maturity/decline phase of the industry.

Five of the firms diversified. Their actions were consistent with this hypothesis. Although Lorillard had acquired three minor candy firms in the mid-1960s, it was acquired by Loews in 1968 and is treated as not applicable, since it was no longer an independent actor before the halfway point of the study was reached.

Hypothesis 7: Firms that undertake a leadership strategy under Hypothesis 2 will diversify into international markets.

The two leaders, Philip Morris and RJR, both diversified their markets internationally. Such diversification was consistent with this hypothesis.

Hypothesis 8: Firms that do not adopt leadership strategies under Hypothesis 2, will not expand inter-nationally.

Lorillard and Liggett sold their overseas rights. These sales were consistent with this hypothesis. B&W, as a BAT subsidiary, is nonapplicable. American did expand overseas (Gallaher in the United Kingdom). Such expansion was not consistent with this hypothesis. However, it should be noted that American had expanded overseas in 1927 with its Wix acquisition, which eventually led to its Gallaher position. In fact, absent being forced into the "White Knight" role by Philip Morris's pursuit of Gallaher, it is questionable whether or not American would have gone overseas. Nevertheless, it did.

Hypothesis 9: Due to (1) the cigarette firms' unique production/technology specificity (hence their lack of transferability), (2) the maturity of closely related industries (in the consumer packaged goods industry) and (3) the absolute size requirement of a new product area for effective diversification, companies in the cigarette industry will choose an acquisition rather than an internal development strategy to achieve product market diversification.

No firm even attempted to devise an internal development strategy. Thus, all firms' lack of activity was consistent with Hypothesis 9.

Hypothesis 10: Cigarette firms will acquire businesses that will be related to their core competencies (i.e., consumer packaged goods marketing).

Since Lorillard was acquired relatively early in the study's time frame and due to B&W's subsidiary status to BAT, they are not applicable. While both Philip Morris and RJR have evolved down a learning curve with respect to acquisition, they are both now squarely focused on the consumer packaged goods industry, which is a clean fit with their core competency. As previously discussed, American's breadth of business juxtaposed against their intangible marketing relations leaves it neither consistent nor inconsistent with this hypothesis.

Hypothesis 11: Because uncertainties over legal liabilities and industry viability impair the perfect market assumption of perfect information (which also impairs any acquiring firm's visualization of future horizontal management capabilities), cigarette firms that will be acquired by firms from outside the industry will be acquired for investment portfolio or financial restructuring reasons.

KKR, an LBO firm, acquired RJR. Lowes, a financial holding company, acquired Lorillard. Although Liggett was originally acquired by Grand Met for its spirits business, it was subsequently purchased by LeBow in an LBO. All three firms acquired by outside the industry firms were purchased for financial engineering rationales. These actions were consistent with the hypothesis.

ANALYSIS

Hypotheses derived from Porter's work are matrixed against the firms' actions shown in Table 6.1. The hypotheses have stood up quite well when tested by the firms' actions. Although case studies do not lend themselves to statistical analysis, the binomial test was performed for each hypothesis that had a frequency of five or more. Because of the case nature of the study, the decision rule was to utilize a 0.1 level of significance to reject the null hypothesis that there is no difference between the probability of obtaining a consistent observation with a hypothesis and the probability of obtaining an observation not consistent with that hypothesis. Figure 6.1 shows that in four (and barely missing in the fifth) out of the five applicable cases, the null hypothesis of chance occurrence was rejected statistically. If the three mutually exclusive set of hypotheses concerning leadership versus niche, international or not, and acquirer versus acquiree are collapsed into single hypotheses, one gain's qualitative support but not statistical significance for these interrelated hypotheses.

Table 6.1
Hypothesis

	HYPOTHESIS	PHILIP MORRIS	R.J. REYNOLDS	AMERICAN BRANDS	BROWN & WILLIAMSON	LORILLARD	LIGGETT & MYERS	PERCENTAGE
1	Market Change	+	+	+	+	+	+	.016*
2	Leader	+	-	+	n/a	n/a	+	
3	Niche	n/a	n/a	n/a	+	o	n/a	
4	Harvest	+	+	+	+	+	+	.016*
5	Exit	+	+	+	+	+	-	0.109
6	Diversify	+	+	+	+	n/a	+	.031*
7	International	+	+	n/a	n/a	n/a	n/	
8	No International	n/a	n/a	-	n/a	+	+	
9	Internal	+	+	+	+	+	+	.016*
10	Acquiror	+	+	o	n/a	n/a	+	
11	Acquiree	n/a	+	n/a	n/a	+	+	

Legend:
+ Consistent
- Inconsistent
o Indeterminable
n/a Not Applicable

WITH WHAT SUCCESS?

If a firm were to achieve what Porter has labeled a "sustainable competitive advantage," at the minimum, it would be expected that the firm remain in business, given that all these firms were in the first Fortune 500. If one has been acquired and other competitors have not, one has not, by the most elemental definition, been successful. Since B&W has always been a BAT subsidiary, there existed five independent firms at the start of this study's time frame in 1950. At the conclusion of the study, only Philip Morris stood as it originally did in 1950—as an independent entity. Liggett & Myers had been acquired first by Grand Met and subsequently by LeBow. Lorillard was taken over by Loews, while RJR had succumbed to KKR. American has exited the business.

An analysis of the firms' activities vis-à-vis Porter's hypotheses gives a rationale to these outcomes. Philip Morris exercised a leadership strategy, diversified its products and markets, and as indicated in Chapter 5, executed the strategy extremely well. Lorillard and Liggett are likewise clearly explained, albeit with opposite results.

Lorillard did not develop a leadership strategy, nor did it have, historically, a successful niche strategy. This market failure eliminated significant overseas expansion, and Lorillard sold its overseas brand rights to Philip Morris. Lorillard did not move to make any significant product acquisitions. Relative to its competitors, it was stagnant and it was acquired by Loews with LBO debt levels in 1968 before the word LBO existed. Liggett & Myers, one of the Big Three leaders in 1950, was consistent with Hypothesis 2 by falling from a leadership position to dead last in 1995. Its domestic market decline inhibited overseas expansion, and international brand rights were sold to BAT in 1977. This same lack of market force prevented it from sustaining its creation and early dominance of the price-value segment. Its diversification into the spirits business attracted the attention of Grand Met, the Philip Morris of its industry. Upon L&M's refusal to sell its spirits operations to Grand Met, Grand Met purchased all of L&M, subsequently disposing of the cigarette operations to LeBow in an LBO. L&M's lack of scope in both its cigarette and spirits markets, relative to its competitor's, extinguished its independence.

RJR was inconsistent with Porter's hypothesis on leadership by having been, and then staying, a leader through the maturity/decline phase. It both expanded overseas and learned to diversify into related businesses, but yet it was acquired by KKR. The problem with RJR was its strategic implementation, as described in Chapter 5. Its overseas expansion, lacking in local market sensitivity, resulted in international sales one third those of Philip Morris's. Its early product diversifications were significantly larger than Philip Morris's (Chapter 5), and due to a lack of fit (e.g., the oil business), management was distracted with subsequent problems in these unrelated businesses. By the time management divested itself of these unrelated acquisitions, it found itself second to Philip Morris in the domestic market. Its related diversification efforts with Nabisco were quickly dwarfed by Philip Morris's acquisitions of Kraft, General Foods, and Suchard. RJR's sloppy strategic execution resulted in KKR's ability to leverage RJR's very own brand names with junk bonds in an LBO purchase.

With its fall from 1950 market leader to fifth position in 1990, American Brands would appear to set the stage for a repeat of the Lorillard and L&M stories. However, as Porter pointed out in Chapter 4 in his description of industry evolution, chance plays a role in strategic management. American's 1927 acquisition of Wix, which led to a passive minority shareholder interest in the United Kingdom's Gallaher, was the difference for American. When Gallaher requested American to act as a "White Knight" to rebuff Philip Morris's acquisition attempt in 1968, American was given a second chance. American took the bitter lessons it had learned in the U.S. market and applied them with a victorious vengeance in the United Kingdom market. Its success in the United Kingdom market and its other product markets (where it now used this same leadership strategy) enabled it to complete a reverse acquisition on E-II when E-II attempted a hostile takeover in 1988. Chance gave American a second possibility, and American exploited the opportunity.

CONCLUSIONS

Statistical significance is found for four of the five applicable hypotheses, and the fifth hypothesis is nearly so. If the three sets of mutually exclusive hypotheses are collapsed into three single hypotheses, qualitative support is found for all the hypotheses. Likewise, it can be found that when Porter's hypotheses are viewed along the dimension of domestic market strategy, coupled with international expansion and product diversification, they serve as a reliable predictor of future success. Philip Morris's, Lorillard's, and Liggett & Myers's results were directly predictable from the related hypotheses. RJR's result required the addition of good strategic implementation skills, while American added the element of chance and learning, both large elements in Porter's description of industry evolution.

DISCUSSION

Given the general perspective of cash-rich cigarette companies acquiring everything in sight, it is interesting to recognize that three of the companies were purchased, two had to fight off hostile acquisition attempts, one has exited the industry, and only Philip Morris has enjoyed a threat-free existence. Only Loews's acquisition has stood the test of time, whereas L&M's fate with LeBow is speculative. KKR's acquisition of RJR had placed KKR more in the role of an operator than it had ever been before. Its ability to extricate itself from RJR was a contest between the free cash flow needed to deleverage versus the growth of the price-value market with its negative effect on that very same free cash flow, aggravated by Philip Morris's Marlboro Friday actions.

The growth of the price-value segment and the sidestream smoke issue are the twin Achilles' heels of the domestic cigarette industry. The price-value segment threatens profits, whereas the sidestream smoke issue could lead to a legal liability financial disaster. However, it is somewhat ironic to consider that the only cigarette firm, Philip Morris, to pursue a leadership strategy during the forty-five year time frame of the smoking and health issue (RJR started with that position) has been the most successful and the only firm never to have been threatened by a takeover. But the next ten years could be significantly different. The issue of fraud (When did the tobacco firms know what about addiction-and/or smoking-related illnesses?) has been softening the American public's unwillingness to find cigarette firms liable for a smoker's right to damages. Heretofore, the public has felt that the smoker knew better and should not profit from his or her continued smoking of a well-known health hazard. However, the expanding perspective, that the cigarette firms have lied—has been conditioning the American public, the potential jury pool, to the argument that the average smoker commenced smoking in childhood before reaching the age of consent, as highlighted by the FDA, and that by the time an individual realized the dangers from smoking, he or she was, as pointed out by the surgeon general, addicted. Hence, a victim deserving of compensatory and punitive damages is being created.

It was in response to this growing negative judicial environment that Liggett reached its settlement. Almost simultaneously with the Liggett settlement, a trial balloon for a "grand" legislative settlement arose from the Washington political scene. In return for congressional immunity from future liability suits, the industry would pay multibillions to the states for the cost of medical care for smoking related illnesses as well as compensation for some individual smokers (Freedman & Hwang, 1996). Funds would also be contributed for antitobacco campaigns at both the state and federal levels. Failure to achieve necessary consensus deflated this balloon. However, at year-end 1996, similar grand settlement discussions were reinflated by the efforts of Washington superlobbyist Thomas Boggs, Jr. Credence was given to his efforts because his lobbying firm had represented both the Association of Trial Lawyers and tobacco interests (Ingersall & Frisby, 1996). Discussions continued into 1997 with Mississippi's Attorney General Michael Moore playing a key role. A memorandum of understanding—the tobacco accord—was signed in June 1997 by Philip Morris, RJR, Brown and Williamson, Lorillard, and UST along with attorney generals representing forty states.

Since the tobacco accord requires enabling legislation it is subject to the approval of both the executive and congressional branches of government.

Congressional leaders and the president will be influenced by an advisory committee consisting of such public health groups as the American Medical, Heart and Cancer Associations. The committee is chaired by former Surgeon General C. Everett Koop and former FDA chief David Kessler. The advisory group, within a week of the memorandum's signing, had indicated that there were some non-negotiable changes required in the accord if the committee's blessing was to be given. The sixty-eight page memorandum, certain to play a significant role as a lawyer's work relief act, requires the industry to pay $368.5 billion in the first twenty-years followed by a $15 billion per annum payment indefinitely. The monies would be utilized to settle the state Medicaid suits (Mississippi was the first state to settle), existing class-action suits, health care, and anti-smoking education and advertising. Future class-action and punitive damages suits would be banned and individual lawsuits would face a total $5 billion per year maximum exposure. Warning labels would be enlarged and state, inter alia, that smoking causes cancer. Billboard advertising as well as the use of human and cartoon characters would be banned. The Tobacco Institute and the Council for Tobacco Research would be dissolved and disbanded. A look-back provision that requires a monetary penalty if youth smoking does not stop by certain percentages over a certain number of years, e.g., 50% in seven years, would be enacted. The FDA is given regulatory control over nicotine but this authority is limited from a total ban until 2009 and the FDA would have to show (1) that its action would significantly reduce a health risk, (2) is technologically feasible, and (3) would not create a black-market effect. It is these two latter features to which the advisory committee immediately reacted. Although the lower court decision (see Chapter 2) is being appealed, the committee feels that the FDA has already been given regulatory authority over nicotine without the restrictions enumerated above. With respect to the look-back provisions the committee's co-chairs have stated that the penalty (five cents a pack in their estimate) for failure to reach certain youth smoke reduction target is not sufficient to act as a disincentive, i.e., the industry would willingly pay five cents a pack to induce youth to smoke.

Aligning the varied interests of the numerous stakeholders will be extremely difficult. Not only does the accord face the initial non-negotiable changes demanded by the advisory panel but it also faces numerous other intervening interests. Illustrative of these conflicts are: (1) the American Lung Association states that the $360 billion payment is both too low and would be tax deductible; (2) ASH Director John Banzhaf states that he will challenge the constitutionality of any provision eliminating punitive damages; (3) Delaware Senator Biden states that the cigarette firms CEOs must testify to the effect that cigarettes are addictive and can kill you and if they do not do so the settlement will be rejected; (4) Senator Lautenberg of New Jersey has his staff drafting legislation that will mirror the conclusions of the Koop-Kessler report; and (5) Elizabeth M. Whelan (1997) President of the American Council on Science and Health utilized Martin Broughton's, BAT's chairman, statement that "[t]hey want to be paid off and we want a peaceful life" to describe the accord as "the biggest drug payoff of the century." The mixture of contingency fees, legal reputation building, rent seeking by the legislatures, the anti-smoking interests and the industry itself, played out on the international, national, state, and local levels, weaves a most intricate web of self- and public- interest. The multiple actors and interests increase geometrically, the complexity of the essential problem enunciated by Surgeon General Dr. Antonia Novello in her 1992 Surgeon General report:

> One of the fundamental paradoxes of market-oriented societies is that some entrepreneurs—even acting completely within the prescribed rules of business practice—will come into conflict with public health goals. The market structure of the tobacco industry constitutes a major threat to public health simply because the product is tobacco. In the tobacco industry, attempts to control a large market share, marketing to target groups, widespread use of innovative promotional techniques, and corporate growth, development, and consolidation—in short, the traditional elements of successful entrepreneurial activity—are ultimately inimical to the public health. (US Department of Health and Human Services [USDHHS], 1992)

When legislators, plaintiff lawyers, activists, and the industry's firms all exercise their own peculiar "traditional elements of successful entrepreneurial activity," the discovery of a common interest becomes difficult at best and impossible at worst.

Given these conflicts and given that historically all firms except Philip Morris have been purchased, normally with significant debt, a potentially more fruitful approach could be a leverage buy-out of the industry by the Koop-Kessler group. Ownership by a quasi-government Koop-Kessler group would not be such a conceptual leap as one might first imagine, once one considers the historic tax situation along with a prospective reduction in transaction costs due to a common ownership. Such action would in economist's terminology internalize the externality. A marriage of the cigarette ownership with the public health agenda setters would allow for a direct resolution not only of the aforementioned conflicts (thus reducing transaction costs), but also of such problems as how to handle international sales—which is not discussed in the agreement. Historically the government has been an implicit co-owner of the cigarette firms with its historical 50% tax (excise, sales, and income) take of the tobacco value chain's sales dollar. A quasi government sponsored LBO makes the co-ownership by the government explicit.

More likely is the probability that the tobacco accord will be legislated into existence in some revised version. All parties to the argument are driven by a fear of class-action suits; either the loss of same or the inability to be certified to bring one. Wall Street desires certainty (see Hypothesis 11) with respect to future earnings which the settlement could give them. In fact, given that many financial analysts believe there will be a wash between monies spent on payments and reductions in advertising, it is quite possible the street will reward the firms with a higher price to earnings ratio, to either market levels or higher, thus increasing the price of the stock. State attorney generals and congressmen visualize their political stock being enhanced as the white knights who have slayed the dragon nicotine. Plaintiffs attorneys who have taken the states' Medicaid cases on a contingency free basis have a bonanza to share. Assuming an accord passes into legislation the question that drove this book starts anew—what will the strategies be for the industry's firms? The industry rules of competition will change just as significantly as they did for the Bonsack machine, the trust busters, the mass marketing of a firm's single brand champion and the brand prolification of segmented filter tips (read safer). Will the industry attempt to market a "safe" cigarette? Will the accord's restrictions on advertising apply to such a safe" cigarette? Will the industry focus even more overseas? Can the smaller resource firms do that? Will RJR, with its history of Premier and Eclipse, attempt a leadership role in a potentially large "safe" cigarette segment? Will Philip Morris with its greater profitability raise its price less than the others (to cover the accord's payment) in an attempt to gain greater market share? Will the price increases necessitated by the accord's payments kill the golden nicotine goose for both the shareholders and the government? Will the anti-smoking movement continue to globalize at Internet speed? The only certainty is that the cigarette saga will continue—an ongoing epic which has, and will be, comprised of numerous, complex, interrelated, and often ironic vignettes.

Appendix

Smokeless Tobacco

Smokeless tobacco was first used by Native Americans in both North and South America. The natives used many forms of tobacco, including nasal and oral snuff, chewing and plug tobacco, and smoked tobacco. Europeans in the New World adopted all of these forms, with snuff being one of the most popular forms. Eventually, tobacco usage spread to the European continent and went through several stages, from being utilized as a medicine to fight the Plague to the image of snuff as a luxury item of the affluent. While tobacco was being manufactured in Europe and in a few plants in the American colonies (including a mill built by the nation's oldest tobacco manufacturer, the P. Lorillard Company), many southerners used homegrown chewing tobacco, often flavored with honey, sugar, licorice, and molasses. The main market for manufactured snuff products became the north-central part of the United States, where people from heavy snuff-using Scandinavian countries settled. It was not until 1950 that smokeless tobacco manufacturers such as UST started marketing their products in the Southwest, and it was not until the mid-1960s that tobacco products were introduced in the Southeast, which is currently the largest market for smokeless tobacco. When snuff was introduced in the South, it was used mostly by workers whose activities prevented them from smoking because of either inconvenience or danger such as foresters or refinery personnel. Today, use of smokeless tobacco seems to start with males when they are young, usually during their high school years. The trend that has been noticed (and companies have been accused of exploiting it) is a form of "graduation" where a young male begins using snuff that contains low nicotine and is mild or fruit flavored and subsequently graduates to harsher snuff that contains more nicotine.

Throughout the 1960's and 1970's, as cigarette manufacturers faced growing criticism, makers of smokeless tobacco remained relatively unscathed, able to avoid laws requiring warning labels. Labeling requirements changed in 1986 when a much-publicized case was brought against UST by Betty Ann Marsee, who sued UST for $147 million, claiming that UST's products caused the mouth cancer that had killed her teenage son. Although UST won the case, the publicity caused by this case prompted Congress to pass the 1986 Smokeless Tobacco Act. The law forced manufacturers of smokeless tobacco to post the same type of warning labels on their products that cigarette makers were required to put on packs of cigarettes. Three warning labels—stating that the products could cause (1) mouth cancer, or (2) gum disease and tooth loss and that (3) smokeless tobacco is not a safe alternative to cigarette smoking—had to be placed on packages of smokeless tobacco on a rotating basis. The law also banned broadcast ads for smokeless tobacco. At the same time, federal and some state excise taxes were being enacted on a per can basis.

In the years after the Marsee case, criticism of smokeless tobacco died down, with greater attention being given to the ill effects of second hand smoke from cigarettes. Interestingly, many recent court cases brought by states, cities, and municipalities fail to mention UST, Conwood, Swisher, or any other manufacturer of (only) smokeless tobacco. For example, in a case filed in August 1996 by the state of Michigan, more than twenty-five companies were sued for $14 billion. The suit alleged "a well-organized campaign of fraud, lies, intimidation and deception" and sought to recoup, among others, state Medicaid costs. Among the defendants were tobacco giants Philip Morris and R.J. Reynolds, in addition to tobacco wholesalers and even the public relations firm Hill & Knowlton. Yet out of all the companies that Michigan Attorney General Frank J. Kelley chose to sue, UST was not among them. In fact, most cases revolve around smoking- and second hand-smoke-related illnesses rather than the cancer that is allegedly caused by smokeless tobacco use.

UST— REAPING THE BENEFITS OF MARKET DOMINANCE

UST was incorporated in 1986 as a holding company for U.S. Tobacco. The original company, Weyman-Bruton Co., was incorporated in 1911 after James Buchanon Duke's tobacco trust was dissolved by the U.S. government. Although the company started as strictly a snuff manufacturer, U.S. Tobacco diversified initially into related tobacco products and accessories (chewing tobacco, cigars, pipe cleaners) and then eventually into unrelated fields. Most of these unrelated acquisitions, including forays into candy and nuts, pet food, and broadcasting, were sold only a few years after being purchased. In addition, UST sold its House of Windsor subsidiary (cigars) to its employees in 1987. UST's long run of acquisitions and divestitures has resulted in a current portfolio consisting of tobacco, wine operations, and entertainment. The wine subsidiary operates through four wineries, Chateau Ste. Michelle, Columbia Crest, Conn Creek and Villa Mt. Eden. Wine operations accounted for 8.3% of UST's revenues in 1995 and 1.9% of operating income. UST's other, unrelated holding is Cabin Fever Entertainment. This subsidiary, which focuses on "American-style" productions, "specializing in home videos for viewers in the heartland," accounted for 5.1% of consolidated revenues and actually posted an operating loss of $5.3 million in 1995.

Despite the performance of its Cabin Fever subsidiary, UST has provided stunning returns for its shareholders. To put UST's success in perspective, consider that a $10,000 investment (dividends reinvested) in UST in 1985 would be worth approximately $190,000 at the end of 1995, an increase of almost 1,800% and an annualized average of 21%. UST's return on assets has grown from 21.3% in 1985 to 56.3% in 1995. Operating and profit margins have risen in the same fashion, resulting in 1995 margins of 53.4% and 32.4%, respectively (with operating margins on tobacco as high as 60%). To account for this impressive profitability, one must look at several factors. First are volume gains. Since 1978, UST's volume (in millions of cans) has risen from 295.1 to 625.8, a compound average of 7% per year. The second factor has been price increases. Since 1978, UST has been able to raise prices an average of 10.4% per year, compounded. While some of these increases have come during periods of high inflation in the late 1970s and early 1980s, UST has passed on huge increases even during years of low inflation (see Figure A.1). UST's ability to increase prices at rates several times that of inflation can be explained by UST's dominance in the smokeless tobacco market, especially moist snuff (to be discussed below).

Figure A.1
UST Price Increases Relative to the PI, 1986–1994

Year	CPI	Price Increase
1986	1.9%	14.4%
1987	3.7%	10.8%
1991	4.2%	10.8%
1992	3.0%	9.5%
1993	3.0%	9.1%
1994	2.6%	10.3%

Source: Author's calculations.

The final value-added factor has been cost controls. From 1985 to 1995, UST increased sales from $478 million to over $1.3 billion—an increase of 177%, truly an impressive rise. But perhaps even more impressive is that UST's cost of goods sold, over the same period of time, increased only 67.2%. This helped to increase operating profits by an extraordinary 300%. UST's ability to keep its raw materials costs down can be explained in the context of Porter's five competitive forces. Perhaps the most important of those forces contributing to UST's success is the power of suppliers—or a lack thereof. The suppliers in the labor-intensive tobacco industry have traditionally held little power for the simple reason that there are a large number of small suppliers with little or no market influence. At the same time, the end users (UST and industry giants Philip Morris and R.J. Reynolds) are limited in number and thus have significant strategic bargaining power when auction season comes around.

In terms of market share, UST has totally dominated the moist, smokeless (snuff) tobacco market for years. But in recent years, UST and its powerful brands Copenhagen and Skoal have begun to show some signs of weakness. From a market share high of 89.1% in 1987, UST has slipped to an estimated 83.5% in 1995. Causing problems for UST has been Conwood Co. and Swisher International. Both Conwood and Swisher manufacture a variety of tobacco products. The most bothersome to UST have been the low-priced snuff brands, such as Silver Creek (Swisher) and Cougar (Conwood), that have been nibbling away at UST's market share. Silver Creek sells in two-for-one packs, while Cougar is about half the price of Skoal. This has allowed price-value brands to grow from virtually nothing in the early 1990s to 2.4% of the market in 1995. Overall, Conwood, UST's closest competitor, has been able to increase its market share from 8.7% in 1985 to an estimated 13.1% in 1995. Meanwhile, UST's chances of expanding internationally (as the cigarette manufacturers have done) are slim. Outside of the United States and Sweden, there is very little market for smokeless tobacco. Besides the fact that snuff and chewing tobacco are virtually unknown in other countries, many countries throughout Europe and the Pacific Rim have placed tough restrictions on snuff. The one area that is being considered is Eastern Europe, which former CEO Louis Bantle considers to be UST's best opportunity for overseas growth.

But some signs of nervousness about UST's ability to maintain past returns are starting to show in Bantle himself, among others. In August and September of 1995, Bantle sold 500,000 shares of his UST stock. In addition, four officers or members of the board sold a total of 151,000 shares in June 1996, including Ralph Rossi, a member of the board of directors and former vice chairman, who sold 75,000 shares in June 1995 in addition to the more than 172,000 shares that he sold in 1995. Could this signal an end to UST's dominance and huge returns? Or are the officers and directors nervous about the mounting lawsuits faced by tobacco companies?

One problem that will only hurt UST's margins are competing discount brands. The increasing pressure on UST's market share by discount brands is similar to the pressure faced by premium cigarette brands in the early 1990s. What remains to be seen is what UST will do to stem the tide of discount brands before they steal even more market share. One possible scenario is a Marlboro Friday–type counterattack. On Friday, April 2, 1993, Philip Morris did the unthinkable: They cut prices on one of the most valuable brands in the world. That day, which has come to be known as "Marlboro Friday," was Philip Morris's reaction to several years' worth of losing market share to the growing numbers of discount brands, which had gained a 30.2% share of the total cigarette market by 1992. In addition, Marlboro's share of the U.S. market had fallen from a high of 26.3% in 1989 to 24.4% in 1992 and seemed to be headed lower. So on Marlboro Friday, Philip Morris announced it was cutting the price of a pack of Marlboros by $.40, an 18% decrease. On that day, Philip Morris's stock fell 23%. As it turned out, the move by the widely-criticized (and eventually fired) Philip Morris CEO Michael Miles turned out to be a stroke of genius. After Marlboro Friday, Marlboro's market share hit a trough of 23.5% for 1993. Since then, Marlboro has regained market share and controlled 31.8% of the U.S. market for the first half of 1996. As for discount brands, they hit their peak in 1993 at 36.8% of the U.S. market and have fallen ever since—to 32.5% in 1994, 30.1% in 1995, and 28.7% for the second quarter of 1996. Marlboro is widely considered to be one of the top two brands in the world, alongside Coca-Cola.

By analogy, UST's premium Copenhagen and Skoal brands are beginning to face increasing competition from Conwood and Swisher as previously discussed. But UST is not only facing competition from other brands of snuff; consumers seem to be realizing the large discrepancy between snuff and chewing tobacco, with most premium cans of snuff averaging around $3.00 a tin, while discount cans of snuff or a pouch of chewing tobacco, like Pinkerton's Red Man, cost around $2.00. In addition, overall smokeless volume is beginning to decline by 1 to 1.5% per year after years of (small) increases in the 1980s (Black, 1995). It is becoming increasingly apparent that UST cannot continue to raise prices by 10% per year. In short, UST, like Philip Morris before 1993, is beginning to see its extremely profitable premium brands lose market share to discount brands. And just as in Marlboro's case, UST's days of 60%-plus margins on tobacco may not be sustainable. With the steady erosion of market share, UST may turn to a Philip Morris strategy and slash prices on Copenhagen and Skoal. Such a strategy of protecting brand name equity has been utilized not only by Philip Morris in its cigarette business but also by its Kraft Foods subsidiary in the cereal business—"Grape Nuts Monday."

The fact remains that UST's brands are very popular but somewhat expensive for UST's target market of young, blue-collar males. Any significant price cut would most likely be seen as a positive to the ex-Copenhagen and ex-Skoal users who have switched on the basis of price. Eventually, UST would be able to regain its market share and subsequently raise prices slowly in order to restore at least some of its lost margins. Cigarette prices, for example, have increased by 3.84% and 2.2% in 1994 and 1995, respectively, after a large 7.8% drop in 1993.

One final possibility for UST to increase demand for its products would be to market smokeless tobacco to former smokers as a method of quitting. This issue was addressed by Brad Rodu and Philip Cole in an article published in *Priorities* (Rodu & Cole, 1997 reprint). The proposal presented is to switch cigarette smokers to smokeless tobacco so that they may receive the nicotine intake they crave without inhaling harmful smoke from cigarettes. The idea is controversial, and UST would probably face opposition if it openly marketed its products as a "safer" alternative to cigarette smoking. Yet the article points out that since "smokeless tobacco use is 98% safer than cigarette smoking," users of smokeless tobacco do not have to worry about "lung cancer nor other diseases of the lung," and "users have no excess risk for heart attacks"(p. 1). While smokeless tobacco is not without its risks, it may be able to be utilized as a method of switching smokers from one harmful product (cigarettes) to a *less* harmful one (snuff). This would allow UST to expand its customer base at a time when many of the estimated 48 million smokers in the United States are quitting. However, current regulations, including the warning labels mentioned above, would prevent direct promotion of smokeless tobacco as an alternative to cigarettes.

Bibliography

Adler, S.J., & Freedman, A.M. (1990, March 5). Smoked Out: Tobacco Suit Exposes Ways Cigarette Firms Keep the Profits Fat. *Wall Street Journal*, p. A1.

Agins, T., & Forman, C. (1990, March 16). Saks Management Teams with Tobu of Tokyo in Bid to Buy U.S. Retailer. *Wall Street Journal*, p. A3.

Alexander, S., & Stipp, D. (1990, August 26). Store Is Kept as Defendant in Tobacco Suit. *Wall Street Journal*, p. B1.

Allen, H. (1988, June 16). Ah, Those Smoking Yesterdays. *Washington Post*, p. C1.

Alsop, R. (1989, June 6). Enduring Bonds Hold Their Allure By Sticking Close to Their Roots. *Wall Street Journal*, p. B4.

Altman, K. (1990, May 29). The Evidence Mounts on Passive Smoking. *New York Times*, p. C1.

American Brands. (1965–1995). *Annual Reports*, and *10K reports*.

American Cancer Society. (1991). *Cancer Facts & Figures–1991*. Atlanta, GA: American Cancer Society.

American Lung Association. (1987). *Tobacco's Toll on America*. New York: American Lung Association.

Amit, R. (1986). Cost Leadership Strategy and Experience Curves. *Strategic Management Journal*, *7*(3); 281–292.

Anders, G., & Lowenstein, R. (1991, February 13). RJR Has New Look; But Still Top Cookie? *Wall Street Journal*, p. C1.

Anders, G. (1988, December 2). RJR Stock Falls in Heavy Trading. *Wall Street Journal*, p. C1.

Anders, G. (1989, April 6). RJR Reaffirms Its Plan to Shed Assets, But Bond Sales May Ease the Time Table. *Wall Street Journal*, p. A10.

Anders, G. (1990a, June 20). RJR and Its Main Shareholders, KKR, Begin $5.3 Billion Refinancing Effort. *Wall Street Journal*, p. A2.

Anders, G. (1990b, June 21). RJR Nabisco's Junk Bonds Rise as Much as 6%. *Wall Street Journal*, p. A5.

Anders, G. (1990c, December 18). RJR Swallows Hard, Offers $5-a-Share Stock. *Wall Street Journal*, p. C1.

Anders, G. (1991a, March 21). Back to Biscuits: Old Flamboyance is Out as Louis Gerstner Remakes RJR Nabisco. *Wall Street Journal*, p. A 1.

Anders, G. (1991b, April 12). Investors Grab Shares of RJR for $1.13 Billion. *Wall Street Journal*, p. C1.

Anderson, J., & Van Atta, D. (1990, August 7). Capitol Clout and "Firesafe" Cigarettes, *Washington Post*, p. B8.

Andrews, K.R., et al. (1965). *Business Policy: Text and Cases*. Homewood, IL. Irwin.

Ansoff, H.I. (Ed.), (1965). *Corporate Strategy*. New York: McGraw-Hill:

Ansoff, H.I. (1979). *Strategic Management*. New York: John Wiley & Sons.

Ansoff, H.I. (1984). *Implanting Strategic Management*. Englewood Cliffs, NJ: Prentice-Hall.

Ansoff, H.I. (1988). *The Corporate Strategy*. New York: John Wiley & Sons.

Apple, R. (1988, April 1). Tobacco Export Ban Would Harm U.S., Not Reduce Foreign Consumption. *Tobacco International*, pp. 31–34.

Arbose, J., & Burnstein, D. (1984, August). BAT Moves Beyond Tobacco. *International Management*, pp. 16–20.

Armstrong, L. (1987, September 14). Where Cigarette and Spirits are Still Booming. *Business Week*, p. 94.

ASH Review. (1987, January). *Smoking and Health Review, 16*(1).

ASH Review. (1989a, April). *Smoking and Health Review, 19*(3).

ASH Review. (1989b May-June). *Smoking and Health Review, 19*(4).

ASH Review. (1990, March). *Smoking and Health Review, 20*(2).

Ashe, R.L., Jr. & Vaughn, D.H. Smoking in the Work Place: A Management Perspective. *Employee Relations Law Journal, 2*(3), pp. 383–406.

Associated Press. (1987, October 6). Smokeless Cigarette May Hurt Cancer Stance. *Washington Post*, p. D3.

Associated Press. (1988, November 3). RJR Nabisco's Board Invites More Takeover Offers. *Washington Post,* p. F1.

Associated Press. (1989a, October 8). Tobacco Export Guarantees Irate Lawmakers. *Washington Post*, p. A15.

Associated Press. (1989b, December 4). Anti-Smoking Groups Fuming Over Philip Morris TV Ads. *Marketing News,* p. 5.

Associated Press. (1990a, May 1). Ask First or Just Light Up? Etiquette Isn't Paramount. *Washington Post Health*, p. 5.

Associated Press. (1990b, June 16). EPA Details Death Toll of Passive Smoke. *Washington Post*, p. A4.

Associated Press. (1990c, September 26). State Panel Seeks Ban on Cigarette Machines. *New York Times*, p. B4.

Atkinson, A.B., & Stiglitz, E. (1980). *Lectures on Public Economics*, New York: McGraw-Hill.

Auerbach, P. (1988). *Competition: The Economics of Industrial Change,* Cambridge, MA: Basil Blackwell Publishing.

Babcock, C.R. (1989, January 26). Congressmen Tee Off for Fun, Profit. *Washington Post*, p. A1.

Babcock, C.R. (1990, August 2). Tobacco Groups' Generosity Unabated in Paying Speech Fees to Lawmakers. *Washington Post*, p. A29.

Bacon, K.H. (1989, November 15). Tobacco Industry Facing Challenge on Contents, Ads. *Wall Street Journal*, p. A28.

Bacon, K.H. (1990, January 21). HHS to Ask Media to Run Free Add against Smoking. *Wall Street Journal*, p. A8.

Baden-Fuller, C.W.F., & Stopford, J.M. (1991). Globalization Frustrated: The Case of White Goods. *Strategic Management Journal, 12*(7): pp. 493–507.

Baker, J.N., & Cohen, A. (1988, April 18). A Big Apple Anti-Smoking Law. *Newsweek*, p. 25.

Barford, M.F. (1991, May). Tobacco to 1995, Consumption Moves South. *Economist Intelligence Unit* (London, England).

Barkley, J. (1989, March). "Don't Smoke That Cigarette or Else" Fear Communication— Is It Effective? *Outlook*, p. 2.

Barnard, C.I. (1938). *The Functions of the Executive*. Cambridge, MA: Harvard University Press.

Barnes, R. (1989, April 7). Md. Senate Endangers Smokers' Rights Bill. *Washington Post*, p. B7.

Barnes, R., & Lancaster, J. (1989, March 16). House Votes Protection to Smokers. *Washington Post*, p. C1.

Bartlett, S. (1988, December 2). RJR Nabisco: $25 Billion Question. *New York Times*, p. A1.

Bates, S. (1989, January 22). Virginia Teachers Question Proposed Smoking Ban. *Washington Post*, p. B3.

BAT Industries. (1985–1995). *Annual Report and Accounts*.

Beerham, J.N., & Grosse, R.E. (1990). *International Business and Governments*, Columbia: University of South Carolina Press.

Bell, J.W. (1988, March 8). SEITA, An Aggressive Marketer Also Helps Unify the Industry. *Tobacco International*, pp. 9–12.

Bell, J.W. (1981, July 24). SEITA: Stirring to Life Over "Les Blondes" Threat. *Tobacco International*, pp. 60–62.

Bell, J.W. (1985, November 15). France the Tobacco Crop In 1985: Situation and Prospects. *Tobacco International*, p. 22.

Bell, J.W. (1986a, February 7). Smokers Told To Look At More Than Tar & Nicotine Ratings. *Tobacco International*, p. 27.

Bell, J.W. (1986b, May 30). Sarlat Plant Helps Power France Onto World Market. *Tobacco International*, p. 42.

Bell, J.W. (1986c, July 25). A Variety of Sources for 1985 French Leaf Imports. *Tobacco International*, p. 22.

Bell, J.W. (1986d, July 25). French Market Shows Steady Growth in 1985. *Tobacco International*, p. 20.

Bell, J.W. (1987, February 2). SEITA Shows Strength In Battle For French Cigarette Market. *Tobacco International*, pp. 5–7.

Bell, J.W. (1987b, February 20). Tabaqueria, Shabby in 1975, Now a Wonder of Processing, Production. *Tobacco International*, pp. 18–22.

Bell, J.W. (1987c, July 24). SEITA's First Quarter Hints At Product Trends. *Tobacco International*, p. 20.

Bell, J.W. (1987d, November 27). Italian Packers to the World: "Come Look; We've Changed." *Tobacco International*, pp. 12–14.

Bell, J.W. (1989, April 15). SEITA: New Faces, Line Extensions Help Brighten Its Image. *Tobacco International*, pp. 18–20.

Benowitz, N.L., Hall, S.M., Herning, R.I. (1983). Smokers Of Low-Yield Cigarettes Do Not Consume Less Nicotine. *New England Academy of Medicine*, *309*, pp. 139–142.

Bickers, C. (1985, October 14). Tobacco's Economic Contribution Discussed at TGIC Annual Meeting. *Tobacco International*, p. 14.

Birnbaum, J.H. (1997, July 21). Tobacco's Can of Worms. *Fortune*, pp. 58–60.

Bliley, T.J., Jr. (1990, July 14). Off the Issue. *Washington Post*, p. A17.

Blum, D. (1986). Strategies to Reduce Cigarette Sales: Excise Taxes and Beyond. *Journal of the American Medical Association*, *255*, pp. 1049–1050.

Bor, J. (1989, April 24). Tobacco Ads Target Black Americans, Conference Is Told By Cancer Specialist. *The Baltimore Sun*, p. B1.

Bordeaux, A.F., & Brannon, R. H., (Ed.). (1972). *Social and Economic Issues Confronting the Tobacco Industry in the Seventies*, Lexington, MA: College of Agriculture and Center for Developmental Change.

Boul, D. (1987, August 23). What's New in Tobacco. *New York Times*, p. 17.

Bowman, E.H. (1990). Strategy Changes, Possible Worlds and Actual Minds. In J.W. Frederickson (Ed.), *Perspectives on Strategic Management* (pp. 9–37). New York: Harper Business.

Brannigan, M. (1989, April 21). RJR's 1st-Period Earnings Sank 62%; Huge Expenses Linked to Buy-Out Cited. *Wall Street Journal*, p. A3.

Breen, T.H. (1985). *Tobacco Culture*, Princeton, NJ: Princeton University Press.

Brody, J. E. (1990, July 12). Personal Health: As Pressures Build The Goal Of A Smoke-Free Society Seems More Real. *New York Times*, p. B8.

Browning, E.S. (1989, June 23). BSN Boss Hustles to Form European Giant. *Wall Street Journal*, p. B12.

Burgess, J. (1990, December 16). Exports Fire Up Tobacco Industry. *Washington Post*, p. H1.

Burns, J.A., Jr. (1988). Review of the Literature. *Employee Relations Law Journal*, *13*, pp. 723–730.

Burrough, B. (1988, November 29). RJR's Outsider Advisors Are Trying to Set $100-a-share Floor in Bidding for Firm. *Wall Street Journal*, p. A4.

Burrough, B., & Helyar, J. (1988a, November 17). Forstman Little, Partners Quit Bidding for RJR, Sales Group Abandons $2.51 Billion Offer for Interco. *Wall Street Journal*, p. A3.

Burrough, B., & Helyar, J. (1988b, November 22). First Boston's RJR Offer Has Tight Timetable. *Wall Street Journal*, p. A4.

Burrough, B., & Helyar, J. (1988c, November 30). KKR Is Apparent Winner of Bidding for RJR Nabisco. *Wall Street Journal*, p. A3.

Burry, R.D., & Nowitz, A. (1996). *Tobacco Outlook*. New York, NY: Oppenheimer & Co., Inc.

Business Week. (1952, December 27). Cigarette Sales: The Kings Shoot Up, p. 44.

Business Week. (1964a, January 18). The U.S. Sums It Up: Quit Smoking, pp. 43–47.

Business Week. (1964b, February 15). It Won't Happen Here, p. 29.

Business Week. (1981, December). How Cigarette Makers Aim to Fire Up Sales. p. 65.

Business Week. (1988, January 18). Where There's Smoke, There's Trouble, pp. 88–89.

Business Week. (1989, November 18). The Rival That Japan Respects, pp. 108–118.

Business Week. (1950–1990). Annual Survey of the Cigarette Industry.

Buzzell, R.D., & Gale, B.T. (1987). *The PIMS Principles: Linking Strategy to Performance*, New York: Free Press.
Canellos, P.S. (1986, September 8). Scott Stapf Comes Out Smokin', He's a Tireless Lobbyist for the Tobacco Industry. *Washington Post Weekly Edition*, pp. 10–11.
Carter, H. III. (1989, July 13). We're Losing the Drug War Because Prohibition Never Works. *Wall Street Journal*, p. A15.
Casson, M. (1987). *The Firm and the Market*, Cambridge, MA: MIT Press.
Casson, M. (1990). *Multinational Corporations*, Brookfield, VT: Edgar Publishing Co..
Chandler, A.D., Jr. (1962). *Strategy and Structure*. Cambridge, MA: MIT Press.
Chandler, A.D., Jr. (1977). *The Visible Hand*. Cambrdige, MA: Harvard University Press.
Chandler, W.U. (1986, June). Banishing Tobacco. *World Health*, pp. 8–10.
Charlier, M. (1988, February 23). Seven-Up Despite Market Glut, Plans to Launch New Soft Drink. *Wall Street Journal*, p. B6.
Charlier, M. (1991, March 13). Big Brewers Will Be Among Wallflowers at the 1991 "Spring Break" Beach Parties. *Wall Street Journal*, p. B1.
Chase Econometrics. (1983). *The Economic Impact of the Tobacco Industry on the United States Economy*. Vols. 1–2, Bala Cynwyd, PA: Chase Econometrics.
Chira, S. (1985, May 13). Japan Opening Up Tobacco Market. *New York Times*, p. D10.
Chrisman, J.J., Hofer, C.W., & Boulton, W.R., (1988). Toward a System for Classifying Business Strategies. *Academy of Management Review*, *13*(3), 413–428.
Cipollone v. Liggett Group, Inc., 822 F. 2d 335 (3rd Cir. 1987).
Clairmonte, F.F. (1980, Fall). World Tobacco: A Study in Conglomerate Structure. *Journal of World Trade Law*, *14*, 23–38.
Clairmonte, F. (1983). The Transitional Tobacco and Alcohol Conglomerates; A World Oligopoly. *New York Journal of Medicine*, *83*, 1322–1323.
Classen, H.W. (1987). Public Areas Whose Rights Should Be Protected? *Syracuse Law Review*, *38*, 831–857.
Cockburn, A. (1990, September 27). The Other Drug War Where the Tobacco Firms Are the Pushers. *Wall Street Journal*, p. A19.
Cohen, L.P. (1988, December 2). Decision on Bid Seemed Likely to Uphold in Court. *Wall Street Journal*, p. A10.
Cohen, L.P. (1990, February 8). Broader Suits over Cigarettes May Be Possible. *Wall Street Journal*, p. A3.
Cohen, M.I., & Metcalf Kelly. (1990). *The Tobacco Handbook*, New York, NY: Sanford C. Bernstein & Co.
Cohen, M.I., & Reidinger, D.E. (1995). *The Tobacco Handbook*, New York, NY: Goldman Sachs.
Cohn, V. (1989, May 2). Commentary. *Washington Post Health*, p. 11.
Cole, R.J. (1988, June 14). American Brands Sets Sale of Nine E-II Units. *New York Times*, p. D1.
Colford, S. (1989, March 27). Tobacco Critic Opens New Front. *Advertising Age*, p. 6.
Coll, S. (1988a, August 13). $1.1 Billion Offered for Kraft, Inc. *Washington Post*, p. A1.
Coll, S. (1988b, October 21). RJR Nabisco Executives Plan Buyout. *Washington Post*, p. A1.
Coll, S. (1988c, December 4). Henry Kravis Turns Buy-Out into Empire Worth Millions. *Washington Post*, p. A1.

Collins, G. (1989, October 29). On Not Going Up in Smoke. *New York Times*, p. F6.

Collins, G. (1996, November 7). Is LeBow Picking Fight with Ichan over RJR? *New York Times,* p. D1.

Collins, G. (1995, November 12). Look Who Wants to be the Shareholder's Friend. *New York Times*, p. 1F.

Comment: Plantiff's Conduct as a Defense to Claims against Cigarette Manufacturers. *Harvard Law Review* (1986) *99*, 809–827.

Comments. Tobacco under Fire: Developments In Judicial Responses To Cigarette Smoking Injuries. *Catholic University Law Review, 36*: 643–660.

Conroy, S.B. (1989, November 10). Fired Up over Philip Morris. *New York Times*, p. D1.

Control of Smoking, Alcoholism and Drug Abuse. (1987). *International Digest of Health Legislation*. 38(1), 65–71.

Cooper, H.M. (1989). *Integrating Research: A Guide for Literature Interviews* (2nd ed., Vol. 2). Newbury Park, CA: Sage Publications.

Cooper, K.J. (1989, November 2). Thirty Million Gift to Aid School Reform. *Washington Post*, p. A21.

Cooper, L. (1989, August 4). Tobacco Industry Surrenders to Ban on Short Flights, Turns To Next Front. *Wall Street Journal*, p. A3.

Corina, M. (1975*). Trust in Tobacco: The Anglo-American Struggle for Power*. London, England: Michael Joseph Ltd.

Coultas, D.B., & Samet, J.M. (1986). Passive Smoking and Health. *Western Journal of Medicine*, *144*(3), 350–355.

Covington & Burlington. (1985). *An Assessment of the Current Legal Climate Concerning Smoking in the Workplace*. Washington, DC: The Tobacco Institute.

Covington & Burlington. (1988). *An Assessment of the Current Legal Climate Concerning Smoking in the Workplace*. Washington, DC: The Tobacco Institute.

Cowan, A.L. (1988, December 2). Losers Get Some Spoils in Fight for RJR Nabisco. *New York Times*, p. A1.

Cowan, A.L. (1990, June 10). The Gumshoe of Annual Reports. *New York Times*, p. F15.

Cox, H. (1989). Growth and Ownership In The International Tobacco Industry: BAT. 1902–27. *Business History, 31*:(1), 44, 64–67.

Cargill, T.F. (1987, Winter). A Perspective on Trade Imbalances and United States Policies towards Japan. *Columbia Journal of World Business*, 22:(4), 55–56.

Crenshaw, A.B. (1990a, March 11). Better Benefits For The Fittest. *Washington Post*, p. H1.

Crenshaw, A.B. (1990b, April 22). Singing the Diversification Blues. *Washington Post*, p. H15.

Crist, P.G., & Majoras, J.M. (1987). The "New" Wave in Smoking and Health Litigation—Is Anything Really So New? *Tennessee Law Review*, *54*, 551–602.

Crossette, B. (1990, March 18). Women in Delhi Angered by Smoking Pitch. *New York Times*, p. 18.

Crovitz, C.G. (1992, January 8). It's Time for Lawyers to Kick the Tobacco Habit. *Wall Street Journal*, p. A11.

Cuff, D.F. (1989a, March 12). "De-Cluttering" a British Conglomerate. *New York Times*, p. F9.

Cuff, D.F. (1989b, June 24). RJR Nabisco Names Chief of a Tobacco Unit. *New York Times*, p. D4.

Dallos, R.E. (1988, December 2). Buyout Spawns Reluctant Millionaires in RJR's Home Town. *Los Angeles Times*, p. G1.

D'Aveni, R.A. (1989). The Aftermath of Organizational Decline: A Longitudinal Study of the Strategic and Managerial Characteristics of Declining Firms. *Academy of Management Journal*, 32(3), 575–605.

Davidson, J., & Freedman, A.M. (1988, June 29). Nestle Faces New Boycott Threat in Distribution of Infant Formulas. *Wall Street Journal*, p. A28.

Davidson, K. (1996). *Selling Sin: The Marketing of Socially Unacceptable Products*. Westport, CT: Quorum Books.

Davis, L.L. (1989, April 9). Philip Morris's Big Bite: Enormous Cigarette Profits Have Spawned a World Food Giant. *New York Times Magazine*, pp. 30–33, 40, 80–84.

De Maria, L.J. (1988, October 21). Bid for RJR Gives Dow 43.92 Surge. *New York Times*, p. D1.

Denev, K. & Freedman, A. M. (1990, July 27). Tobacco Warnings Don't Pre-empt Claims, Court Rules. *Wall Street Journal*, p. B1.

Dess, G.G., & Davis, P.S. (1984). Porter's (1980) Generic Strategies as Determinants of Strategic Group Membership and Organizational Performance. *Academy of Management Journal*, 27, 467–488.

Deutsch, C.H. (1988, October 23). The Philip Morris Kraft Merger: Why Business May Not Matter. *New York Times*, p. F1.

Deveny, K., & Bacon, K.H. (1990, May 24). Tobacco Is Facing New Attacks. *Wall Street Journal*, p. B1.

Deveny, K., & Freedman, A.M. (1990, July 27). Tobacco Warnings Don't Pre-empt Claims, Court Rules. *Wall Street Journal*, p. B1.

Deveny, K. (1990, May 23). Study Says Minors Buy $1.25 Billion of Tobacco a Year. *Wall Street Journal*, p. B6.

Deveny, K. (1990, June 25). Philip Morris Seeks to Gain in Europe with $3.8 Billion Bid for Suchard State. *Wall Street Journal*, p. A3.

Dewar, H. (1989, September 14) Tobacco Allies Delaying Tactics Hit. *Washington Post*, p. A9.

Dillow, G.L. (1981). *The Hundred Year War against the Cigarette*. New York, NY: Heritage Publishing Co..

Dodsworth, T. (1980, July 25). SEITA: A Tobacco Monopoly Rewritten at the Stroke of a Pen. *Tobacco International*, pp. 49, 54–55.

Donahue, C. (1988, June 20). The Anti-Tobacco Lobby May Be More Smoke Than Fire. *Adweek's Marketing Week*, pp. 31–32.

Dorfamn, J.R. (1990, February 27). Philip Morris's Strength Results in Admirers Galore, But Skeptics See Long-run Squeeze. *Wall Street Journal*, p. C2.

Dorfamn, J.R. (1991, March 11). Grand Metropolitan Shares Win US Friends; Easier Access to Stock, Good Brand Names Help. *Wall Street Journal*, p. A6B.

Doz, Y.L. (1979). *Government Control and Multinational Strategic Management*, New York, NY: Praeger Publishers.

Drucker, P.F. (1954). *The Practice of Management*, New York, NY: Harper & Rowe.

Dullea, G. (1989, October 10). Matchbooks with X-Rated Messages Are Adding to Some Smokers' Woes. *New York Times*, p. D5.

Edell, M.Z. (1986, Fall). Cigarette Litigation: The Second Wave. *Tort & Insurance Law Review*, *22*, pp. 90–103.

Eichenwald, K. (1988a, June 14). Analysts See No Significant Setback for Tobacco Industry in Wake of Ruling. *New York Times*, p. B4.

Eichenwald, K. (1988b, November 3). Talking Deals: Kraft Takeover: Swift and Smooth. *New York Times*, p. D2.

Fanning, D. (1990, March 18). Humiliating Times for a Boss Who Smokes. *New York Times*, p. F18.

Farhi, P. (1988, November 4). RJR Managers Raise Bid to $20.7 Billion. *Washington Post*, p. F1.

Feder, B. J. (1989, March 5). Hanson's Meteoric Rise. *New York Times*, p. F1.

Ferst, S.L. (1995). *RJR Nabisco Holdings Corp.—Company Report*, S. G.: Warburg & Co., Inc.

Fiegenbaum, A., & Thomas, H. (1990). Strategic Groups and Performance: The US Insurance Industry, 1970–1984. *Strategic Management Journal*, *11*(2), 197–215.

Finger, W.R., (Ed.). (1981). *The Tobacco Industry in Transition*, Lexington Books: Lexington, Mass.

Fiore, M.C. (1989, January 6). Trends in Cigarette Smoking in the United States: The Changing Influence of Gender and Race. *JAMA*, 261, 49–55.

Flotz, K. (1990, August 7). Old Joe Is Paying Off for Camel. *New York Times*, p. D1.

Forman, C., & Kamm, T. (1989, October 2). Axa to Continue Bid to Purchase BAT Insurer. *Wall Street Journal*, p. A9E.

Forman, C., & Smith, R. (1989, July 17). Chairman Optimistic Company Can Defeat Offer Made by Goldsmith. *Wall Street Journal*, p. A4.

Forman, C. (1989a, July 12). BAT–Man Caper: Predator Becomes Prey Goldsmith Seeks British Conglomerate. *Wall Street Journal*, p. A1.

Forman, C. (1989b, July 14). BAT Holders Seek Higher Bid But Preferably Cash. *Wall Street Journal*, p. A3.

Forman, C. (1989, October 20). BAT Holders Approve Plan to Restructure. *Wall Street Journal*, p. A11.

Forman, C. (1990, February 20). Drexel's Problems Create New Obstacle for Goldsmith's Tobacco Bid for BAT. *Wall Street Journal*, p. B11.

Foust, D. (1987, July 27). Big Tobacco's Fortunes Are Withering in the Heat. *Business Week*, p. 47.

Fowler, G. (1990, July 19). Dr. Richard M. Overholt, Surgeon and an Anti-Smoking Pioneer, 88. *New York Times*, p. D19.

Fowler, K.L., & Schmidt, D.R. (1988). Tender Offers, Acquisitions, and Subsequent Performance in Manufacturing Firms. *Academy of Management Journal*, *31*(4), 962–974.

Frankel, G. (1989, Sep. 10). BAT Battle A Clash of Styles, Values, Wills. *Washington Post*, p. H1.

Freedman, A.M. (1990a, April 19). Philip Morris Profits Rose 31% in First Quarter. *Wall Street Journal*, p. A6.

Freedman, A.M., & Gibson, R. (1988, October 31). Kraft Accepts Philip Morris Sweetened Offer Totaling $13.1 Billion, or $106 a Share in Cash. *Wall Street Journal*, p. A3.

Freedman, A.M. (1987a, April 23). Harmful Habit: Cigarette Smoking Is Growing Hazardous to Career in Business. *Wall Street Journal*, p. A1.

Freedman, A.M. (1987b, August 26). Liggett & Myers Wins Ruling on Liability In Latest Legal Victory For Tobacco Firms. *Wall Street Journal*, p. B7.
Freedman, A.M. (1988, June 8). Philip Morris Ads Tout Demographics of Smokers to Alter "Low–Class" Image. *Wall Street Journal*, p. 28.
Freedman, A.M. (1989a, June 15). High Stakes for Low Nicotine. *Wall Street Journal*, p. B1.
Freedman, A.M. (1989b, June 15). Past is Ominous for Substitute Smokes. *Wall Street Journal*, p. B1.
Freedman, A.M. (1989c, August 4). "De-Nicotined" Next Gets Pitched by Philip Morris Just Like Decaf. *Wall Street Journal*, p. B3.
Freedman, A.M. (1990b, October 26). Philip Morris Cos. Ousts Executives at Tobacco Unit. *Wall Street Journal*, p. B4.
Freedman, A.M. (1989d, November 1). Philip Morris to Launch Image Ads. *Wall Street Journal*, p. B1.
Freedman, A.M. (1989e, November 14). Rebelling Against Alcohol, Tobacco Ads. *Wall Street Journal*, p. B1.
Freedman, A.M. (1989f, December 1). Cigarette Firms Roll Out Budget Brands. *Wall Street Journal*, p. B1.
Freedman, A.M. (1991, March 26). New Smoke Signals at Philip Morris? *Wall Street Journal*, p. B1.
Freedman, A.M. (1990c, November 13). Tobacco's Slide Trips Even Philip Morris. *Wall Street Journal*, p. B1.
Freedman, A.M., and S.L Hwang (1996, August 26). Legislation Plan on Tobacco Advances. *Wall Street Journal*, p. A2.
French, H.W. (1987, November 1). Anti-Smoking Campaign is Planned for NY. *New York Times*, p. B4.
Frendenheim, M. (1990, July 21). American Brands in Deal for Moen. *New York Times*, p. 31.
Friedman, K.M. (1975). *Public policy and the smoking-health controversy*. Lexington, MA: Lexington Books.
Fritschler, A.L. (1975). *Smoking and Politics: Policymaking and the Federal Bureaucracy*. Englewood Cliffs, NJ: Prentice-Hall.
Galbraith, C.S., & Stiles, C.H. (1983). Firm Profitability and Relative Firm Power. *Strategic Management Journal*, *4*(3), 237–249.
Galvin, L. (1988, May). Medical Express: Are You an Ulcer Candidate? The Acid Test. *Mademoiselle*, p. 118.
Garrington, T. (1989, August 8). Goldsmith Asks BAT Chairman to Discuss Bid. *Wall Street Journal*, p. B4.
Gartner, M. (1990, May 24). Government Smoke Alarms May Save Teens Lives. *Wall Street Journal*, p. B1.
Geyelin, M. (1989, April 21). The Job is Yours Unless You Smoke. *Wall Street Journal*, p. B1.
Gibbs, N.R. (1988, April 18). All Fired Up Over Smoking. *Time*, pp. 64-71.
Gitenan, E. (1989, January 9). Beverages & Tobacco. *Forbes*, pp. 100, 173.
Glaberson, W. (1987, August 16). Tobacco Goes Back On Trial. *New York Times*, p. F1.
Gladstone, R. (1988a, November 19). Bidding Ends for Takeover of Nabisco. *Washington Post*, p. D12.

Gladstone, R. (1988b, November 30). New Bids Are Made for Nabisco. *Washington Post*, p. F1.

Gladwell, M. (1988, June 19). Who Will Be the Next Rose Cipollone? *Washington Post*, p. H2.

Gladwell, M. (1989, March 11). Smokeless Cigarette Sales Halted. *Washington Post*, p. F1.

Gladwell, M. (1990, March 3). Jury Rules in Cigarette Price War. *Washington Post*, p. C1.

Glantz, S.A. (1996). *The Cigarette Papers*. Berkeley and Los Angeles: University of California Press.

Gloede, W.F. (1985, May 6). Upscale Cigarette Brands Smokin' for Morris, RJR. *Advertising Age*, p. 1.

Glynn, T.J., Pearson, H.W., & Sayers, M. (Eds.). (1983). *Women & Drugs* (pp. 252–255*)*. Research Issues 31. Washington, DC: US Department of Health & Human Services.

Gold, A.R. (1988, October 2). One State Says No Smoking for Police and Fire Departments. *New York Times*, p. E4.

Goldman, D.A. (1989, June). *Philip Morris*. New York, NY: Nomura Research Institute.

Goldman, E. (1995). *Philip Morris Companies, Inc.* New York, NY: PaineWebber

Gooch, P. (1987a, March). ATI Reenters Leaf Market to Gain Lost Shares. *Tobacco Reporter*, p. 29.

Gooch, P. (1987b, March). EC Financial Crisis Strains Tobacco's Competitiveness. *Tobacco Reporter*, p. 26.

Gooch, P. (1989, March). Burley Quality Rebounds, But Falling Dollar Hurts. *Tobacco Reporter*, pp. 26–27.

Goodin, R.E. (1989). *No Smoking*, Chicago, Illinois: The University of Chicago Press.

Goodman, E. (1987, February 28). Smoking Ads: A Matter of Life. *The Boston Globe*, p. D16.

Grant, J. (1978, December 11). Kicking the Habit. Barron's, p. 9.

Gras, N.B.S. (1969). *Industrial Evolution*, NY: Augustus M. Kelley Publishers.

Green, M. (1990, July 1). Let's Stop Selling Cancer to Children. *New York Times*, p. F11.

Greenhouse, L. (1991, March 26). Court to Say if Cigarette Makers Can Be Sued for Smoker's Cancer. *New York Times*, p. A1.

Greenhouse, S. (1989a, January 1). Nestle's Time To Swagger. *New York Times*, p. F1.

Greenhouse, S. (1989b, June 7). 5 RJR Nabisco Units Sold for $2.5 Billion. *New York Times*, p. D1.

Greenhouse, S. (1989c, July 13). Institutions Balk at Bid for BAT. *New York Times*, p. D1.

Grefe, E.A. (1981). *Fighting to Win: Business to Political Power*. New York, NY: Harcourt Brace Jovanovich.

Gur, M. (1988, May). Spotlight on Turkey: Changes In The Making. *Tobacco Reporter*, pp. 28–29.

Hadzista, V.C. (1988, April). Greece: Quantity, Varietal Restructuring Critical Issues; USSR Vanishes. *Tobacco International*, pp. 5–8.

Hambrick, D. (1983). High Profit Strategies in Mature Capital Goods Industries: A Contingency Approach. *Academy of Management Journal*, *26*(1), 687–707.

Hambrick, D., & Mason, P.A. (1984). Upper echelons: The Organization as a Reflection of its Top Managers. *Academy of Management Review*, *9*, 193–206.

Hambrick, D.E. (1990). The Adolescence of Strategic Management, 1980–1985; Critical Perceptions and Reality. In J.W. Frederickson (Ed.), *Perspectives on Strategic Management* (pp. 237–261). New York: Harper Business.

Hammer, J. (1988, August). The Kick-the-Habit Business. *Newsweek*, pp. 42–43.

Harrigan, K.R. (1980a). Strategies for Declining Businesses. *Journal of Business Strategy*, *1*(2), 20–34.

Harrigan, K.R. (1980b). *Strategies for Declining Businesses*. Lexington, MA: Lexington Books.

Harrigan, K.R. (1981). Deterrents to Divestiture. *Academy of Management Journal*, *24*(2), 306–323.

Harper, S. (1980, October 27). Top 20 Cigarette Brands Hiked Ads 15.8% in '79. *Advertising Age*, pp. 49–50.

Hay, D., & Vickers, J. (Eds.). (1987). *The Economics of Market Dominance*, New York, NY: Basil Blackwell Ltd..

Health Scene. Smoking: How to Unhook Yourself. (1989, Fall). p.1.

Heath, T. (1991, November 18). Fairfax Follows Area Smoke Signals, Weighs Limits on Tobacco Use, Sales. *Washington Post*, p. H3.

Helyar, J., & Burrough, B. (1988a, October 31). RJR Nabisco Partners Pursue Talks For Competing Bid to Kohlberg Kravis's. *Wall Street Journal*, p. A 6.

Helyar, J., & Burrough, B. (1988b, November 21). RJR Nabisco, Despite Firm Offers, Sets Up Second Round of Bidding. *Wall Street Journal*, p. A3.

Helyar, J. (1988a, August 16). RJR, By Inviting Scientist to Review "Smokeless" Cigarette, Walks a Fine Line. *Wall Street Journal*, p. B4.

Helyar, J. (1988b, August 30). RJR Plans to Market Smokeless Cigarette as Breakthrough with Hefty Price Tag. *Wall Street Journal*, p. B25.

Helyar, J. (1988c, October 21). Blockbuster Deal: RJR Nabisco Buy-Out Would Fit The Pattern of A Restless Chief. *Wall Street Journal*, p. A1.

Helyar, J. (1988d, November 30). In Winston-Salem, Worker's Good Will Goes Up in Smoke. *Wall Street Journal*, p. A1.

Helyar, J. (1988d, December 6). RJR Tobacco Unit Shuffles 3 Officials, Timing May Be an Effort to Impress KKR. *Wall Street Journal*, p. A3.

Helyar, J. (1988f, December 12). R.J. Reynolds Low-Smoke Cigarette To Begin Test Marketing Next Month. *Wall Street Journal*, p. B5.

Hentoff, N. (1987, February 28) ... And Liberty. *Washington Post*, p. A12.

Herbert, T.T., & Deresky, J. (1987). Generic Strategies: An Empirical Investigation of Typology Validity and Strategy Content. *Strategic Management Journal*, *8*(2), 135–147.

Herman, R. (1989, January 3). Western Life Styles Take Their Toll Abroad: Diseases of Affluences. *Washington Post Health*, pp. 12–15.

Hershey, R.D., Jr. (1988, June 14). Cuomo Panel Urges Growth of Federal Role in Economy. *New York Times*, p. D1.

Hevesi, D. (1990, July 27). Warning Labels Don't Protect Cigarette Makers, Court Says. *New York Times*, p. A1.

Hilder, D.B. (1990, May 2). RJR Nabisco Junk Bonds Presents Conundrum for Would-Be Profiteers in Volatile Papers. *Wall Street Journal*, p. C2.

Hill, C.W. (1988). Differentiation Versus Low Cost or Differentiation and Low Cost: A Contingency Framework. *Academy of Management Review*, *13*(3): 401–412.

Hilts, P.J. (1990a, February 14). U.S. Health and Job Costs of Smoking is Put at $52 Billion a Year. *New York Times*, p. A18.

Hilts, P.J. (1990 April 11). Sullivan Would End Tie of Sports and Tobacco. *New York Times*, p. B13.

Hilts, P.J. (1990c, May 18). Health Department Softens Stance on Cigarette Exports. *New York Times*, p. A14.

Hilts, P.J. (1990d, May 25). Sullivan Urges Ban On Cigarette Sales to Children. *New York Times*, p. A16.

Hilts, P.J. (1990e, September 26). Major Gains Are Cited For Those Who Smoke. *New York Times*, p. B4.

Hilts, P.J. (1990f, October 4). Thailand's Cigarette Ban Upset. *New York Times*, p. D1.

Hilts, P.J. (1996). *Smokescreen*. Reading, MA: Addison-Wesley.

Hinden, S. (1988b, December 2). KKR's Next Task: Cut Up Nabisco and Find Buyers for the Pieces. *Washington Post*, p. G3.

Hinden, S. (1988a, December 2). Congress Urged to Help Curb LBO's. *Washington Post*, p. G3.

Hofer, C.W., & Schendel, D. (1978). *Strategy Formulation: Analytical Concepts*. St. Paul, MN: West.

Hoffman, H. (1991, March 11). Several Universities Kick Tobacco Habit By Snuffing Out Their Cigarette Stocks. *Wall Street Journal*, p. A6B.

Holland, M., & Novack, V. (1989, October 22). LBO's: Enough Already: While On Capitol Hill, Lobbyist and Loopholes Keep Congress in Line. *Washington Post*, p. C1.

Holland, M. (1989, April 23). How to Kill A Company. *Washington Post*, p. C1.

Hood, N., & Vahlne, J., (Eds.). (1988). *Strategies in Global Competition*. New York, NY: Croom Helm.

Hooper, C. (1988, November 3). Doctor's Group Tries to Block Sale of Smokeless Cigarettes. *Washington Post*, p. F1.

Hudson, R.L. (1987, November 24). BAT Post Rise of 21% in Pretax Income for Quarter. *Wall Street Journal*, p. A4.

Huebner, A. (1985, Spring). Tobacco's Lucrative Third World Invasion. *Business and Society Review*, pp. 49–53.

Hugel, C.E. (1987, October 18). Tackling the Top Job at Two Companies. *New York Times*, p. F6.

Hussey, D.E. (Ed.). (1990). *International Review of Strategic Management*. NY: John Wiley & Sons.

Hutchinson, D. (1986, September 15). The Drive to Kick Smoking at Work. *Fortune*, pp. 42–43.

Hwang, S.L. (1996, October 21). Tobacco Firms May Shift Tack on Cancer Link. *Wall Street Journal*, p. B1.

Hwang, S.L., and Parker-Pope, T. (1996, October 9). American Brands to Cut Tobacco Ties. *Wall Street Journal*, p. A3.

Hwang, S.L. (1992, May 14). RJR Sees Its Cigarette Sales Recovering. *Wall Street Journal*, p. B1.

Ibrahim, Y.M. (1990, March 29). French Plan to Restrict Ads Less Wine and No Smoking. *New York Times*, p. D1.

Ingersall, B., and Frisby, M.K. (1996, December 19). Smoke Signals: Omens of Tobacco Truce Are in the Air. *Wall Street Journal*, p. A16.

Isikoff, M. (1989, February 28). Bennett Keeps Pledge and Kicks the Habit. *Washington Post*, p. A21.

Jackson, E.L. (1955). *The Pricing of Cigarette Tobacco.* Gainesville, FL: University of Florida Press.

Jacobson, D.N. (1989). After Cipollone v. Liggett Group, Inc.: How Will the Floodgates of Cigarette Litigation Open? *American University Law Review*, (38), 1021–1059.

Janson, D. (1988a, March 13). Data on Smoking Revealed at Trial. *New York Times*, p. B8.

Janson, D. (1988b, June 14). Cigarette Maker Assessed Damages In Smoker's Death. *New York Times*, p. A1.

Jefferson, D.J. (1988, August 26). BAT to Stress Farmers' Internal Growth In Expanding U.S. Finance Services. *Wall Street Journal*, p. B2.

Jefferson, D.J. (1990, January 1). BAT Farmers Unit Outlines Agreement for Hearing on Hoylake Purchase Plan. *Wall Street Journal*, p. A5B.

Jennings, V.T. (1991, January 16). Montgomery County Jail to Ban Smoking— But Not Cold Turkey. *Washington Post*, p. A21.

Johnson, P.R., & Norton, D. (1983). The Social Costs of the Tobacco Program. *American Journal of Agricultural Economics*, *65*(1), 117–129.

Karnani, A. (1984). Generic Competitive Strategies: An Analytic Approach. *Strategic Management Journal*, *5*(4): 367–380.

Karnani, A., & Wernerfelt, B. (1985). Multiple Point Competition. *Strategic Management Journal*, *6*(1): 87-96.

Kepko, W. (1985, Fall). Products Liability—Can it Kick the Smoking Habit? *Akron Law Review*, *19*(2), 269–292.

Kerr, P. (1991, February 20). Smokers' Bill Test Tobacco's Strength and Florio's Future. *New York Times*, p. A1.

Kilpatrick, J.J. (1990, April 26). Smoking "Facts" Go Up in Smoke. *The Baltimore Sun*, p. A13.

Kim, J. (1988, June 19). In Asia, a Challenge to Tobacco Imports. *New York Times*, p. E28.

Kim, L., & Lim, Y. (1988). Environment, Generic Strategies, and Performance in a Rapidly Developing Country: A Taxonomic Approach. *Academy of Management Journal, 31*(4), 802–827.

King, T. R. (1990, January 1). Benson & Hedges to Shed Image as Yuppie Smoke. *Wall Street Journal*, p. B1.

Kinsley, M. (1986, October 9). A Puff Piece for the Tobacco Companies. *Wall Street Journal*, p. B35.

Kluger, R. (1996). *Ashes to Ashes*. New York: Alfred A. Knopf.

Knight, J. (1988a, August 8). Smoking Issue Is Smothered In BAT Deal. *Washington Post,* p. D1.

Knight, J. (1988b, November 18). Insurance Companies Sue RJR. *Washington Post,* p. D11.

Knight, J. (1988c, November 29). RJR Nabisco Chief Says He Bidded Low for Firm. *Washington Post*, p. D1.

Knight, J. (1988d, December 2). KKR Using Only $15 Million of Its Own in Nabisco Buyout. *Washington Post*, p. A1.

Koepp, S. (1988, June 27). Tobacco's First Loss. *Time*, pp. 48–50.

Koeppel, D. (1990a, January 29). In Philadelphia, R.J. Reynolds Made All the Wrong Moves. *Adweek's Marketing Weekly*, pp. 20–22.

Koeppel, D. (1990b, May 28). An Ethical Plan for Tobacco. *Adweek's Marketing Week*, pp. 18-22.

Konolige, K. (1988, August 28). Supporting the Habit. *New York Times Book Review*, p. 13.

Kotha, S., & Orne, D. (1989). Generic Manufacturing Strategies: A Conceptual Synthesis. *Strategic Management Journal*, *10*(3), 211–231.

Labation, S. (1988, June 19). Denting the Cigarette Industry's Legal Armor. *New York Times*, p. E28.

Lacayo, R. (1988, April 18). Smoke Gets in Your Rights. *Time*, p. 72, 75.

Lait, M. (1989, June 18). Smokers Breathing Fire At Sponsor of City Ban. *Washington Post*, p. A8.

Landro, L., & Kneala, D. (1990, April 11). Time and Viacom Talks to Merge Comedy Networks. *Wall Street Journal*, p. B1.

Langley, M. (1986, November 14). Lagging Lobby: The Tobacco Institute Loses Political Power As Attitudes Change. *Wall Street Journal*, p. A1.

Lawson, D.S. (1989). Canada's Tobacco Products Control Act. *Food Drug Cosmetic Law Journal*, *44*, 291–295.

Lazzareschi, C. (1988, May 15). Pitching Pharmaceuticals to the Public. *Washington Post*, p. H7.

Leary, W.E. (1988, December 11). Critics Say It's No Cigarette: Pardon Me—Can I Bum a Nicotine Delivery System? *New York Times*, p. E4.

Lengnick-Hall, C.A., & Lengnick-Hall, M.L.(1988). Strategic Human Resources Management: A Review of the Literature and a Proposed Typology. *Academy of Management Review, 13*(3): 454–470.

Lesly, E. (1995, April 3). "Barbarians" Revisited. *Business Week,* pp. 46–47.

Levine, B. (1988, April). Confessions of a "Nicomanic." *Vogue,* p. 62.

Levy, C. (1988, August 29). Tobacco Firm Fuels Flight Against Howard Anti-Smoking Proposal. *Washington Post*, p. D3.

Lewin, T. (1990, May 24). Harvard and CUNY Shedding Stocks in Tobacco. *New York Times*, p. A1.

Lieb, C.W. (1953). Can the Poisons in Cigarettes be Avoided? *The Reader's Digest*, *63*, 45–47.

Lieberman, M.B. (1989). The Learning Curve, Technology Barriers to Entry, and Competitive Survival in the Chemical Processing Industries. *Strategic Management Journal*, *10*(5), 431–447.

Liggett Group, Inc. (1960-1995). *Annual Reports and 10K Reports*.

Lipman, J. (1989, July 25). Model Says Cigarette Ads Targeted Youth. *Wall Street Journal*, p. B4.

Lipman, J. (1990a, February 27). Foes Claim Ad Bans Are Bad Business. *Wall Street Journal*, p. B1.

Lipman, J. (1990b, March 15). Critics Use New Soapbox to Assail Ads for Infant Formulas, Tobacco. *Wall Street Journal*, p. B6.

Lipman, J. (1990c, June 6). Decline of Tobacco Sales in Canada Fuels Ad Debate. *Wall Street Journal*, p. B1.

Lipman, J. (1990d, July 9). Marlboro Just Says No on Logo. *Wall Street Journal*, p. B1.

Lipman, J. (1991, March 28). Tobacco Concerns Are Hopeful About "De-Nicotined" Cigarettes. *Wall Street Journal*, p. B13.

Loews, Inc. (1970–1988). *Annual Reports and 10K Reports.*

Lorillard, Inc. (1965–1968). *Annual Reports and 10K Reports.*

Lowenstein, R. (1989, July 13). Investors Analysts Are Cold to Bid for BAT But Many See Goldsmith Sweetening Terms. *Wall Street Journal*, p. C2.

Lowenstein, R. (1990, December 30). Why Some Holders of Tobacco Firm May Feel Burned. *Wall Street Journal*, p. C1.

Lublin, J.S., & Smith, R. (1989, July 13). BAT Fights Goldsmith Bid with Words But Lines Up U.S. Firepower Just in Case. *Wall Street Journal*, p. A3.

Lublin, J.S. (1989a, July 12). Speculative Fever Sweeps London Following Goldsmith's BAT Bid. *Wall Street Journal*, p. A14.

Lublin, J.S. (1989b, July 17). BAT Head to Face Raider on 4 Continents. *Wall Street Journal*, p. B12.

Luciano, L. (1989, August). The Rewards of Sin Tax. *Money*, p. 133.

Mahar, Maggie. (1990, July 9). Going Up in Smoke? The Tobacco Industry's Image Grows Increasingly Tarnished. *Barron's*, p. 8.

McAllister, B. (1987, November 4). Tobacco Officials Tell of Hiring Deaver. *Wall Street Journal*, p. A3.

MacAllister, B. (1990, August 9). Philip Morris's Hometown Lobbyist. *Washington Post*, p. A21.

Mackay, J. (1988, October). The Tobacco Epidemic Spreads. *World Health*, pp. 11–12.

Mansneurs, L. (1988, April 24). Smoking Becomes Deviant Behavior. *New York Times*, p. E1.

Manus, P. (1987, December). A Market of Taxation and Tradition. *Tobacco Reporter*, pp. 32–33.

Marcus, A. (1990, October 18). Parent's Smoking Becomes Issue in Parent Custody Case. *Wall Street Journal*, p. B1.

Marriott, M. (1988, April 13). Smoking Curbs To Begin Wednesday. *New York Times*, p. B8.

Mascarennas, B. (1988). Strategic Group Dynamics. *Academy of Management Journal*, *32*(2), 333–352.

Mascarennas, B., & Aaker, P.A. (1989). Mobility Barriers and Strategic Groups. *Strategic Management Journal*, *10*(5), 475–485.

Maxwell, J.C., Jr. (1983). *The Maxwell Fact Book*, NY: Lehman Brothers Kuhn Loeb Research.

Maxwell, J.C., Jr. (1987b, November 16). Cigarette Sales Expected to Drop by 2.5% This Year. *Advertising Age*, p. 16.

Maxwell, J.C., Jr. (1987a, January). Maxwell Report: Cigarette Industry Maintains Strength. *Tobacco Reporter*, p. 36.

Maxwell, J.C., Jr. (1988, January). Maxwell Report: Cigarette Sales to Drop 2.5 Percent. *Tobacco Reporter*, pp. 36–37.

Maxwell, J.C., Jr. (1989). Maxwell Report: 1988 Year End Sales Estimates for the Cigarette Industry. Richmond, VA. *Wheat First Securities.*

Maxwell, J.C., Jr. (1996). Historical Sales Trends in the Cigarette Industry. Richmond, VA. *Wheat First Securities.*

McAvoy, C. (1990, November 13). Yankee Traders Agents of Influence in Japan. *Wall Street Journal*, p. A14.

McCarthy, C. (1989, June 25). Koop & the Cigarette Hustlers. *Washington Post*, p. F2.

McCarthy, M.J. (1988, December 12). RJR's Premier Is Off—But Not Running. *Wall Street Journal*, p. B1.

McCarthy, M.J. (1989, June 2). Winston Hopes "Winning Taste" Scores. *Wall Street Journal*, p. B10.

McCarthy, M.J. (1990, May 3). Tobacco Critics See A Subtle Sell To Kids. *Wall Street Journal*, p. B1.

McGee, J., & Thomas, H. (1986). Strategic Groups: Theory, Research and Taxonomy. *Strategic Management Journal*, *7*(2), 141–160.

McGee, J., & Thomas, H. (1988). Making Sense of Complex Industries. In N. Hood & J.E. Vahlne (Eds.), *Strategies in Global Competition*, (pp. 40–78). New York: Croom Helm Ltd.

McGowan, R. (1988). *Business, Politics and Cigarettes: An Analysis of Public Policy Interventions on Cigarette Sales*. Unpublished Doctoral Dissertation, Boston University.

McGowan, R. (1995). *Business Politics and Cigarettes*. Westport, CT: Quorum Books.

McGowan, R., & Mahow, J.F. (1992). Multiple Games, Multiple Levels: Gamesmanship and Strategic Corporate Response to Environmental Issues. *Business and the Contemporary World*, *5*(4), 162–177.

McNamee, P., & McHugh, M. (1990). The Group Competitive Intensity Map: A Means of Displaying Competitive Position. *International Review of Strategic Management*, *1*, 73–100.

Melcher, R., Schedon, S., & Tarpey, J. (1985, June 24). BAT Industries: Moving to Cut Its Independence on Cigarettes. *Business Week*, pp. 65–66.

Melloan, G. (1989, November 17). U.S. Senate Insurance Regulators Could Decide BAT's Fate. *Wall Street Journal*, p. A31.

Miles, R. H. (1982). Coffin Nails and Corporate Strategies. Englewood Cliffs, NJ: Prentice-Hall.

Miller, D. (1986). Configurations of Strategy and Structure: Towards a Synthesis. *Strategic Management Journal*, *7*(3): 233–249.

Miller, D. (1988). Relating Porter's Business Strategies to Environment and Structure: Analysis and Performance Implications. *Academy of Management Journal*, *31*(2), 280–308.

Miller, D., & Friesen, P.H. (1986a). Porter's (1980) Generic Strategies and Performance: An Empirical Examination with American Data—Part 1: Testing. *Organization Studies*, *7*(1), 37–55.

Miller, D., & Friesen, P.H. (1986b). Porter's (1980) Generic Strategies and Performance: An Empirical Examination with American Data—Part 2: Performance Implications. *Organization Studies*, *7*(3), 255–261.

Miller, L.M., & Monahan J. (1954, July). Facts Behind the Cigarette Controversy. *Reader's Digest*, 65:1.

Milligan, S. (1987, June). Eyes on the Lies. *Washington Monthly*, pp. 39–42.

Milloy, C. (1990, April). Ethics Go Up in Smoke. *Washington Post*, p. D3.

Mintz, M. (1985, July 28). Tobacco Industry Seen on Defensive. *Washington Post*, p. D4.

Mintz, M. (1986, November 13). Cigarette Makers Lose Court Test: N.J. Judge to Allow Access to Records. Washington Post, p. E1.

Mintz, M. (1987b, August 8). Tobacco Firms Win Court Victory. *Washington Post*, p. F1.

Mintz, M. (1987c, October 18). Canadian, U.S. Papers Split on Tobacco Ban. *Washington Post*, p. F5.

Mintz, M. (1987d, December 20). Tobacco Press Kit Ignites Controversy. *Washington Post*, p. K2.

Mintz, M. (1988a, January 3). New Tobacco Trials to Begin: 2 Product Liability Suits to Pose Challenge to Industry. *Washington Post*, p. F1.

Mintz, M. (1988b, April 22). Judge Says Tobacco Industry Hid Risks. *Washington Post*, p. A1.

Mintz, M. (1988c, May 1). Tobacco Firms' Attorneys Reconsider After Setbacks. *Washington Post*, p. H1.

Mintz, M. (1988d, June 14). Jury Finds Tobacco Firm Shares Blame in Death. *Washington Post*, p. A1.

Mintz, M. (1988e, June 19). Winning Lawyer Hasn't Quit Fight Against Tobacco Firms. *Washington Post*, p. H4.

Mintz, M. (1990, April 8). Insurers' Hazy Relationship with Tobacco. *Washington Post*, p. H3.

Mintz, M. (1990, Sep. 2). Issue of Blame in Smoker's Death Smoldering Again. *Washington Post*, p. H3.

Morin, R. (1989, January 26). Tobacco Institute Ads Shaded Truth. *Washington Post*, p. A16.

Morris, B., & McCarthy, M.J. (1989, August 11). RJR in Long-Awaited Move, to Dismiss About 12% of Workers in Tobacco Unit. *Wall Street Journal*, p. A3.

Morris, B., & Waldman, P. (1989, March 10). The Death of The Premier. *Wall Street Journal*, p. B1.

Morris, B. (1988, December 2). Defeated RJR Chief Johnson Won't Be Short of Consolation. *Wall Street Journal*, p. A10.

Morris, B. (1989, July 21). Philip Morris Jabs at its Weakened Rival. *Wall Street Journal*, p. B1.

Mufson, S. (1989, November 30). More Firms Launching Buybacks. *Washington Post*, p. D1.

Murray, A.I. (1988). A Contingency View of Porter's Generic Strategies. *Academy of Management Review*, *13*(3), 390–400.

Nath, U.R. (1986a). *Smoking: Third World Alert*. New York, NY: Oxford University Press.

Nath, U.R. (1986b, June). Smoking in the Third World. *World Health*, pp. 6–7.

National Center for Health Statistics. (1996) *Heath, United States, 1995*. Hyattsville, MD: Public Health Service.

Nazario, S. L. (1990, October 31). California Anti-Smoking Cigarette Ads Seem to Reduce Smoking. *Wall Street Journal*, p. B1.

Neff, R., Magnunson, P., & Holstein, W.J. (1989, August 7). Rethinking Japan: The New Harder Line Toward Tokyo. *Business Week*, pp. 44–52.

Nelk, L. (1987). No Butts About It. Smokers Must Pay for Their Pleasure. *Columbia Journal of Environmental Law*, *12*:291, pp. 317–341.

Nelson, R.R., & Winter, S.G. (1982). *An Evolutionary Theory of Economic Change*, Cambridge, MA: The Belknap Press.

New York Times. (1987, August 26). Tobacco Industry Wins Case: Packs' Warning Held Adequate; Stocks Climb. p. D1.

New York Times. (1988a, February 28). No Smoking or No Work. p. E7.

New York Times. (1988b, April 3). Where You Can Light Up under New York's New Law, p. B8.

New York Times. (1989a, February 5). Miscellanea, p. F14.

New York Times. (1989b, May 5). Court Rules Cigarette Warnings Do Not Block Suit, p. D3.

New York Times. (1989c, May 7). Ban on Smoking Sparks a Promise of Challenge, p. E3.

New York Times. (1989d, June 15). No Heart Aid Seen in Mild Cigarettes, p. A1.

New York Times. (1989e, June 23). RJR Nabisco Names Chief of Tobacco Unit, p. D4.

New York Times. (1989f, July 13). Behind Film's Warnings on Cigarettes, p. D19.

New York Times. (1989g, August 7). The Surgeon vs. Foreign Smoke, p. A14.

New York Times. (1989h, August 20). Exsmokers Don't All Overdose on Caffeine, p. A22.

New York Times. (1989i, August 25). Son of Loews Chairman Advances at Lorillard, p. D3.

New York Times. (1989j, December 31). New York Restricts Smoking as of Tomorrow, p. B9.

New York Times. (1990a, June 7). French Ban on Tobacco Ads, p. D2.

New York Times. (1990b, June 27). A.M.A. Assails Nation's Export Policy on Tobacco, p. A12.

New York Times. (1990c, August 29). In Moscow, Cigarette Addicts Will Just Get Half Pack a Day, p. A2.

New York Times. (1990d, October 14). Unhealthy Patriotism, p. A18.

New York Times. (1990e, December 24). A Clamor in Norway to Ban All Smoking, p. 4.

New York Times. (1991a, March 15). Study Finds Big Weight Gain In Those Who Quit Smoking, p. A21.

New York Times. (1991b, March 25). Study Finds Big Weight Gains in Those Who Quit Smoking, p. A21.

New York Times. (1991c, March 28). Fair Warning on Cigarettes, p. A24.

New York Times. (1991d, April 8). Philip Morris Is Criticized, p. D4.

Newsweek. (1988, April 18). A Big Apple Anti-Smoking Law: The Latest Measure in a Growing National Trend, p. 25.

Nicholls, W.H. (1951). *Price Policies in the Cigarette Industry*. Nashville: Vanderbilt University Press.

Niederkorn, W.S. (1989, August 27). Week In Business. *New York Times*, p. F12.

Nobuaki, N. (1988, Spring). Japanese Trade Barriers: How Big a Problem. *Business Forum*, pp. 23–27.

Nordby, N. (1987, December). Business & Finance: Stock Market Meltdown. *Tobacco Reporter*, pp. 42–43.

Norr, R. (1952. December). Cancer by the Carton. *Reader's Digest*, *61*: 7–8.

Norris, F. (1989, July 13). Closer Scrutiny of Bid for BAT. *New York Times*, p. D6.

Notes. (1988). The Smoldering Issue in Cipollone vs. Liggett Group, Inc.: Process Concerns in Determining Whether Cigarettes Are a Defectively Designed Product. *Cornell Law Review*, *73*:1-3, pp. 606–627.

O'Connor, J. (1980, September 8). Barclay Launch Largest Ever. *Advertising Age*, p. 1.

Okie, S. (1990a, May 5). Cigarette Ads, Smoking Rise Abroad Linked. *Washington Post*, p. A3.

Okie, S. (1990b, July 4). Botany: Extracting Protein from Tobacco Leaves. *Washington Post*, p. A2.

Oldenberg, D. (1990, June 29). A Smoky Ethical Issue. *Washington Post*, p. B5.

Olesker, M. (1990, April 26). Cigarette Ads That Target Blacks Are Catching Heat. *The Maryland Sun*, p. B1.

Oster, S.M. (1990). *Modern Competitive Analysis*, New York, NY: Oxford University Press.

Ostroff, G.M. (1990). *Investment Research: Philip Morris Companies*, NY: Goldman Sachs.

Ostroff, G.M. (1991). *Research Brief: RJR Nabisco*, NY: Goldman Sachs.

Ourusoff, A. (1992, September 1). What's in a Name? *Financial World Magazine*, pp. 32–48

Overton, J. (1981). Diversification and International Expansion: The Future of the American Tobacco Manufacturing Industry with Corporate Profiles of the "Big Six." In W.R. Finger (Ed.), *The Tobacco Industry in Transition*, (pp. 159–195). Lexington, MA: Heath.

Peers, A., & Forman, C. (1989, July 14). BAT Withdraws $400 Million Issue of Eurobonds in Wake of Hostile Bid. *Wall Street Journal*, p. C14.

Peers, A., & Sesit, M.R. (1989, July 13). Securities Concerns Are in a Quandary over BAT's Devalued Eurobond Issue. *Wall Street Journal*, p. A6.

Phillips, D. (1990, January 21). 8-State Airline Smoking Ban Nears Reality. *Washington Post*, p. A1.

Philip Morris Companies, Inc. (1988). *The Philip Morris Story*. Richmond, VA: Philip Morris Companies, Inc.

Philip Morris, Inc. (1960–1996). *Annual Reports and 10K Reports.*

Philip Morris, Inc. (1988–1989). *Philip Morris Magazine.* Monthly Editions.

Pierce, J.P. (1989a, January 6). Trends in Cigarette Smoking in The United States: Projections to the Year 2000. *JAMA*, pp. 61–65.

Pierce, J.P. (1989b, February). International Comparison of Trends in Cigarette Smoking Prevalence. *American Journal of Public Health*, *79*:2, pp. 152–157.

Pierce, J.P., et al. (1989c, January 6). Trends in Cigarette Smoking in The United States: Educational Differences Are Increasing. *JAMA*, pp. 56–60.

Porter, M.E. (1980). *Competitive Strategies*. New York: Free Press.

Porter, M.E. (1981). Strategic Interaction: Some Lessons from Industry Histories for Theory and Anti-Trust Policy. In S.C. Salop (Ed.), *Strategy, Predation and Anti-trust Analysis,* (pp. 449–506). Washington, DC: Federal Trade Commission.

Porter, M.E. (1985). *Competitive Advantage*. New York: Free Press.

Porter, M.E. (1986a). Competition in Global Industries: A Conceptual Framework. In M.E. Porter (Ed.), *Competition in Global Industries*, (pp. 15–60). Boston, MA: Harvard Business School Press.

Porter, M.E. (1986b). *Competition in Global Strategy*. Boston, MA: Harvard Business School Press.

Porter, M.E. (1987). From Competitive Advantage to Corporate Strategy. *Harvard Business Review*, 65(3), 43–59.

Porter, M.E. (1990). *The Competitive Advantage of Nations*, New York: Free Press.

Porter, M.E. (1991). Towards a Dynamic Theory of Strategy. *Strategic Management Journal*, *12*(5):95–117.

Porter, M.E. (1996). What is Strategy? *Harvard Business Review*, 74(6), 61–89.

Post, J.E. & Andrews, P.N. (1982). Case Research in Corporation and Society Studies. *Research in Corporate Social Performance and Policy*, *6*, 1–33.

Prahalad, C.K., & Doz, Y.L. (1987). *The Multinational Mission*, New York, NY: Free Press.

Preston, L.F., & Post, J.E. (1975). *Private Management and Public Policy*. Englewood Cliffs, NJ: Prentice-Hall.

Putterman, L. (1986). *The Economic Nature of the Firm*. NY: Cambridge University Press.

Quimpo, M.G. (1990, November 18). Smokers Fume About Bans At The Office. Washington Post, p. H-3.

Quinn, J.B., Mintzberg, H., & James, R.M. (1988). *The Strategy Process*. Englewood Cliffs, N J: Prentice Hall.

Quint, M. (1988, April 3). Peril In Trading Rooms: $1,000,000 Cigar Break. *New York Times*, p. B28.

Ramirez, A. (1990a, January 14). A Cigarette Campaign Under Fire. *New York Times*, p. D1.

Ramirez, A. (1990b, May 30). Price Blind Smoker Loyalty Defies Economics and Critics. *New York Times*, p. D1.

Ramirez, A. (1990c, June 3). From Coffee to Tobacco, Boycotts are a Growth Industry. *New York Times*, p. 2E.

Ramirez, A. (1990d, June 12). Lower Cigarette Sales Links to Tax Rise. *New York Times*, p. D1.

Ramirez, A. (1990e, June 22). Liggett To Change Its Focus With Shift From Cigarettes. *New York Times*, p. D1.

Ramirez, A. (1990f, June 23). Philip Morris Will Buy Suchard's Europe Units. *New York Times*, p. 31.

Ramirez, A. (1990g, September 9). Smoking Is Ruled Cause of a Death. *New York Times*, p. B4.

Ramirez, A. (1990h, September 14). 2 American Makers Agree to Sell Soviets 34 Billion Cigarettes. *New York Times*, p. A1.

Ramirez, A. (1990i, September 17). Tobacco Industry Sees Boom in Soviet Sale. *New York Times*, p. D5.

Ramirez, A. (1990j, September 27). Talking Deals: Fast Russian Sale by Philip Morris. *New York Times*, p. D2.

Ramirez, A. (1990k, October 2). Budget Package Regarded As Mixed Bag of Business. *New York Times*, p. A25.

Ramirez, A. (1990l, October 24). RJR Nabisco Trims Loss to $86 Million. *New York Times*, p. D5.

Ramirez, A. (1991a, January 18). New Cigarette Raising Issue of Target Market. *New York Times*, p. D8.

Ramirez, A. (1991b, March 27). Philip Morris Says Maxwell Will Retire. *New York Times*, p. D5.

Ramirez, A. (1991c, March 28). New Chief for Philip Morris. *New York Times*, p. D1.

Ramirez, A. (1991d, April 13). Slide in Tobacco Sales Hurting RJR Nabisco. *New York Times*, p. 37.

Ramirez, A. (1991e, August 28). Jury's Award to Liggett Overturned. *New York Times*, p. D4.

Rashy, S.T. (1990, February 25). For Tobacco's Lobbyists, No Nice Days At The Office. *New York Times*, p. 4E.

Ravenscraft, D.J., & Scheres, F.M. (1987). *Mergers, Self- Offs, & Economic Efficiency*. Washington, DC: The Brookings Institution.

Reed, R., & DeFillippi, R.J. (1990). Causal Ambiguity, Barriers to Imitation and Sustainable Competitive Advantage. *Academy of Management Review*, *15*(1), 88–102.

Reinhold, R. (1990, August 15). In A Smoking Ban Some See Ashes. *New York Times*, p. A22.

RJR Industries. (1965–1985). *Annual Reports and 10K Reports*.

RJR Nabisco. (1986–1995). *Annual Reports and 10K Reports*.

Ridder, K. (1990, October 4). Surgeon General Sharply Criticizes Tobacco Ads Targeted At Young Women. *Washington Post*, p. A19.

Robinson R.B., Jr., & Pearce, J.A. II. (1988). Planned Patterns of Strategic Behavior and Their Relationship to Business Unit Performance. *Strategic Management Journal*, *9*(1), 43–60.

Robinson, W.A. (1985, May 30). Virginia Slims Comes a Long Way in 17 Years. *Advertising Age*, p. 30.

Rodu, B., & Cole, P. (1997, reprint). *Priorities*. American Council on Science and Health Internet.

Roper, J.E. (1971). The Man Behind the Ban on Cigarette Commercials. *Reader's Digest Reprints*.

Rosewicz, B., & Karr, A.R. (1990, June 25). Smoking Curbs Get a New Lift from EPA Plan. *Wall Street Journal*, p. B1.

Ross, C.S. (1987). Judicial and Legislative Control of the Tobacco Industry Toward A Smoke-Free Society ? *Cincinnati Law Review*, *56*, pp. 317–341.

Rossant, J. (1988, February 15). Can Asia's Four Tiger Be Banned? *Business Week*, pp. 46–47.

Rothenberg, R. (1988, October 9). The Big New Pitch For Old Ads. *New York Times*, p. F1.

Rothenberg, R. (1991, April 8). Study Shows Power of Public-Service Ads. *New York Times*, p. D8.

Rothstein, M.A. (1987). Refusing to Employ Smokers: Good Public Policy Health or Bad Public Policy. *Notre Dame Law Review*, *62*:910, pp. 940–968.

Rothstein, M. (1990, December 18). Uneasy Partners: Arts and Philip Morris. *New York Times*, p. C15.

Rowan, C.T. (1990, January 25). Sullivan's Crusade. *Washington Post*, p. B7.

Rowen, H. (1989, July 25). Despite the Risks, U.S. Should Expand Soviet Ties. *Washington Post*, p. H1.

Ruffenach, G. (1989, June 6). RJR Nabisco Sells Food Units to France's BSN. *Wall Street Journal*, p. A4.

Ruffenach, G. (1990a, February 6). RJR Posts Loss for 4th Quarter and All of 1989. *Wall Street Journal*, p. A3.

Ruffenach, G. (1990b), July 24). RJR Posts Loss, But Operating Profit Advances. *Wall Street Journal*, p. A3.

Ruffenach, G. (1990c, October 11). RJR Tobacco Unit Appoints Schroer Chief of Sales Among Falling Market Shares. *Wall Street Journal*, p. B7.

Rumelt, R.P., Schendel, D., & Teece, D.C. (1991). Strategic Management and Economics. *Strategic Management Journal*, *12*, pp. 5–29.

Rundle, R.L. (1990, January 14). U-Haul Puts High Price On Vices of Its Workers. *Wall Street Journal*, p. B1.

Russell, C. (1988, June 14). Risk vs. Reality: How The Public Perceives Health Hazards. *Washington Post Health*, p. 14–17.

Russell, C. (1989, September 5). Finding Out Who Smokes. *Washington Post Health*, p. 17.

Rustin, R.E. (1990, April 24). Goldsmith Ends Attempt to Buy BAT Amid Public Worries on Leveraged Bids. *Wall Street Journal*, p. A3.

Salwen, K.G. (1988, October 21). Tobacco Stocks Soar, Bolstered by Narrowing of Litigation Cloud, Mania for Big Cash Flow. *Wall Street Journal*, p. C2.

Salwen, K.G. (1988, November 7). Staid Institutions Seek Takeover Play Profits. *Wall Street Journal*, p. C1.

Schmalensee, R.L. (1972). *The Economics of Advertising*. Amsterdam: North Holland Publishing Co.

Schmeisser, P. (1988, July 10). Publishing Cigarettes Overseas. *New York Times Magazine*, pp. 16–22, 66.

Schmitt, E. (1987, September 27). The Last Refuge of Smokers May Be No Place But Home. *New York Times*, p. H1.

Schroeder, D.M. (1990). A Dynamic Perspective on the Impact of Process Innovation Upon Competitive Strategies. *Strategic Management Journal*, *11*(1), 25–41.

Schwadel, F. (1989, October 2). Marshall Field's Miller Leaps on Stage With Plan to Buy Firm From BAT. *Wall Street Journal*, p. A9E.

Segev, E. (1989). A Systematic Comparative Analysis and Synthesis Of Two Business-Level Strategic Typologies. *Strategic Management Journal*, *10*(5), 487–505.

Seligman, D. (1987, August 7). Don't Bet Against Cigarette Makers. *Fortune*, pp. 70–77.

Selznick, P. (1957). Leadership in Administration. Berkeley, CA: University of California Press.

Seth, A. (1990). Value Creation in Acquisitions: A Reexamination of Performance Issues. *Strategic Management Journal*, *11*(2), 99–115.

Shapiro, E. (1990, September 17). Market Place: Finding A Buyer for Dole Food. *New York Times*, p. D1.

Shelton, A. (1986, February). Spotlight on Thailand: Economic Downswing Creates Rough Times. *Tobacco Reporter*, pp. 24–28.

Shelton, A. (1987, February). Spotlight on Korea: Cigarette Imports Off to Slow Start. *Tobacco Reporter*, pp. 34–35.

Shelton, A. (1988, March). Credit Programs Enhance Export Prospects. *Tobacco Reporter*, pp. 22–23.

Shelton, A. (1988, May). Editor's Memo. *Tobacco Reporter*, p. 4.

Shepherd, P. (1989). Transnational corporations and the Denationalization of the Latin American Cigarette Industry? In A. Teichoua, et al. (Eds.), *Historical Studies in International Corporate Business* (pp. 201–28). New York, NY: Cambridge University Press.

Siconolfi, M. (1990, May 3). Salomon Chief Tells Meeting His View on Liars Poker. *Wall Street Journal*, p. C16.
Sinclair, M. (1990, September 27). More D.C. Residents Giving Up Cigarettes, Studies Find. *Washington Post*, p. D1.
Sklansky, J. (1989, September 7). Howard County Approves MD's Toughest Anti-smoking Law. *Washington Post*, p. B1.
Slade, J. (1989, June 15). Lots of Smoke, No Fun. *Wall Street Journal*, p. B1.
Smith, R., & Forman, C. (1989, July 14). BAT Focuses on Staying Independent But A Friendly Suitor May Still Surface. *Wall Street Journal*, p. A3.
Smith, R., & Freedman, A.M. (1988, December 27). Possible Bid Lifts American Brands Stock. *Wall Street Journal*, p. B5.
Smith, R., & Helyan, J. (1988, December 5). KKR Gets to Work Lining Up Money for RJR Nabisco. *Wall Street Journal*, p. A3.
Smith, R. (1988, November 21). RJR Legacy LBO Lenders Grow Cautious. *Wall Street Journal*, p. C1.
Smith, R. (1989, July 12). Legendary Raider Sir James Goldsmith Adds To Lore With His Bid For BAT. *Wall Street Journal*, p. A4.
Smith, R. (1990, July 23). Moen Purchase By American Brand Agreed. *Wall Street Journal*, p. A3.
Smith, R. (1989, September 7). RJR Nabisco To Sell Assets of Del Monte. *Wall Street Journal*, p. A3.
Smith, R., and Shapiro, E. (1993, Mar. 26). KKR's Luster Dims as Fall in RJR Stock Hurts Investors' Take. *Wall Street Journal*, p. A1.
Smoking Is Drag on Job Search, Survey Says. (1990, January). *Modern Office Technology*, p. 149.
Solomon, L.C. (1983). The Other Side of the Smoking Worker Controversy. *Personnel Administrator*. (Reprint).
Soper, F.A. (reprint). John Banzhaf and the Giants. *Listen Journal of Better Living*, *21*:7, (Reprint).
Specter, M. (1989, January 12). Death Toll From Smoking Revised Upward. *Washington Post*, p. A1.
Squires, S. (1988, June 28). Smoking: The Evidence Mounts. *Washington Post*, pp. D14.
Standard & Poor's. (1960-1995). *Industry Surveys: Food, Beverages & Tobacco.*
Stasinopoulos, J.G. (1988, May). Spotlight on Greece: Can the Industry Get Back On Track? *Tobacco Reporter*, pp. 34–35.
Steinmetz, G. (1994, Sep 13). Borden Deal May Be White Flag by KKR on RJR Investment. *Wall Street Journal*, p. A3
Sterngold, J. (1988a, October 21). RJR Nabisco Executives Propose $17 Billion Takeover, Biggest Ever. *New York Times*, p. A1.
Sterngold, J. (1988b, November 21). RJR Nabisco Gets $26.8 Billion From First Boston Plan. *New York Times*, p. A1.
Sterngold, J. (1988c, November 27). Why the RJR Nabisco Deal Means so Much to Wall Street. *New York Times*, p. E8.
Sterngold, J. (1988d, December 2). The Nabisco Battle's Key Movement. *New York Times*, p. D15.
Sterngold, J. (1988e, December 5). The Board Room Battle For RJR Nabisco. *New York Times*, p. A1.

Stevenson, R.W. (1989, July 13). State Insurance Laws Could Slow BAT Bid. *New York Times*, p. D6.

Stewart, J.B. (1983, May). No Smoking on Duty. *Journal of the Law Society Scotland, 28*, p. 215.

Sticht, J.P. (1983). *The RJR Story: The Evolution of a Global Enterprise*. Princeton, NJ: Princeton University Press.

Stigiltz, J.E., & Mathewson, G.F. (1986). *New Developments in the Analysis of Market Structure*. Cambridge, MA: MIT Press.

Stone, M. (1987, October). Spotlight on the United Kingdom: Competitions as Intensive As Ever. *Tobacco Reporter*, pp. 24–27.

Stout, D. (1996, October 18). Direct Link Found Between Smoking and Lung Cancer. *New York Times*, p. A1

Stout, H. (1988, June 12). Cigarettes: Still Big Business. *New York Times*, p. F4.

Stout, H. (1990, July 10). Selling American: In A Major Turnaround U.S. Is Posting Surplus In Trade With Europe. *Wall Street Journal*, p. A1.

Studer, M., & Federman, D. (1988, November 11). Switzerland's Nestle Fights To Stay On Top. *Wall Street Journal*, p. A12.

Sullivan, A., & White, J.A. (1988, December 8). Texaco Pressed By Big Investors For Wider Role. *Wall Street Journal*, p. A4.

Sullivan, D. (1989, September). Testing Hypothesis about Firm Behavior in the Cigarette Industry. *Journal of Political Economy, 93*, pp. 586–598.

Sumner, M., & Ward, R. (1981, December). Tax Change and Cigarette Prices. *Journal of Political Economy, 89*, pp. 1261–1265.

Sun, L.H. (1988, July 3). Nestle's Arrival Heats Up Formula Mix. *Washington Post*, p. H1.

Sun, L. H. (1988, October 21). Three in Running to Buy Woodies. *Washington Post*, p. A1.

Swardson, A. (1989, August 4). Bentsen Offers Bill to Curb Tax Advantages of Mergers. *Washington Post*, p. D1.

Tamburri, R. (1989, March 3). Two Tobacco Firms To End Billboard Ads Over Canadian Rules. *Wall Street Journal*, p. B6.

Taylor, S.A. (1989, Winter). Tobacco and Economic Growth in Developing Nations. *Business in the Contemporary World, 1*(2), 55–70.

Tedlow, R.S., & John, R.R., Jr. (1986). *Managing Big Business* Boston, MA: Harvard Business School Press.

Tedlow, R.S. (1990). *New and Improved: The Story of Mass Marketing in America*. New York, NY: Basic Books Inc.

Teece, D., Jr., (Ed.) (1987). *The Competitive Challenge*, Ballinger Publishing Co.: Cambridge, Mass.

Tell, L.J., & Rhein, R., Jr. (1988, May 30). The Smoking Problem Needs Radical Solutions—Here's One. *Business Week*, p. 31.

Tennant, R.B. (1950). *The American Cigarette Industry*. New Haven, CT: Yale University Press.

Ten Year Lobbying Effort Results in Smoking Ban on Most U.S. Flights. (1989, October 23). *Aviation Week & Space Technology*, p. 71.

Tesler, L.G. (1962, October). Advertising and Cigarettes. *Journal of Political Economy, 72*, pp. 471–499.

The Economist. (1992, May 16–22). The Search for El Dorado, pp. 21–24.

The Economist. (1988a, March 26). Trade Liberalization's Dark Shadow, pp. 70-71.

The Economist. (1988b, April 2). Passive Smoking: Emission of Guilt, p. 76.

The Economist. (1989a, May 13). Mania Questioned, p. 67.

The Economist. (1989b, August 26). Tobacco and the bid for BAT: Good Stuff, Nicotine, pp. 54–56.

The Economist. (1989c, September 23). The Third World: Trial and Error, pp. 3–58.

The Economist. (1989d, September 30). Learning The Hard Way. pp. 70–71.

The Economist. (1989e, November 4). Nice Day, Nice Smoking, p. 94.

The Economist. (1990a, January 20). American Business: Just For Fun, p. 102.

The Economist. (1990b, April 21). Selling Tobacco: Defending the Rights of the Marlboro Man, p. 84.

The Economist. (1990c, June 30). Cadbury and Philip Morris Sh-h-h-h., You Know Who, p. 68.

The Economist. (1997, June 28). The Passing of a Hero, p. 32.

The Tobacco Institute. (1988-1995). *The Tax Burden on Tobacco*. Vol. 23:23–30, Washington, D.C: The Tobacco Institute.

The Tobacco Institute. (1988b). *The Tobacco Industry Profile*. Washington, DC: The Tobacco Institute.

The Tobacco Institute. (1989). *The Anti-Smoking Campaign: Enough Is Enough*. Washington, D.C: The Tobacco Institute.

Thomas, L.G., III. (1986). *The Economics of Strategic Planning*. Lexington, MA: Lexington Books.

Ticer, S., & Jacobson, G. (1988, October 10). Smoke, Smoke, Smoke, That, Um....GIZMO ? *Business Week*, p. 145.

Tilley, N.M. (1985). *The R.J. Reynolds Tobacco Company*. Chapel Hill, NC: The University of North Carolina Press.

Timberlake, C. (1989, September 22). British Government Clears Goldsmith's Bid for BAT. *Washington Post*, p. G3.

Time. (1952). Smoking and Cancer. p. 34.

Time. (1988, December 5). If I Fail, I'm on the Hook. p. 71.

Tobacco Advisory Council. (circa 1987). Smoke and the Non-Smoker. Washington, DC: Tobacco Advisory Council.

Tobacco-Free Young America Project. (1987). *Tobacco-Free Young America Project Legislative Handbook*, Washington, DC: American Cancer Society, American Heart Association, American Lung Association.

Tobacco International. (1978, July 21). A New French Cigarette in Wake of Tougher Government Controls, pp. 52–55.

Tobacco International. (1979, June 15). SEITA Plays a Troubled Role in France, p. 16.

Tobacco International. (1980a, April 4). A Brief History of SEITA, p. 48.

Tobacco International. 1980b. August 22). SEITA Goes Public to Stem the Trade, p. 24.

Tobacco International. (1982, June 11). SEITA introduces Anew Blond, pp. 16–18.

Tobacco International. (1982, December 24). SEITA Presents a Low-Tar and Nicotine Cigarette—Gauloises Light, p. 90.

Tobacco International. (1983, July 22). In France: Blond Sales, Growth & Processing of Light Tobaccos Gain, pp. 42, 44, 46, 48.

Tobacco International. (1985, July 26). SEITA Still Dominates French Market; Gauloises Blondes Soars, pp. 11–12.

Tobacco International. (1986, May 30). France Tabac Markets Expanding French Flue-Cured, Burley, p. 45.

Tobacco International. (1987, August 21). Thailand: Despite Growers' Chagrin, Early Crop Output Up; Smoking Increasing, pp. 7–8, 50.

Tobacco International. (May, 1996). The World According to BAT, pp. 39–46.

Tobacco Quarterly. (1988). Review, 10(1), pp. 3-63.

Tobacco Reporter. (1985a, March 22). Male Japanese Smoking Less, But Female More, p. 88.

Tobacco Reporter. (1985b, March 22). RJR awards second $1 million grant to NSCU; $26,000 to Virginia Tech, p. 88.

Tobacco Reporter. (1986c, February). Taiwan: Monopoly Opens Market to American Cigarettes, pp. 16–20.

Tobacco Reporter. (1987a, January). Singapore: Government Aims to Eliminate Smoking, p. 16.

Tobacco Reporter. (1987b, February). Thailand: Leaf Curers Ask Government to Act Against Smuggling, p. 26.

Tobacco Reporter. (1987c, February). Monopoly Seeks Improved Quality and Efficiency, pp. 35–37.

Tobacco Reporter. (1987d, February). Leaf Output on the Decline, p. 37.

Tobacco Reporter. (198e7, February). World Summary: Leaf Output Falls Five Percent in 1986, p. 42.

Tobacco Reporter. (1987f, March). Editor's Memo, p. 4.

Tobacco Reporter. (1987g, March). Singapore: Government Aims to Eliminate Smoking, p. 22.

Tobacco Reporter. (1987h, March). Taiwan: Local Market Opened for U.S. and E.E.C. Cigarettes, p. 22.

Tobacco Reporter. (1987i, March). Monopoly Hopes New Brand Will Replace Imports, p. 29.

Tobacco Reporter. (1987j, April). Korea: United States Agrees To Import Two Korean Brands, pp. 13–16.

Tobacco Reporter. (1987k, June). Korea: Prices Set for Two New High-Quality Cigarettes, p. 18.

Tobacco Reporter. (1987l, April). Taiwan: Three More Countries Given Access To Tobacco Market, pp. 18–20.

Tobacco Reporter. (1987m, June). International Briefs, p. 21.

Tobacco Reporter. (1987n, June). Spotlight on Turkey: An Eye To The Future, pp. 22–25.

Tobacco Reporter. (1987o, July). Japan: Foreign Cigarettes Attain 3.9 Percent Market Share, p. 12.

Tobacco Reporter. (1987p, July). Korea: Komoco Exports Reach U.S. Smokers, p. 12.

Tobacco Reporter. (1987q, September). World Leaf Output Up Eight Percent, p. 36.

Tobacco Reporter. (1987r, October). Topline Report, p. 8.

Tobacco Reporter. (1987s, December). Taiwan: Well-Known Foreign Brands Drive Competition Away, pp. 18–19.

Tobacco Reporter. (1988a, January). Korea: Both Domestic and Import Cigarette Sales Increase, p. 13.

Tobacco Reporter. (1988b, January). Taiwan: Imports Still Growing as Group Launches New Drive, p. 16.

Tobacco Reporter. (1988c, January). WHO Conference Attacks Advertising, p. 27.

Tobacco Reporter. (1988d, February). Topline Report, p. 8.

Tobacco Reporter. (1988e, February). World Leaf Trade Exports Fall to 1.35 Million Tons, pp. 36–40.

Tobacco Reporter. (1988f, March). Topline Report, p. 6.

Tobacco Reporter. (1988g, May). International News, pp. 8–26.

Tobacco Reporter. (1988h, May). Topline Report, p. 6.

Tobacco Reporter. (1988i, June). Korea: Government Announces Plan to Cut Cigarette Duties, p. 18.

Tobacco Reporter. (1988j, June). Singapore: Airline Starts Non-Smoking Flights Due to Demand, p. 20.

Tobacco's Smoking Game? (1988, June). *Harpers Magazine*, p. 25.

Tollison, Robert, D. (1988). *Clearing the Air*. Lexington, MA: Lexington Books.

Tollison, Robert, D. (1988). *Smoking and the State*. Lexington, MA: Lexington Books.

Toman, B. (1988, July). BAT Industries Faces Battle to Win Farmers Group With Stiff Upper Lip. *Wall Street Journal*, p.A12.

Trachtenberg, J.A. (1990, April 19). Dayton Hudson Said to Be Front-Runner To Buy BAT's Marshall Field's Chain. *Wall Street Journal*, p. A4.

TRB. (1990, April 26). Tobacco Anomalies Abound. *The Baltimore Sun*, p. A15.

Uhlig, M.A. (1987, December 27). Again New York Tries To Quit Smoking. *New York Times*, p. 6E.

U.S. Department of Agriculture. (1985–1995). *Tobacco Situation and Outlook Report*. Washington, D.C.: Quarterly Reports.

U.S. Department of Health, Education and Welfare. (1979–80). *Smoking and Health: A Report of the Surgeon General*. Washington, DC.

U.S. Department of Health and Human Services. (1980). *The Health Consequences of Smoking For Women. A Report of the Surgeon General*. Rockville, MD.

U.S. Department of Health and Human Services. (1982). *The Health Consequences of Smoking: Cancer, A Report of the Surgeon General*. Rockville, MD.

U.S. Department of Health and Human Services. (1983). *The Health Consequences of Smoking: Cardiovascular Disease. A Report of the Surgeon General*. Rockville, MD.

U.S. Department of Health and Human Services. (1984). *The Health Consequences of Smoking: Chronic Obstructive Lung Disease. A Report of the Surgeon General*. Rockville, MD.

U.S. Department of Health and Human Services. (1985). *The Health Consequences of Smoking : Cancer and Chronic Lung Disease in the Workplace: A Report of the Surgeon General*, Rockville, MD.

U.S. Department of Heath and Human Services. (1986). *The Health Consequences of Involuntary Smoking: A Report of the Surgeon General*. Rockville, MD.

U.S. Department of Health and Human Services. (1989). *Reducing the Health Consequences of Smoking: 25 Years of Progress. A Report of the Surgeon General, Executive Summary*. Rockville, MD.

U.S. Department of Health and Human Services. (1992). *Smoking and Health in the Americas: A 1992 Report of the Surgeon General, in Collaboration With the Pan American Health Organization*. Atlanta, GA.

U.S. Department of Health and Welfare. (1964). *Smoking and Health: Report of the Advisory Committee to the Surgeon General of the Public Health Service. A Report of the Surgeon General*. Washington, DC.

U.S. News & World Report. (1988, April 18). Environment: Big Apple Smoke Lift, p. 17.

U.S. News & World Report. (1990, March 5). Where There's Smoke, pp. 57–58.

Wald, M.L. (1988, February 14). Using Liability Law to Put Tobacco on Trial. *New York Times*, p. F11.

Waldholz, M., & Heylar, J. (1988, October 21). FDA Feels Heat on Smokeless Cigarette. *Wall Street Journal*, p. B1.

Waldholz, M. (1988, December 5). Influential Congressman Presses FDA To Decide Status of New RJR Cigarette. *Wall Street Journal*, p. B4.

Waldholz, M. (1989, June 15). Notion of "Safer" Cigarette is Assailed by Large Study. *Wall Street Journal*, p. B1.

Walker, S. (1985). Media and Broadcasting Law. *Australian Business Law Review*, *13*, pp. 112–118.

Waldman, P. (1989a, August 11). KKR's Staff Cuts for Tobacco Unit Have Many Fuming. *Wall Street Journal*, p. A3.

Waldman, P. (1989b, December 19). Tobacco Firms Try Soft, Feminine Sell. *Wall Street Journal*, p. B1.

Waldman, P. (1990a, January 30). Tobacco Lawsuit Accusing Reynolds Dismissed By Court. *Wall Street Journal*, p. B7.

Waldman, P. (1990b, April 25). RJR Reports 1st Period Loss of $222 Million. *Wall Street Journal*, p. A3.

Wall Street Journal. (1988a, July 28). Wasserstein Perella Rockets to the Fore of Merger World With Nomura Alliance, p. 6.

Wall Street Journal. (1988b, November 29). Philip Morris Says Plan to Acquire Kraft is Cleared by FTC, p. A6.

Wall Street Journal. (1988c, December 2). RJR Takeover Could Hurt Marketers and Consumers, p. A10.

Wall Street Journal. (1988d, December 2). Skaddem Arps Partner Played Key Role of Auctioneer in Battle for RJR Nabisco, p. A10.

Wall Street Journal. (1988e, December 2). Will Others Follow as KKR Tames Megadeal Frontier, p. C1.

Wall Street Journal. (1989a, May 14). Lorillard Unveils Cigarette That Has Lemon Flavor, p. B3.

Wall Street Journal. (1989b, May 14). Tobacco Advertising, p. B3.

Wall Street Journal. (1989c, July 13). Smokers Don't Mind These Longer Flights, p. B1.

Wall Street Journal. (1989d, July 14). Here's The Pointless History of BAT's Industries Name, p. A3.

Wall Street Journal. (1989e, August 8). BAT Units Petition to Intervene in Suit By Goldsmith Denied, p. A4.

Wall Street Journal. (1989f, August 21). Philip Morris Starts Tests of New Luxury Cigarette, p. B4.

Wall Street Journal. (1989g, August 25). Loews' Lorillard Unit Names Andrew Tisch New Chief, Chairman, p. B8.

Wall Street Journal. (1989h, September 26). Merrill-Led Group to Buy RJR's Del Monte Business, p. A10.
Wall Street Journal. (1989i, November 11). House Unit Plans to Query Philip Morris on Ad Series, p. B6.
Wall Street Journal. (1989j, November 28). R.J. Reynold's Spending, p. B6.
Wall Street Journal. (1988a, June 14). Liggett Ordered to Pay $400,000 In Damages for Smoker's Death, p. A3.
Wall Street Journal. (1988b, November 22). First Boston Group's Proposal for RJR Is Product of Diverse Cast of Characters, p. A4.
Wall Street Journal. (1990a, April 17). Ad Notes: Anti-Smoking Campaign, p. B7.
Wall Street Journal. (1990b, July 27). Liggett Group Inc.'s Name Changed Cleared; New Directors Elected, p. B10.
Wall Street Journal. (1990c, October 2). Liquor, Luxury Levies Trouble Firms, p. B1.
Wallace, A.C. (1990a, June 14). Junk Bonds of RJR Holdings Surge. *New York Times*, p. D4.
Wallace, A.C. (1990b, June 21). Refinancing Plan Sought for Nabisco. *New York Times*, p. D1.
Wallace, A.C. (1990c, June 27). Kohlberg Renegotiates $500 Million Loan to RJR. *New York Times*, p. D1.
Wallace, A.C. (1990d, July 2). Capital Spending Cut By RJR. *New York Times*, p. D1.
Wallace, A.C. (1990e, Jul 4). Banks With Stakes in Borrowers Are in Spotlights. *New York Times*, p. 47.
Wallace, A.C. (1990f, July 17). Refinancing Lifts Prices of RJR Bonds. *New York Times*, p. D1.
Wallace, A.C. (1990g, July 27). Investors Struggle to Value RJR Nabisco's New Issue. *New York Times*, p. D1.
Warburg. (1996, May 7). *BAT Industries—Company Report*.
Washington Post. (1984, September 27). Hill Presses Cigarette Labels, Presses Toward Adjournment, p. A1.
Washington Post. (1987, October 6). "Smokeless" Cigarette May Hurt Cancer Stance, p. D3.
Washington Post. (1988, January 3). Toting Up Tobacco's Scorecard, p. F5.
Washington Post. (1988, May 1). Defense Deploys an Army of Lawyers, p. H1.
Washington Post. (1988, November 26). Round Up, p. D11.
Washington Post. (1988, December 13). 25 Years of Hanson Summed Up in One Line, Imperial Tobacco, p. B12.
Washington Post. (1989, May 8). Smokers' Rights Measure Snuffed, p. B4.
Washington Post. (1989, November 10). Acquisitions: Philip Morris, p. F2.
The Washingtonian. (1990, May). Capitol Commitment: Information Please, p. 13.
Waxman, H.A. (1990, June 26). Tobacco Exports: Why the Silence? *Washington Post*, p. D21.
Wayne, L. (1990, May 20). RJR Nabisco's Disgruntled Bondholders. *New York Times*, p. F15.
Weisskopf, M. (1990, May 11). Passive-Smoking Curbs Weighed. *Washington Post*, p. A25.
Weisskopf, M. (1990, November 23). EPA Struggles Over How to Assure Smoking Panel's Independence. *Washington Post*, p. A29.

Wessel, D. (1988, December 2). This is for Sure: Buy-outs May or May Not Increase IRS Revenue. *Wall Street Journal*, p. A10.

Wessel, D. (1989, November 21). Tax Rise on Liquor, Tobacco is Studied by Federal Group. *Wall Street Journal*, p. A8.

Wessel, D. (1991, March 12). Exports Won't Pull U.S. Out of Recession. *Wall Street Journal*, p. A2.

Whalan, E.M. (1997, June 26). "...Or a Payoff to Purveyors of Poison." *Wall Street Journal*, p. A18.

White, H.E. (1990, October 2). Thailand, Bowing to Foreign Pressure, Will End It's Ban On Cigarette Imports. *Wall Street Journal*, p. B4.

White, J.A. (1989, June 1). Metropolitan Life is Set Back in Suit Over RJR Bonds. *Wall Street Journal*, p. B89.

White, J.A. (1988, November 17). ITT Sues RJR, Saying Buy-out Devalues Bonds. *Wall Street Journal*, p. C1.

White, R.E. (1986). Generic Business Strategies, Organizational Context and Performance: An Empirical Examination. *Strategic Management Journal*, *7*(3), 217–231.

Whitten, I.T.(1979, June). *Brand Performance in the Cigarette Industry and the Advantage of Early Entry, 1913–1973*. Washington, DC: Federal Trade Commission.

Will, G. F. (1990, January 25). Tobacco's Targets. *Washington Post*, p. B7.

Williams, L. (1987, January 17). Blacks Debate The Influence of Tobacco Industry. *New York Times*, p. 1.

Winer, L. (1988, August 4). Puff Pieces: The World According to Philip Morris. *Wall Street Journal*, p.18.

Winkler, M., & Burrough, B. (1988, November 7). RJR Nabisco Buy-Out Sets The Stage for a Drexel-Salomon Duel. *Wall Street Journal*, p. C1.

Winslow, R. (1990, March 6). Some Firms Put A Price On Smoking. *Wall Street Journal*, p. B1.

Wollenberg, S. (1989, September 29). Low-Smoke Cigarette Announced. *Washington Post*, p. C13.

Wootten, H.M. (1957, December). Cigarette Series, Printers' Ink, p. 231.

Yin, R.K., (1989). *Case Study Research: Design & Methods*, (Vol. 5), Newbury Park, CA: Sage Publications.

Yip, G.S. (1982). Internal Development Versus Acquisition. *Strategic Management Journal*, 10(3): 285-293.

Yoder, E.M., Jr. (1989, April 16). The High-Living Barons of Tobacco Road. *Washington Post Book World*, p. 3.

Yoshihashi, P., & Hilder, D.P. (1988, August 26). BAT's Accord to Buy Farmers Angers Anti-Smoking Groups, Some Politicians. *Wall Street Journal*, p. P2.

Yudof, M.G. (1983). *When Government Speaks: Politics, Law and Government Expressions in America*. Berkley, C: University of California Press.

Zajac, E.J., & Shortell, S.M. (1989). Changing Generic Strategies: Likelihood, Direction, and Performance Implications. *Strategic Management Journal*, *10*(5): 413-430.

Zoutewelle, L.J. (1987, January). New Year Promises More Grey Skies. *Tobacco Reporter*, pp. 32–34.

Zoutewelle, L.J. (1988, January). Economic and Monetary Troubles Ahead. *Tobacco Reporter*, pp. 20–22, 27.

Index

About the Author

RAYMOND M. JONES is Assistant Professor of Strategic and Organizational Studies at The Sellinger School of Business, Loyola College. Professor Jones has held executive positions with Occidental Petroleum and has served on the boards of numerous U.S. and international corporations.

ISBN 1-56720-158-X
90000>
EAN
9 781567 201581
HARDCOVER BAR CODE